LIVING TWICE

By the same author

Biography

Héloïse
Charles of Orleans, Prince and Poet
The Order of the Rose: The Life and
Ideas of Christine de Pizan

Translations of:

Colette
Creatures Great and Small
My Mother's House and Sido
The Vagabond
Break of Day

Maurice Goudeket
Close to Colette

Jules Supervielle
Selected Short Stories

LIVING TWICE

MEMOIRS

Enid McLeod

Hutchinson Benham
London

Hutchinson Benham Limited

An imprint of the Hutchinson Group
17-21 Conway Street, London W1P 6JD
London Melbourne Sydney Auckland
Wellington Johannesburg and agencies
throughout the world

First published 1982

© Enid McLeod 1982

Set in Baskerville by V & M Graphics Ltd, Aylesbury, Bucks
Printed in Great Britain by The Anchor Press Ltd
and bound by Wm Brendon & Son Ltd
both of Tiptree, Essex

ISBN 0 09 149600 4

CONTENTS

1	Legacies of Childhood and Schooldays	7
2	A Feminine Oxford	18
3	Pastures New	30
4	Out of Bondage	43
5	Pontigny	55
6	The Student World in Geneva	67
7	Foreign Fields	78
8	More Travel, Change and Politics	88
9	Héloïse	100
10	The Ministry of Information	114
11	The British Council	135
12	Slow Approach to Paris	149
13	Feeling my Way: Paris 1955-1956	162
14	Mission Accomplished: Paris 1957-1959	185
15	A Richly Varied Retirement	210

Some years ago, John Weightman, then Professor of French at Westfield College, a friend and near neighbour of ours, used to say to Ethel Whitehorn and me that we really ought to write something about those French writers, the founders of the *Nouvelle Revue Française*, whom we knew so intimately, for he thought there could be few Englishwomen who had had that experience. But at that time we felt unable to do this, thinking we hadn't enough material to make any sort of publication.

After Ethel died, our Genevese friend Roger de Candolle wrote to say he felt strongly that I ought to put on record what he considered a remarkable fact: that Ethel, so deeply English and with no special knowledge of the French, not an intellectual although she was acutely perceptive of human character, should instantly have captivated and been accepted by that closed circle of sophisticated Frenchmen, one of whom, Roger Martin du Gard, referred to her as *'l'incomparable amie insulaire'*.

In these memoirs I have tried not only to do as John Weightman and Roger de Candolle suggested, but, in recalling the events of my own life, to paint as full a portrait as I can of the rare being who shared so many of them.

Enid McLeod

Chapter One

LEGACIES OF CHILDHOOD AND SCHOOLDAYS 1896-1915

The moment of my birth was sudden, swift, and rather startling for my mother, as she told me when I was old enough to hear it. For the doctor who had come to our house to attend her in labour was seized with an uncontrollable attack of diarrhoea at the vital minute and had to rush to the lavatory. While he was there I popped out, safe and sound. As I grew into childhood, this first act of mine was amusedly thought by my parents to be characteristic, for I always rejected offers of help with my lessons, saying 'I can dood it myself', a statement with which the family used to tease me. Another family phrase which they felt might have applied to my determined entry into the world we acquired a few years later when we were on holiday in a farmhouse. The farmer's stubborn little daughter, Dora, attached herself to my brother and me and whenever we tried to shake her off, took no notice but merely replied, 'I'm tummin, so dere!'

Lest anyone should fear that the chronicling of this first event of my life means that I am going to go on telling in detail all the happenings of my youth, let me say at once that such is not my intention. I want rather to try and see, looking back now with the perspective of time, something of the character that I was born with and what were the early influences that gave me the tastes and interests that I subsequently developed.

First and foremost was the habit of reading. Happily for me, both my parents were much given to this. They had married latish in life, and though far from being intellectuals, they had between them collected a sizable library of all the main nineteenth-century novelists and many poets. One of these last was a volume of Wordsworth which my mother, a short dark-haired woman with some French and Italian blood in her otherwise English veins, had won as a school prize for quite a wide range of subjects, including history, which, I suspect, was chiefly a matter of dates. Her addiction to these she retained and passed on to me, together with a sense of chronology, which gave me a love of synoptic tables of historical and artistic events, which I later found of help in my work, as well as of interest in themselves.

Dotted about among this nineteenth-century literature, were a dozen or so thin, green-bound volumes of a cheap series called Morley's Universal Library, price one shilling each, covering a very wide range of titles, such as Locke's *Civil Government*, Hobbes's *Leviathan*, Defoe's *Journal of the Plague*, Bacon's *Essays*, Chapman's *Homer* and Dryden's *Aeneid*, the plays of Molière and Voltaire's *Candide*. I have them still, silent witnesses of my father's frustrated youth. He had been a pupil, and I believe a good one, at the Manchester Grammar School, then as now an excellent public school. But whatever career he was destined for, the sudden bankruptcy of his father made him abandon it and, as the eldest son, he had to leave school to help the family financially by taking the first job that came to hand. This was that of a commercial traveller, something to which no social stigma was attached in the industrial north, but which was despised in snobbish towns like Bath and Bristol, where we lived. I remember my father's dislike of the many vulgarian members of his occupation he came to know, and the slight sense of shame I suffered because of it. (For a long time I hated the sight of a form on which I had to fill in my father's profession.) He must therefore have collected these shilling volumes later, although his humdrum business-life gave him little time to read them. He was a kindly, rather heavily built, very patient man, after whom I took physically, though not in patience.

To come back to myself, it was natural that with such parents I should have been taught reading early, and fortunately it was one of the subjects I learnt at the Kindergarten round the corner from our house at 82 Cotham Road, Bristol, to which I went when I was about four or five. There I recollect the moment I realized the thrilling world that learning to read was to open for me. Among other things we were taught to sew hems, a skill that involved much blood-letting from my clumsy fingers. But what helped to numb the pain of this was that the mistress who presided over our efforts told us an enthralling fairy tale while we laboured. I say 'told' because I did not then realize she was reading it and thought she was making it up. As the end of the autumn term approached and I realized that the story was coming to an end, I felt increasing despair that I should never hear it again. But my mother had found out that the story was in fact George Macdonald's entrancing tale, *The Princess and the Goblins*, and on Christmas Day it was on my plate. I could hardly believe that, if I stuck to my reading, I could hear it all over again. I have that volume still, and have read it many times since then.

After this, what to give me for presents was never any problem: fairy tales! And little by little I collected all I could get: the Andrew Laing coloured fairy books, Perrault's old French fairy tales, Hans Andersen and Grimm. So much did I feel myself to belong to that enchanted world of princesses that I persuaded Alice, a buxom country girl from Porlock Weir in Somerset, who came to us when I was three, stayed for forty years of devoted service and was always ready to play with me, to make me a crown of cardboard painted gold, fastened at the back with one of those brass clips with pointed ends that you pierce through and open out. I hung this on the hall hatstand and on returning from school I always took off my school hat and put on the crown before settling to my homework. Sometimes my brother would steal up behind me and tweak it off, often bringing a tuft of hair with it; but apart from such moments it gave me great satisfaction.

Later I progressed to the world of Greek mythology and later still to King Arthur and his knights, and tales of chivalry. But I remained a denizen of the fairy world, as my first school prizes attest, when at the age of seven we moved from our house in the Victorian part of Bristol to another in the newer suburb of Redland, and I was sent to the Redland High School, nearer our house though still a good mile's walk - a long journey for young legs four times a day.

This school was housed in a medium-sized but noble-looking dwelling that a prosperous Bristol merchant had built for himself in the first half of the eighteenth century. It had the beauty of symmetry, for on each side of the small entrance hall two splendid staircases led to the upper storey. This beautiful house had fine grounds too. A very broad terrace flanked by a pillared balustrade stretched in front of the façade of the building. From the middle of the balustrade twin flights of stone steps led to the sloping garden. If I have dwelt in detail on this building it is because I feel sure that during the eleven years of my schooling there it influenced me in several ways which later enriched my life. First, it gave me a sense of the past, and of the pleasure and privilege of living surrounded by some of its attributes. Secondly, although our teachers never taught us anything about the history of the house, I think that merely by passing my days there I gradually absorbed a life-enhancing interest in architecture. Thirdly, and more subtle than either of these things, was the deep satisfaction that I derived from the beautiful balance of the building, and the symmetry of its design, so that ever since then I always feel that basic, widespread, human need for symmetry, which the ancients considered was bred in us by our own bodies and limbs.

But all that of course came very slowly during those eleven years, when perhaps only the seeds of it were sown. Meanwhile the classroom where I spent the summer days of my first term was also well-suited to my needs. It was in one of the side wings of the building, and it looked on to a small Dutch garden with neatly trimmed box hedges. At the far corner of it a large syringa bush marked a door in the high wall of rosy bricks that separated it from the terrace, and I was at once seized by the magic that a door in the wall holds for many people, even after you have discovered what lies beyond it. I can still feel the appeal of it.

So I fear I must have spent much time dreaming in that first term. But I must also have attacked my lessons with gusto, for although I cannot remember anything about them, it seems that I was already good at English and French, so much so that on my first school report our plump and kindly old headmistress, Miss Cocks, had contented herself with the comment 'Bravo!' For those first French lessons we used the classic little *Early French Lessons* by Henri Bué, which had just come out and was later, I think, to be called *French Without Tears*. I have it still. This early proficiency in French and English developed throughout my school days, though I don't think I was an outstanding pupil and that dreary remark 'Good on the whole' appeared only too often in my reports.

LEGACIES OF CHILDHOOD AND SCHOOLDAYS 1896-1915

I don't of course remember much of the lessons, but I have a vivid memory of the appearance and character of many of the mistresses who gave them, and of what, looking back, I now see was the wholehearted devotion they gave to their tasks. This was particularly evident during the period of the annual Christmas play for which I was often chosen and for which they would not only coach us but even, in their own time, make the costumes themselves. One outstanding instance of that was when we 'did' Beaumont and Fletcher's *The Knight of the Burning Pestle* and I was chosen for the part of the citizen's wife. For this they made me a replica of the black velvet costume worn in Rembrandt's *Portrait of an Old Woman* in the National Gallery, including not only the white bonnet with its two rounded ear-flaps but the intricate Elizabethan ruff. What hours of delicate work that must have taken! This quite short play was an excellent choice, full of fun as it is, and my part of the citizen's wife, good-natured but garrulous, always butting in with remarks, suited me down to the ground, as no doubt my teachers, casting me for it, slyly thought it would. Such was my ease and naturalness on the stage that I dimly remember our headmistress and some London critic she had invited down for the occasion discussing with my parents the possibility of my thinking of a career as an actress. But I had four years schooling still to get through, and by the end of that time, circumstances had changed.

That was when I was fifteen and beginning to take an interest in Elizabethan drama and of course especially Shakespeare. This was fostered in me by an inspired teacher, Elizabeth Rendall, to whom I owe that lifelong enrichment that the love of his plays gives one's mind and language. This must have started earlier than that for at the age of nine I received as a prize (for English) a book that I have never seen mentioned since then. It was called *The Shakespeare Story Book*, by Mary Macleod, with a long and first-rate introduction by Sidney Lee. Her lively and straightforward telling of the plots of sixteen of the plays seems to me much superior to Charles and Mary Lamb's *Tales*, and the many delightful black-and-white line illustrations, which again have stood the test of time, became my visual image of the characters portrayed for long afterwards.

The year after I won this I saw my first professional

performance of a Shakespeare play: *Henry V*. It was a near thing that I got to it, for I believe that some piece of naughtiness on my part had made my father decide that I should not go. But he relented in time and I must have been so uplifted by the experience that on returning home I wrote a note to 'my dear darling Dad' thanking him for letting my mother take me and ending with a post-script 'I will try and be very much better in future'. Not long after this the upper forms of the school began to be taken to the Shakespeare performances by E. F. Benson's company, which in those days travelled to schools all over England. With them I saw *The Merchant of Venice* in which Portia and Bassanio were played by two such beautiful creatures that I have never been able to forget them. Her name was Dorothy Green, and his (which has only this moment swum up from my memory) was Murray Carrington. But the crowning Shakespearean performance I saw in those days was by Forbes Robertson, with his deep and thrilling voice, as Hamlet, after which it was a long time before I could bear to see anyone else in the part.

This was only one of many theatrical experiences in my youth, for my mother in particular had a great love of the theatre, which she passed on to me. My brother and I were in fact taken regularly to the pantomime, the first occasion being to *The Babes in the Wood* when I was four, when I distinctly remember inhaling with relish the intoxicating theatre smell of mingled dust and grease-paint which the descending curtain blew out over the stalls. This was followed by *Peter Pan*, and at the end of my school days I was taken to see Sarah Bernhardt; but I fear that I was so aware of her wooden leg that I failed to fall under the spell of the alleged golden voice, which by then had grown rather high and shrill. I saw Pavlova as the Dying Swan too.

A less exotic but more satisfying theatrical experience of those last school years was provided by an excellent repertory company which had taken over the eighteenth-century Theatre Royal, one of the glories of Bristol. In those days it was far from being the elegant playhouse which, as the Bristol Old Vic, it has now become. Where the orchestra stalls are now was in those days a bare floor with wooden benches where, when one stood up, one could lean one's elbows on the protecting ledge of the dress-circle and talk to those sitting there. But to me this shabbiness was transformed by my sense of the past that it had known. The Administrator of the company was Bridges Adams and the main actors Clive Carey and Muriel Pratt. They had a wide range of plays and either with my parents, or sometimes even alone, I saw nearly all of them, including many of Shaw's plays and also the plays of the Manchester Horniman School, then much in vogue, as well as Masefield's *Tragedy of Man* and *Philip the King*, and many more.

If it was to my mother that I owe my love of the theatre and my addiction to dates and chronology, it was my father who revealed to me country joys. In those days the countryside lay all about the part of Bristol where we lived and my father, who was a great walker, often took my brother and me for week-end rambles. One of my favourite walks took us through Westbury-on-Trym to the beautiful little village of Henbury. Here there were many exciting things, a water-splash across the road for one. I was fascinated too by the long yew hedge in the garden of the old Manor House, and more still by the graveyard of the Church, where was the tomb of Scipio Africanus, a negro slave of the Earl of Suffolk, who was buried there in 1720 at the age of eighteen with an inscription which read:

'I WHO WAS BORN A PAGAN AND A SLAVE
NOW SWEETLY SLEEP A CHRISTIAN IN MY GRAVE.'

an inscription that never failed to stir my imagination. Since then I have always liked graveyards.

Not far beyond this village we came to a gate in the wall bordering the road - once again the magic of a gate in the wall. This led to a path romantically called the Arbutus Grove, which wound up to Kings Weston Down, a vast stretch, splendid to scamper over. I fear that much of that part of the country has since been built over so that now it is, alas, a case of 'farewell happy fields'. But a different haunt that cannot have been spoiled was when we crossed the splendid Suspension Bridge over the Avon to Leigh Woods and picnicked by the Abbot's Pool. Another joy was the Saturday summer afternoons when my father hired a boat at Keynsham on the other side of the city to row us up the Avon, towards Bath, between banks of wild flowers and I lay in the bows lulled by the 'thrilling-sweet and rotten river-smell', and tasted for the first time the spell of rivers, which I have never ceased to feel.

Although we often went to Bath, I didn't then appreciate its eighteenth-century beauty, nor that of the quarter of Bristol that dates from the same period. I found the centre of the city more thrilling in those days, when tall-masted ships came up the river and docked in the very heart of the town, reminding us that Bristol was once a great port from which Sebastian Cabot and his fellow Merchant Adventurers sailed to the western lands - stories that all we children knew. The memory of those things, and our holidays in the neighbouring country, often in the beautiful Quantock Hills, near Holford and Alfoxton Park, make me feel that, in spite of Scottish, English, French and Italian ancestors, my roots are in that most beautiful part of England, the West Country.

This carefree home and school life continued on its even way until the early part of 1914 when I was seventeen and in what, it had been decided, was to be my last school-year. The head-mistress then began to harry me as to what I wanted to do when I left. As I had no ideas of my own she suggested what was then almost the only possible career, that of a teacher, and proposed that I should there and then try my hand at it by teaching pupils in the first form. The mere idea of this filled me with panic. For one thing I had never known any small children, except my one brother, only eighteen months older than myself; and I was not by nature drawn to them, or at ease with them, a thing that they are always quick to realize. During my first attempt to teach them I felt so self-conscious that I could make no contact with them, so I thankfully obtained relief from this task at once.

I think it was that summer that the idea occurred to both my parents that I might go to Oxford. My brother at Clifton College had that year won a scholarship to Sidney Sussex at Cambridge and was to go up in the autumn. My parents had always felt strongly that their daughter should have the same opportunities as their son, than whom I was in any case more studiously inclined. It was already too late for me to pass the necessary college entrance examinations before the following autumn, so that I should be obliged to remain at school for another year. While all this was hanging in the balance, that July I took the Higher School Certificate exam which is, I suppose, the equivalent of the modern A Levels. My results in this were such as to lead the Headmistress to say that, if I decided to remain for another year, I should be Captain of the School - a purely honorary title, as far as I remember, based chiefly on seniority, with no duties attached, except perhaps for the occasional exercise of a little mild authority, which may have helped to increase my self-confidence. This settled the matter and gave me an exhilarating sense of being reprieved.

After the school holidays, my father went to talk over the Oxford plan with my Headmistress. In those happy far-off days it was one's elders who made all the necessary arrangements, a memory that makes me sympathize acutely with the young today, who have to strive so hard by themselves to win the university places they crave. For me St Hugh's was chosen, I expect at the suggestion of the French mistress, Miss Alison Dobbs, whose college it was. Application was at once made and accepted, subject to my passing the college entrance exam, of which more in a moment.

I was naturally overjoyed at the prospect of putting off the choice of a career for another three years, and in the meantime of being allowed to continue the school life which I so much enjoyed. I think my teachers must have enjoyed teaching me too, for I had always been a jolly child, full of fun, but by now I believe I was developing a more adult sense of humour and some wit, as well as wider interests. Whatever the reason, two of them at once volunteered to help me in their spare time, the classics mistress with extra coaching in Greek and Latin for Responsions, then the essential entrance exam for Oxford, as Littlego was for Cambridge; while Alison Dobbs, a noble-looking Irish woman (whom I met again forty years later, when she became a great friend) helped me with my French for the college entrance exam.

It seems strange, looking back, to realize that the decision to let me go to Oxford was made a month after the outbreak of the First World War. But I think it took a long time for ordinary families, like mine, to understand the terrible event that was then beginning. The only one of us who was affected was my brother, who instantly decided in August that he must join up and went off to the local barracks to do so. But without wishing to belittle his motive I can't help thinking that he may have been inspired by an opposite wish of mine, to escape from a life of further study to one of

15

activity. There is also the fact that he was by nature of a very quarrelsome and irascible temperament, not at all an easy person to live with in a small family, as his tempers only too often upset us all. In the event he was at once sent to an officers' training camp at Conway and was to spend the next year or so in what sounded like a pleasant camp life. My mother and I went to see him and his fellow trainees in the following January, and as he seemed popular with them perhaps this form of life had improved him. As we had no other close relations in the services, the war still seemed remote from us.

So my last school year followed much the same pattern as the previous ones. At the end of June I went to Oxford to take Responsions. Although the final Schools were then taking place, the only undergraduates to be seen, where once there had been a throng, were those unfit for the Services. The only notables pointed out to me were Aldous Huxley, who was one of these, and Dorothy Sayers, whom I saw bicycling past Wadham wearing long dangling earrings that looked oddly at variance with her gown. When the exam, which I duly passed, was over, I reported to St Hugh's, as I had been instructed to do, that my school had not been notified of the date of their own entrance exam, which consequently I had not taken. Rather taken aback by this, they promised to send the papers to Redland, for me to take before the end of the school term. But even this they forgot too, so when we broke up I still had not taken it. How odd such casualness seems today!

That summer there was no question of a country holiday, but some cousins had lent us their house in Wandsworth Common for seven weeks, so I had a wonderful opportunity to taste the wider world of London, with all its fine buildings and theatres, in between my provincial life and that of Oxford. When we returned to Bristol at the end of September there was just a fortnight for me to prepare for the great new venture ahead. I presume that my Headmistress must have written during that time to remind the College authorities that I had not taken their exam and perhaps to reassure them about my abilities. As I learnt later from a fellow undergraduate, there was no need for me to worry about this, if indeed I did, for she told me that, although she had not been up to the standard of the exam herself, she was admitted on the strength of her brilliant athletics record at school, as being likely to enhance the reputation of the college in a similar way, as indeed she did.

So I duly went up on 16 October, a month after my nineteenth birthday, was admitted without question and took up residence with my fellow freshers.

Chapter Two

A FEMININE OXFORD
1915-1919

The actual residence which I took up in that first term was far from desirable. A new building for St Hugh's was then under construction at the corner of Banbury Road and St Margaret's Road. Until it was completed we were lodged in Wycliffe Hall, a theological college at the end of Banbury Road near the Parks, whose students had left at the end of the previous term. It was a gloomy, undistinguished building in the Victorian Gothic style, of which the only thing I remember is that the chapel was a long way from my room. As in those days all undergraduates were obliged to attend a certain number of early morning prayers, known as 'keeping chapels', and as I always had great difficulty in getting up in the mornings, I began this part of my Oxford life badly; so much so in fact that on one occasion, when I had to sit next to the Principal, Miss Jourdain, at lunch she remarked that she had not often seen me in chapel. I made some lame excuse about its being a long way from my room, and how I often found the doors closed when I got there. She countered this by saying that I could always go into the gallery, which unfortunately prompted me to say that I was afraid this would interrupt the service because the stairs creaked. 'Do they?' she asked in her dry humourless voice, and changed the subject. After lunch I went to inspect those stairs. They were of stone.

Miss Eleanour Jourdain, better known as one of the authors of the well-known book *An Adventure*, describing the ghostly experience that she and Miss Moberly claimed to have had at Versailles, had only just been appointed Principal. She was a short, plump, white-haired, pink-and-white complexioned woman, whose twinkling but cold blue eyes betrayed neither humour nor much interest in her students. The Versailles story had given us the feeling that she was a slightly spooky person, who just might have second sight. As for her remoteness from us, I think this may have been due to a lack of confidence in herself, which used to manifest itself in an odd way. When she was expecting some important visitor to lunch, even though she had spent the morning working at her desk, and would be returning to it afterwards, she would put on a large flowery hat for the meal, as if to shelter under it.

I found most of the dons rather inhuman, as in those days academic women tended to be, unmarried as they generally were. Except for the history tutor, Miss Cecilia Ady, a jolly woman and outstanding don, with an infectious chuckle, they were in strong contrast to the friendly mistress I had known at school. My own tutor, Miss Wardale, was one of the most academic-looking of them all, and though I dare say she meant well, even her aspect chilled me, as she was rather withered-looking, with tiny eyes behind thick glasses and no warmth of manner. The fact that her subject was language rather than literature perhaps had something to do with the choice I made in this matter.

The English School of Language and Literature was at that time a very new discipline, with which Sir Walter Raleigh, then the Professor of English Literature and an adviser to the University Press, had had much to do. In the latter capacity he had persuaded the press to bring out editions of the English classics, which they had previously despised, thus providing those who were reading English with the texts they needed. The Language side of the School's syllabus was under the philologist Dr Joseph Wright, author of the *Dialect Dictionary*. We were from the outset faced with the choice of which side of the subject we wished to take, but all I knew was that Language entailed a detailed study of Anglo-Saxon, Old English; and Middle English with difficult books like *Beowulf*, whereas Literature meant reading for work just what I wanted to read for pleasure. No wonder I choose Literature. What in practice this choice meant I still do not know, for we all had to attend the same number of lectures and do as much individual work on both aspects of the subject. When it came to our final Schools, it turned out that I had made the wrong choice; but of that later.

Our first weeks in that building seem in retrospect to have been a time of suspended animation, as we felt unable to settle in our temporary cells. But we had time to observe our fellow freshers, whom we met at those traditional cocoa parties at which we entertained each other in the evenings, and to single out those to whom one felt instinctively drawn by some inexplicable attraction, as mysterious as the opposite slight aversion to others.

On our return from the Christmas vacation we had the excitement of moving into our new building, ready at last. This was a pleasant, long, three-storeyed, neo-Georgian building at right-angles to the Banbury Road, with most of its rooms looking south. The fact that it was built at one end of an old tree-planted garden made it look as if it had always been there, as did the wide crazy-paved terrace below the ground-floor windows, which the endearingly eccentric old classics tutor, Miss Rogers, at once began to cram with a myriad small plants, grubbing happily away there in any spare moment.

To my pleasure I was given one of the first-floor rooms near the middle of the building (not far from the chapel this time!). This new little white-walled room, the only one of my own I had ever had except an attic bedroom at home, was adequately furnished with a desk, divan bed and chest of drawers of no particular style. But it gave me a new-born interest in interior decoration, which remained a life-long interest, and I began at once to try and beautify the room. I achieved this with generous help from my brother, now a captain in the Welsh Fusiliers, and over the next two years made an elegant little room of it, with more distinguished furniture, an easy chair, plenty of silk cushions and a few bits of the flame-coloured Ruskin pottery then in vogue.

But there were other things to think about in the first Hilary term, in the shape of two exams. One was Pass Mods, an essential preliminary for those reading English. It consisted of a few Greek and Latin texts, and some Logic, for which we had to take a crash course which I enjoyed but afterwards naturally completely forgot. The other exam, which it may be of some historical interest to mention, was a divinity exam universally known in Oxford slang as 'Divvers'. There was no time-limit for the taking of this and therefore many went on doing so, and failing throughout their years at Oxford. But it had to be passed before final Schools. It entailed a concentrated study of certain books of the New Testament and of the journeys of St Paul. It demanded a parrot-like memory but little else. The actual exam consisted of only one or two papers followed by an oral, at which I remember my slight apprehension was quickly removed by the jovial presence among the examiners of Joseph Wright, the philologist whose acquaintance I had already made and who became a staunch friend. I had decided to get this exam over early, and I duly passed it.

It was while we were sitting those first two exams that the almost undiluted ranks of women undergraduates brought home to me the fact that we were living in a very feminine Oxford, where a male undergraduate was a very rare bird indeed, who presumably had been pronounced medically unfit for the forces.

I don't think the lack of masculine society worried any of us very much, for after all we had never known a normal Oxford life. But I dare say the distraction it would undoubtedly have caused helped to keep us as immature as we were, living as we did in an atmosphere rather like that of a high-grade finishing school, in which a good deal of liberty was allowed and where our interests and affections were centred on each other. The kindred spirits I had found in our first term, as soon as we returned from the Christmas vacation ran together like blobs of quicksilver, growing bigger as time went on until we included not only others of our year but some of the second and third years too, so that we gradually became the dominant group of our year.

Two of those seniors were destined for illustrious careers, ending in Damehood, although at the time we were not aware of their particular distinction. One was Margery Perham, who was reading history. Her life had been saddened at the end of the academic year before by the death of her favourite brother, who had been up with her. I think the gaiety and vitality of our group helped to cheer her, for she sometimes joined in our nonsense; but it was not until she had gone down and we heard that she had immediately been asked to lecture on history to the troops in camp on Salisbury Plain that we realized her brilliance, which continued thereafter to shine more and more brightly. She became a friend for life.

The other was Joan Evans, who was two or three years older than we were and in a privileged position. She was the god-daughter of the Principal, and although she had not taken her B.A. she was reading for her B. Litt. in what we all thought a fascinating subject: medieval jewellery, of which she already had a small collection. This she generously lent us to adorn ourselves when we were acting plays like Yeats's *Countess Cathleen*, for Yeats was then one of our gods. Joan was the only daughter of very elderly parents (and sister of her much older half-brother Sir Arthur Evans, who excavated Cnossos). I think she too was attracted by our abundant vitality. She was in fact one of the rare students whom I kept in touch with in later life, when she showed me much kindness, partly perhaps because I shared her interest in the Middle Ages. But apart from personal generosity to me and many others, she later became a tremendous benefactor to the College in most imaginative and understanding ways, always anonymously, never known to any of us until after her death.

In such pleasant company, then, with those two preliminary exams behind us, we were free to enjoy to the full both the work and pleasures of our University life for the next sixteen weeks, beginning with the Trinity term, heralded on May morning by that moving ceremony on the top of Magdalen tower, when the choristers greet the dawn. I said that we enjoyed our work as well as our pleasures. I at any rate even managed to enjoy lectures. It has always been the fashion at Oxford, especially among the men, to cut these, but women tend to be more conscientious about that kind of thing. What I felt was that one could not possibly read all day long and it was pleasant to go out and about in the mornings. Then, being a slow reader, I often found even a dull lecture useful and provocative in some way. I enjoyed too seeing something of my fellow-undergraduates from the other women's colleges. Most enjoyable of all, perhaps, was the custom of repairing between lectures to the Cadena in Cornmarket Street, for coffee and gossip.

Picturesque personages were not wanting among our lecturers. One such was Dr A. J. Carlyle of New College, who spoke to us from notes so dropping to bits with age where he had folded them over the years that he had difficulty in reading the sentences that had been worn away in the folds.

At the other end of the scale was the Sir Walter Raleigh, who had the enviable gift of so enthralling his audience with his eloquence that one hung on every word in his rich voice and came away filled with a kind of exaltation. On the language side we followed the lectures of Dr Wright, whose subject most of us found boring in the extreme. But we attended them partly because he would jovially threaten us with dire penalties if we did not take down every word he said (and as his books were not then published we had to), partly because we found him an endearing figure with his shabby clothes, his stubby pipe and his Yorkshire accent, and partly because of his goodness and kindness to us at those Sunday tea-parties which he gave with his charming, delicate-looking wife and where we were always welcome.

But the part of our lives that was most enjoyable, especially for those reading literature, was when after lunch in the summer term we took our books to the river and spent long afternoons lying in punts and reading, with a picnic tea to refresh us and sometimes even a picnic supper too, lulled by those unforgettable river-smells and the scent of beanfields in flower drifting over us. More strenuous but no less enjoyable were the occasional afternoons when we scoured the countryside on our bicycles and learnt to love the beautiful villages of the Cotswolds. The expedition that I remember most vividly was the one when we discovered Burford. Among the novels which had come out just before that time, our favourites were Compton Mackenzie's *Sinister Street* followed by *Guy and Pauline*, a romantic tale that appealed to us particularly, partly because it was set in a Cotswold village called Wychford. This was described with so much precision that we felt it must exist, and that we must find it. Could it possibly be Burford? So off we went to see, and when we got to the bottom of the broad and beautiful High Street there, and were leaning on the parapet of the bridge over the Windrush, we were struck by the likeness of the house on the river bank below to the house in the novel. A man was working in the garden and we felt impelled to call out and ask him its name. He looked up at us, immediately grasping from our faces the question in our minds, and said 'In novels it's called "Plashers Mead".' Ever since that day Burford has held a special place in my affections and been the scene of several important happenings in my life.

We had to make do with such country pleasures, for there were few intellectual or aesthetic enjoyments in Oxford in those years. No Union of course, no OUDS and (in those pre-Oxford Playhouse times) little at the Oxford theatre except the annual visit of the D'Oyly Carte Opera Company, when there was a mad scramble to get seats for the Gilbert and Sullivan operas, most of which I saw at that time. Nothing in the way of concerts either, though we enjoyed the beautiful singing of the choristers, especially at the candle-lit evensong at New College. And there was the Bach choir. Many of my friends belonged to this, as they happened to have pleasant voices, and they always returned from the Monday evening practices full of the fun they had had under the conductorship of Dr (later Sir) Hugh Allen, of New College, then Professor of Music; a man cast in Beecham's mould. As I felt left out of all this I went with them on one occasion to ask him if I could join the choir, although I knew I had no voice and couldn't sing in tune. He asked me whether I was sure about this and gave me a short test. After a bar or two he agreed that I was right, but noting my disappointment he said I could come with the others, as long as I didn't open my mouth. What the result of these rehearsals can have been, with a choir in which there were hardly any male voices, I cannot imagine.

I remarked earlier in this chapter how immature we all were when we first went up; we remained so right up to the end of our three years at Oxford. Not only immature but entirely ignorant of what are so curiously called the facts of life, as though there were no others. At any rate I am sure this was true of my closest friends, all of whom happened to be daughters of mothers who were either frigid, like mine, or very elderly and so remote from such matters, or hard and worldly and not interested in their daughters. For all these reasons none of us knew 'what happened', and being, at our age, understandably curious about it we had a talk one evening when we told each other what we supposed occurred.

I think I came nearest the mark as I had derived a few vague ideas from my reading. In the lewder of the *Canterbury Tales*, for instance, there was a good deal about 'swyving', though the glossary was not very explicit about the meaning of the word. I remember one bold character who 'swyved the miller's daughter bolt upright', which sounded rather uncomfortable and not at all voluptuous. Then when I was struggling to read *Genesis* I came across a character called Onan, who was forced to marry his brother's widow, in order to 'raise up seed' to his brother; but as he did not want to do this, when he 'went in unto her', he 'spilled it on the ground'. Now what on earth did all this mean, I wondered? So there we were, with no way of satisfying our natural curiosity, certainly not by questioning our tutors, most of whom I can well believe were as ignorant as we were. We should just have to wait until perhaps one of these days some man would appear and fall in love with us, and explain it all. I thought my chances of this were slim, for though rather witty, vivacious and popular, I was plump, and in spite of my curly, bracken-coloured hair and a good complexion I was not pretty, which in my inexperience I thought one had to be to attract a man. We were all in a highly-charged though innocent state and our feelings occasionally expressed themselves in devotion to the more approachable of our dons.

It so happened that at the beginning of my third year, a new Secretary to the college was appointed. This was a post about equivalent in importance to that of Bursar. She was, I believe, a most efficient secretary, but not an academic and with nothing outstanding about her in the way of looks or anything else. But I immediately developed a real school-girl crush on her. I don't think this displeased or astonished her, as she was used, as I discovered later, to having that sort of effect on young women. She may even have been flattered, for I and one of my friends had just been elected, by the votes of our fellows, joint senior students of the year. But though I think she enjoyed my company, she kept me very much in my place. She told me nothing about her life before she came to the college, I never met any of the friends she talked about, I had no idea of her age and was never allowed to use her Christian name; so Miss H. she always remained and her letters were always signed with her initials. Though she admired my brain, not having that sort herself, she found much fault with my character, especially the jealousy and possessiveness which my passion for her had inspired.

I had never previously given my character much thought, so to learn of these ugly streaks that had suddenly appeared in it was something of a shock. I knew of course that my absorption in her was making me less aware of others and that my friends were puzzled by it, but this did not seem to me actually sinful. However, something that happened during that Christmas vacation did produce a definite guilt feeling. I was staying up for a day or two after term, in order to see as much of her as I could, when I heard from my mother that my brother, who had at last got to France the previous August, was missing. I stifled the thought that I ought to have rushed home at once and stuck to my plan to go two days later. And I fear I may not have been as sympathetic with the grief of my parents as I should have been. My guilt-feeling persisted even after we heard a week later that my brother was safe and well, though a prisoner, as his whole battalion had been captured a month before.

So when I returned at the beginning of the Hilary term I was still in a remorseful state and therefore receptive when she began to tell me about her Anglo-Catholic faith and to try to convert me to it. I had been brought up as a Congregationalist which, as far as I was concerned, merely meant walking on Sunday morning, dressed in my best clothes and wearing an often uncomfortable Sunday hat, to attend a simple little service in a church in Sneyd Park, where I enjoyed the singing and the often eloquent sermons. And that was that. But in her I discovered one who was impregnated with what seemed to me a deeply sentimental adoration of Christ and an agonized awareness of His sufferings, which I simply could not feel. But it appeared that, if I would only confess, all that would change. So chiefly to please her I agreed to go and make the acquaintance of the Cowley Father who was her confessor. He had the romantic name of Lucius Cary and he was a charming man, aristocratic, good-looking and full of humour, just the sort of man I found seductive. I think he must have understood the situation at a glance, knowing her well as he presumably did. But he took to me and I suppose his priestly duty obliged him to support her persuasions. So he lent me books that would enlighten my ignorance, and saw me from time to time to prepare me for confession.

The upshot of all this was that by the summer term I was in a somewhat confused state, not knowing which was the more important, Schools, which I was due to take in the last fortnight of June, or my first confession, which was fixed for the end of that month. But at least I had enough sense to spend the first half of the term concentrating on the essential revision for Schools and then on the ten days of the exams themselves. I don't know what class I hoped or was expected to get, a second I rather think, but I still remember the pang with which I saw my name among the thirds in the lists posted up outside the Sheldonian. It would not be true to attribute this disappointing result entirely to my state of mind at the time, but it was some consolation, when I went to take leave of Professor Wright, and he asked me why I had chosen to specialize in literature rather than language, that he told me my language papers would have got me a first, whereas my literature ones were not at all outstanding. I was distressed to have to tell my parents my results, but if they were disappointed they never said so. And in after life I have never found that my third hampered me in any way, for it was enough to say one had been to Oxford to quell any further questioning.

But in that June I had little time to repine, for the day when I was to make my first confession was near. I had had no guidance as to how I should set about preparing it, so I decided to tackle it as I did my essays, taking a theme and developing different aspects of it. I chose as my theme the seven deadly sins, and tried to fit my little faults, envies, meannesses, selfishness and so on, not forgetting my tendency to jealousy and possessiveness, in under the appropriate headings. But important-sounding sins like lust presented something of a problem where I had to make do with a few impure thoughts, as I had no physical actions to report. What my confessor thought of it of course I do not know, but he duly gave me absolution and I left the church with a sense of relief, but also with that same flat feeling I had experienced after my confirmation, because my hope that I would find myself in some way changed was not realized.

More acute was my realization that now my university life was over and I must leave the city where I felt so much at home, and return to Bristol, which now seemed to me a dull, provincial town where I knew few people and where, because my father had had a stroke the year before, our home life would be quiet and uneventful. There could be no chance of a job as I still did not know what I wanted to do. And, most painful of all, I would have to say good-bye to Miss H. But before I left Oxford in the first days of July I had the good fortune to hear of some work that would keep me there for another year. I had met a girl called Alice Cathrall who was secretary to Dr Charles Singer, a specialist in Greek medicine and biology. His wife Dorothea had conceived a rather half-baked plan of compiling a catalogue of medieval manuscripts on medicinal herbs and flowers. To this end she had got the Radcliffe Camera to reserve a corner in the gallery of the library for her, and was recruiting a team of six or eight graduates with a knowledge of Latin to go through the catalogues of manuscripts and, when they spotted a likely-sounding one, to make a detailed card of it. Anything more hit-and-miss could hardly be imagined, but she was willing to pay what was then a good salary, £3 a week. Alice introduced me and she took me on without question. So after a few days at home I returned to Oxford, got a room at a pleasant lodging-house in the Banbury Road, Mrs Hunter's, and began work.

It must have been this first experience of working in the ordered calm of a great library that gave me the idea that perhaps librarianship would be the ideal career for me, bookish as I was. So I consulted a certain Dr Bannister, whom I do not remember but who may have been the Librarian there. But he took a gloomy view of the idea. Undaunted, I then asked the advice of Dr Percy Simpson who was working on his great edition of Ben Jonson and who had been one of my tutors on Spenser's *Faerie Queene*. He promised to speak to Falconer Madan, the Librarian of the Bodleian, about me, but he got the same answer, this time more forcibly, for Madan said he 'very emphatically' never recommended librarianship to any 'lady' unless she had private means, as it was impossible to make a living at it. In fact he seems to have found the whole idea of having women in a library distasteful! How odd to think that now it is largely a feminine profession. All the same, looking back I feel glad that I was thus frustrated or I would have missed the richer life that awaited me.

My days thus filled with congenial work in splendid surroundings, I spent a happy last year in Oxford. I was still completely infatuated by Miss H., living for the moments of my free time when I could see her. As she was now lodged in rooms outside the College she often needed my services with domestic matters. She obviously enjoyed my company, and my invitations to tea in the town or on the river, where I hired a canoe, chiefly for her. But it always remained very much a *de haut en bas* relationship and she still seemed to regard herself as one appointed to chide me for faults in a way which it never occurred to me to question. Fortunately Father Cary, to whom I continued occasionally to confess, was always ready to see me in the Cowley Mission House where his wise, understanding and amusing conversation restored the balance, because he obviously thought well of me.

Apart from these two I had no friends, but in my last month there came to lodge at Mrs Hunter's a French girl, Hélène Humbert, who was there to learn English, which she already spoke rather well. She had with her several volumes of French poetry, nineteenth-century poets such as Verlaine, Baudelaire and Samain, for which last she had a special devotion. She had a most musical voice, rich and low, and she took to reading this poetry to me in our leisure evening hours, gradually passing on to me her own enthusiasm, not only for the poets but for French literature in general, thus unconsciously opening a door through which I passed into a whole world that was to become a second home for me throughout my life.

For the rest I was deeply happy to be still in Oxford where I fell more and more under the spell of that beautiful city so full of the 'last enchantments of the Middle Ages', which were beginning to be the period of history I loved best. But I knew in my bones that it was now time to go and I was perhaps already looking forward to the wider life I hoped to lead in London, where it was decided that I should go that September, when I would be twenty-three, to learn those secretarial skills that so many young women with vague literary leanings but no precise ideas hope may lead them to the kind of career they crave.

Chapter Three

PASTURES NEW
1919-1921

The establishment at which St Hugh's had suggested I should acquire these skills was a slightly amateur one that two of their graduates, Miss Greig and Miss Gibson, had set up in offices in Southampton Row. Someone, I don't remember who, had booked me a room in one of those small private hotels, little better than boarding-houses, that lined the streets of Bloomsbury in those days, but have now largely disappeared.

Both Father Cary and Miss H. had feared that I might feel terribly lonely in London, where I had only a few distant relations I hardly knew. Father Cary had therefore given me the address of the Church, St Mary Magdalen, Munster Square, where he went at regular intervals to hear confessions and, as this was not far off, I managed to go and see him there on my twenty-third birthday. Throughout the ensuing six months his affectionate letters helped much to make me feel truly befriended.

As the school had only recently been set up there was still only a handful of pupils, ranging from a few school-leavers, then called flappers, to two university graduates, myself and a girl called Phyl Lowe, who had been at Girton and with whom I made friends. As we were too few to divide into more than two classes, the heads did all the teaching themselves. The course covered the usual subjects, but instead of Pitman's shorthand, which even good brains find laborious to learn, we were taught a much simpler system, invented I think by a Cambridge don, which would never have enabled one to get a job with a really rapid speaker but, backed up by my good memory, it served me well enough with hesitating dictators, which I was to find most people are.

All this occupied me fully from Monday to Friday of each

week and gave me a delightful sense of freedom at the weekends, which I spent happily getting to know the parts of London that attracted me - never the City - in solitary rambles. I would take a different district each time and, with the aid of a good map and some guide books, wander slowly along the streets, examining the houses and every now and then resting on a bench to read it up. Such pottering is by far the best way of getting to know a strange city, as I found many years later in Paris.

It must have been on those Saturdays too that I spent part of my time in the Reading Room of the British Museum, though what I was doing there I do not remember. It was Miss H. who had inspired me with the idea of going there, for she frequented it herself in the vacations and had written to me earlier that year, 'I wish you knew this place. It would excite you beyond all things. The sound of leaves being turned over, and faint footsteps, and coughing occasionally, and whispers in this huge place is gorgeous.' I felt the same about it when I got there myself. It was easy enough to get a ticket in those days, as one was not obliged to state what one was studying. And it was always easy to get a seat. I never knew what she was reading there, but when I asked her to suggest what I should, she prophetically mentioned the subject of Abélard and Héloïse, though I don't remember we had ever talked of them and I certainly didn't pursue the idea at that time. From then on, the hours I spent in the Reading Room were to be amongst the happiest in my life and the memory of them came vividly back to me not long ago when I went to the office there, where one has to renew one's ticket at regular intervals. The official in charge, the same man who had been there when I first went, looked at me and said 'You've been coming here a long time, haven't you? Would you like to know the record we have of you?' Whereupon he went to his filing cabinet and, bringing out my card, proceeded to tell me all the addresses from which I had applied in the intervening forty-five years.

My leisure time was also filled with letter-writing, letters home and constant letters to Miss H. As I was beginning to enjoy myself by going to theatres and the Russian Ballet (always in the gallery of course) I had plenty to tell her about; and to my surprise these letters called forth unexpected praise from her, for what she called the beauty of my style.

This made her urge me to work at it as she now felt sure that I might be a writer. Like many young people I had long cherished a hope of that kind myself, though always hampered by the feeling that I had nothing to write about, having no creative imagination. I realized that there is all the difference in the world between letter-writing and creative writing, but all the same her praise was encouraging and made me feel that perhaps at last she was beginning to treat me as an equal rather than as a younger person for whom she was morally responsible. I was to find later that I was mistaken.

In any case I had no leisure to pursue her suggestion, for the secretarial course finished at the end of February, and for the rest of that year I was caught up in a series of fascinating short-term posts. I was in fact what the agencies now call a 'temp', though the posts did not come to me through agencies - there was I think only one, the Women's Employment Bureau - but through fortunate chance meetings which in my case led me so effortlessly from one thing to another that I began to feel there was no need to struggle to find jobs.

The first trifling one came while I was still at the secretarial school, to which Buckingham Palace had applied for someone to undertake a small piece of work in, I think, the Office of the Privy Purse. As I was one of their two senior pupils they sent me. I was given exact instructions how to get into the Palace and then how to find the little room in which I was to work. On a desk there was a mass of documents which I was asked to find some way of classifying. They did not seem to be of any particular interest, though each was about some particular person; but, as it was left to me to decide, I hit upon the brilliant idea that alphabetical order was the thing, and proceeded to arrange them. The job was perhaps a little more complicated than I now remember, but it is difficult to believe that one of the clerks could not have done it; it only took two or three days, and I appear to have given satisfaction. So I returned to the office, well pleased with my first experience and my first fee, with which I immediately bought a pair of antique brass candlesticks from the Old Curiosity Shop in Portsmouth Street, which I thereafter carried round with me to adorn the various lodgings which I inhabited.

It was, I think, also through the school that I heard of my next job, which lasted all March. This was with Bertrand Russell, who was then living in a flat in Prince of Wales Mansions, Battersea. He had a few bits of work which he had to finish by the end of the month. He was rather taken aback when he found that I was scribbling down his dictation in a mixture of shorthand and abbreviated longhand, and said good-naturedly 'I thought you knew shorthand', to which I could only reply that I thought so too, but that as I found his matter difficult to understand I was sure I should never be able to read it back if I took it down in shorthand; but that if he could go a bit more slowly I thought I could manage. So we got along together by these joint efforts. Apart from the work, I enjoyed his company greatly, as I stayed to lunch and often to supper there too, and he often walked home with me. It was on one of these walks, as we leant over Battersea Bridge and I saw him in profile, that I innocently asked whether he had ever thought of wearing a beard, as that was the way I imagined philosophers. He replied 'It's because I have a weak chin that you thought of that, I suppose', and I said it was. But he took it in good part as a piece of youthful sauciness. Apart from such interchanges, never in my life had I had such entertaining conversation. When I told him my main interest was literature, he talked much of books and I remember that he suggested I might enjoy Max Beerbohm's *Seven Men*, which I at once bought and greatly relished.

At the end of the month he told me that he was shortly going to China for a year, but that he had been invited by Trinity College, Cambridge to take up there the Fellowship from which he had been dismissed during the war, when he had been imprisoned as a conscientious objector. He therefore suggested that, before he returned from China, I should go to Cambridge, stay at the Blue Boar at his expense, call on the Master of Trinity to tell him what I was doing and ask to see the rooms he would have, after which I would buy any items I thought he might need and which weren't already there. Presumably he also hoped that by then my shorthand would have improved. Was there such a shortage of good secretaries at that time, I wonder, that he should have been satisfied with me? It sounded a headily responsible programme to the green young creature I still was, though I think I was beginning to combine my ignorance of the world with an unwarranted self-confidence that perhaps took people in. All the same I did not instantly accept his plan, saying I would think it over and write to him about it. When I went home for a little holiday, I found my parents were against the idea, chiefly because they thought it was a long time to wait and might perhaps in the meantime prevent me from getting the good permanent job for which they hoped the expensive secretarial course had fitted me.

I was given the same advice when I went to Oxford in April, but rather on the grounds of his reputation and unreliability, of which I knew nothing; so I obediently wrote and refused the offered post and heard from him no more. I was in Oxford at that time because I had heard, I don't know from whom, that Gilbert Murray wanted some temporary secretarial help, so I applied, was accepted, and began work with him at once. I say 'with him' but in fact for the first fortnight I was almost completely at the beck and call of his wife, Lady Mary. She was a typical aristocratic espouser of good causes, a dominating character, and the cause for which she was then working was 'Save the Children', a charity which had, I suppose, sprung up at the end of the First World War. Her daughter, the handsome Rosalind, married to Arnold Toynbee, was helping her mother with it, and before I knew where I was I was swept in too. At Lady Mary's bidding I had immediately to go and do a day or two's work at Brasenose for Michael Holroyd*, who was I think helping her in some way. There again I had the pleasure of occasional talk about literature, and when I had finished my job he gave me a copy of the poems of William Cory, whose lovely lyric 'They told me, Heraclitus' I have ever since connected with those Brasenose days.

Much less to my taste was Lady Mary's demand that I should help her with a flag day she was organizing in Oxford. Shy of young men as I was, for I still knew none and was in any case self-conscious, the mere idea of standing at the corner of Folly Bridge, as she wanted me to, and approaching groups of undergraduates then just assembling for the summer term filled me with fright. So I tried to refuse but Gilbert and I were overborne and I had to spend the day

*Footnote: He was the son of Sir Charles Holroyd, the Director of the National Gallery, and no relation at all of Michael Holroyd, the present well-known biographer.

in Oxford with my box. After one or two unsuccessful attempts I gave up, hid the box, and spent a happy day in the town, returning to their house at evening with the empty box and saying I had had no luck. Whatever she thought of this there was nothing she could do about it. But I was greatly relieved when, a fortnight later, she left for Vienna, taking with her a large quantity of chocolate for the starving children; unfortunately it was stolen on the journey. I then, much more happily, began work for the professor, whose courtesy and consideration made it a delight to work for him.

But there was one jarring note in that otherwise harmonious period, and that was caused by the strange and, to me, inexplicable behaviour of Miss H. She had at first seemed to welcome the idea of my return and had sent me addresses of houses where I might get rooms. In early May she asked if I would like to take her to the OUDS, which I gladly did, as I always took her to things, or gave her things, she wanted. But ten days later, after I had been one day to Eights Week with a friend and seeing her there asked her, perhaps a shade jealously, whom she was with (for it will be remembered that I was never allowed to meet her friends,) I suddenly got the first of a series of cruel letters, harshly upbraiding me for going back to Oxford at all, and saying I must go away at once. What could have caused this? Was the friend she was with another of the freshers she was taking up (I knew I already had a successor) and was her behaviour in this way, and perhaps her friendship with me, getting her a bad name with the College although I never went near it at the time? I was given no explanation. This treatment of course made me wretchedly miserable but curiously enough did not alter my devotion, though I was still her slave rather than the equal friend I had hoped I had become. All the same I never dreamt of obeying her command that I should leave Oxford before the job ended (she clearly gave no thought to my work.)

I was sad when, at the beginning of July, those two months of work ended and, as nothing else had turned up, I went back to Bristol for my first holiday break since the summer before. My mother must have been glad of my help, for our faithful Alice had had to leave us temporarily to look after her own dying mother. But I can't have been unhappy then for in Miss H.'s letters, which had become normal again as soon as I left Oxford, she said things like 'Your letters always make me laugh aloud' and 'Your faithfulness and absurdity are alike comforting'. But although I was clearly enjoying some leisure I was always on the lookout for possible jobs, and one day went up to town to consult the one and only employment agency which neither then nor indeed ever, had anything to offer me. So I continued to trust in my chance-meeting system through the few friends I had made and who once again did not fail me.

My fellow-student at the secretarial school, Phyl Lowe, had in the meantime become secretary to Canon Tom Pym, the Head of the Cambridge House Settlement in the Camberwell Road, and she asked me if I could take her place while she had her month's leave in September. This was a very different experience from my two former jobs, but what might have been the perhaps boring 'good works' side of it was enlivened and even made funny by the personality of Canon Pym, a tall, fair-haired, ruddy-faced, youthful man, full of humour and very easy to get on with. The large Mission House occupied premises at the corner of the Camberwell Road and a side street leading to Addington Square, where there was a women's hostel called Talbot House, which was, I think, connected with the Mission and where I lived for that month. At the end of the month I went home to spend my twenty-fourth birthday.

In October I got another temporary job at the League of Nations. The secretariat was then housed in Sunderland House* in Curzon Street. My friend Alice Cathrall had left Dr Charles Singer and become a member of the League's Personnel Department, or perhaps even the head of it, as it was she who had written to offer me a job helping with the preparations for their move to the new Palais des Nations in Geneva in October. I thoroughly enjoyed this and met there many of the officials whom I was to see again later in Geneva. Less enjoyable were the quarters which were all I could find to live in: a really horrible hostel in Warwick Square, Pimlico, where I had appalling meals, and a bedroom in a neighbouring house with a grim bathroom. Towards the end of October I saw the secretariat off at Victoria, where they all arrived in a great fluster, and then went back to Sunderland House to help Alice tidy up.

*Footnote: Now the Curzon Cinema

When that was over, I had no time to feel abandoned in any way, for I had already heard that both Canon Pym and Mrs Taylor had some work they wanted me to do. I returned at once to Talbot House, which now seemed friendly and homelike to me. It proved a fortunate as well as a happy return, for I had there another of those meetings that led to my being offered another temporary job, which I found fascinatingly different from any work I had previously done. This encounter was a social one at which I met Lorna Southwell, that very distinguished graduate of St Hugh's, who was a friend of Tom and Dora Pym. She was at that time secretary to Dr Crichton Miller, the psychoanalyst, and apparently saw in me the right person to take the place for two months of the secretary at his nursing home Bowden House, in Harrow, while she was on leave. I of course accepted Lorna's suggestion, and it was immediately settled that I should go to Bowden House for the following January and February.

But before that there was a very exciting event; the first degree-conferring ceremony in which women had ever been allowed to participate in Oxford. They had been officially recognized as women students since 1910, and could be entered for University examinations, but they were not considered eligible for degrees until 1920. Many days must, I suppose, have been devoted to this ceremony, to deal with all the past women students. My day was 25 November. The ceremony itself was in the Sheldonian Theatre, where it is still held. For all of us it was a most exciting occasion, a revival of our happy undergraduate days, but I doubt whether we realized fully what a historic moment in the lives of women in Oxford we were celebrating.

I enjoyed life at Bowden House from the start, but particularly enjoyed working for Dr Crichton Miller, a shrewd Scot with a great sense of humour. His idea was that the patients and the staff should all live and eat together, so that the former - not a great many of them - should have the impression of life in a normal country house. This worked very well and, as we all had some idea of the degree of illness of the patients, we all had some sense of responsibility for them, even when Crichton Miller himself was not there, either working in Harley Street or at home.

My own work there was very different from any of the

other jobs I had done, for this was no mere shorthand and typing affair. I had charge of all the files of the patients, which I found absorbing reading. The parts of the notes which the doctor wrote in Latin were especially illuminating, and I remember how taken aback he was when he found I could read them. But after all one could hardly have worked for a psychoanalyst, a profession of which I had previously known nothing, without becoming acquainted with a wide range of sexual practice, let alone perversions. So what with all that and the reading of such classic works as the six volumes of Havelock Ellis, I soon became more informed, theoretically at least, on those questions that had so puzzled me at Oxford. But there was one thing I always resisted and that was the doctor's suggestion that I myself should be analysed, as all the rest of the staff had been. As I was not aware of any inhibitions in myself and couldn't think of any problems I had, I saw no reason for this.

After that was over, and since nothing else was in the wind, this seemed the right time to concentrate on my personal interests instead of thinking of other secretarial work. In the fourteen months since I finished at the secretarial school I had after all had six most interesting jobs, enlarging my knowledge of the world in various directions, superficially but enough to give me more self-confidence; but no holiday. So I was quite happy to return to Bristol for a few weeks which I found an ideal time for plunging once again into that reading of French, chiefly modern novels, which I had much neglected since my first enthusiasm for the language had been roused by Hélène Humbert in Oxford nearly two years before. My reason for this concentration at that moment was that I had been invited to go to Paris for the first time in my life on 1 June. I stayed first with Hélène in her parents' flat at the top of the Boulevard St Michel and she showed me some of the sights of Paris, after which I went on to stay for a month in Neuilly, where one of my Oxford friends, Joyce Chapman, was living with her husband, Elliott Felkin, who was then working with the Disarmament Conference. They took me to many of the main museums - the Louvre, Cluny etc. - as well as for leisurely days at Versailles. I revelled in it all and especially in the first faint whiff I got of life in Paris.

Back in England in mid-August I returned to Talbot

House, where Tom had suggested to me a job of a different kind from any I had done before. He thought it would add to the importance of Cambridge House if an economic bulletin were issued there. He had secured the services of a young economist, John Rowe, who would write it, and he needed a research assistant. We would work in a basement room below the library and I of course would continue to live at Talbot House. Although I knew nothing of economics and the work did not tempt me greatly - it would mean going to various ministries, such as the Board of Education, for the material he needed - I felt so at home in Talbot House and Cambridge House that I accepted, and returned to Camberwell to begin work there in November. It was a kind stroke of fate that I did, for I met there the friend who gradually changed the course of my life and made it the happy existence it ever afterwards remained.

Working in the library there at that time was a young woman called Ethel Whitehorn, two and a half years older than I. She had been looking for some voluntary work when Dora Pym, whom I think she knew slightly, had suggested that she might help there one or two afternoons a week, and also on the same evenings at the club. The rough boys and girls who came there scared me, who merely thumped the piano for dancing, but Ethel had just the right knack of dealing with them, knowing how to keep trouble-makers in order by a mixture of kindliness, understanding and presence. I had already met her once or twice in August, but in November I began to see more of her, for she used to pop down from her library to cheer me up when there were no visitors there, hurrying back up when she heard footsteps. We had taken to each other at once, each realizing that we were of the same breed, as it were, unlike the other residents of Talbot House, where she stayed on to supper on club nights. What she saw in me I don't know, unless it was my fun and enjoyment of life; but what attracted me to her was not only those same qualities but her looks, for she was tall, slim and well-built, with a noble head with wavy rich brown hair, fine features and very expressive grey-green eyes. Looking at her it occurred to me that never previously in my life had I known anyone who was really beautiful as opposed to merely pretty. And of her splendid looks she was quite unaware.

When she discovered in our snatches of talk that I knew no one in London, she invited me one Sunday in November to tea at her parents' house in Hampstead, where she lived with her two sisters. It was a large house at the corner of Chesterford Gardens and Langland Gardens. I was made very welcome by her charming distinguished mother, whom Ethel adored, and who seemed pleased that her daughter had made an English friend after many foreign ones. As a result I was invited frequently to spend whole Sundays in December and January, and in the long conversations which Ethel and I enjoyed we gradually learnt more about our past lives. She had the most to tell and quite dazzled me with the stories of her adventures over the last nine years, always told with wit and point and excellent mimicry.

Her parents had sent her to Swanley Horticultural College in 1912 as she had always had a great love of the land and would like to have been a farmer. There were several foreign students there and she instinctively took to one called Elizabeth van Rysselberghe, always known as Beth, three years older than herself who took to her too and became her closest friend. The two-year course had ended just as the 1914 war broke out, and Ethel, first with Beth but later alone, spent a great part of the war years in Scotland, sometimes working in a famous private garden of a house called Charleton, but also in farms in bleak Fifeshire and once on another in Buckinghamshire where, she said, she had one of the happiest times of her life, helping the farm labourers in all their tasks, even the dirtiest jobs, and sometimes going with the farmer to the local hunt.

But the first two years of this tough work in the bitter cold of Scotland began to tell on her health, so she got a doctor's certificate which enabled her to accept Beth's invitation to go and recuperate for six months at her parents' home at St Clair near Le Lavandou in the South of France. There she was welcomed like an extra daughter by Beth's father Théo van Rysselberghe, a strong, dark, virile Flemish painter, and his keen-minded, literary, small and elegant wife, Maria, whose house was a centre for their intellectual friends and some of their children. Ethel must have seemed like a breath of fresh air to them and it was clear to me that they must all have taken to her at once, appreciating her humour and uncomplicated character. She fitted in well too, for though no intellectual herself, she had an instinctive ability to seize the quality of the books they put before her – as one of them said later *'elle a toujours le sens des choses'*. I know that the children too adored their young-old playmate, for much later on, two of them, Monique Schlumberger and Maiène Copeau, told me how they called her the Commander because she turned them into sea-dogs and taught them to sing *'Britannia Rules the Waves'*, and sea shanties.

The friendships she formed during that visit were to endure and be among the most important in her life. But it was time now to leave and return to her Scottish farms. Before coming back, however, as she felt now so much at home in France, she worked for a time as an ambulance driver at the Scottish Women's Hospital which had been established in the magnificent Abbey of Royaumont, outside Paris, founded by Saint Louis; and also on a farm in Normandy belonging to Jean Schlumberger. But the end of the war was now approaching, so she had only a short time to spend in her Scottish farms again before the Armistice. After that she returned to her French friends, since they now regarded her as part of their family and wanted to take her with them to visit their Belgian and Luxembourg friends whom they had not seen for four years. She must have been as great a success in Luxembourg as she had been in France, for during the next two years she made frequent visits to different friends there as well as to Paris and on one occasion André Gide took her to see Berenson in Florence. Wherever they took her she was never self-conscious, quite ready to speak the odd mixture of French she had picked up by ear from peasants, *poilus* and intellectuals, which never failed to amuse the French. Though never strong on tenses and genders, as time went on she learnt by means of her quick ear to speak excellent idiomatic French, while always retaining her ability to be funny in it, as she was in English too.

Compared with all that I felt I had nothing interesting or amusing to relate, for my stories of undergraduate life in Oxford, and even my subsequent jobs seemed tame and unadventurous by contrast, as indeed they were. But to her, who had neglected her studies at school, my pursuit of literature seemed admirable and my Oxford degree a wonderful achievement. For although she was no bookworm, she must have had a real love of English poetry, as I was to discover many years later when I came across three black notebooks, their pages thickly covered with poems she had copied out in her youthful but already beautiful hand, and obviously much read. So when I told her of my lately-born enthusiasm for French literature and my desire to know more of it, I felt I had fallen into the right hands, for she could tell me so much of the writers she had met, who were among the most important of the *avant-garde* group which had just founded the *Nouvelle Revue Française*, which dominated the French literary world for years to come.

Those times of talk on my visits to Chesterford Gardens were enlivened by many other pleasures too. I found Ethel had a charming singing voice, a mezzo soprano, and a host of songs: English and French folksongs, the Elizabethans and Purcell, Schubert and Schumann and Negro spirituals.

Then suddenly one day Ethel told me that towards the end of February she and her younger sister Peggy were going to the South of France to meet her brother Roger at Marseilles, on his way back from Ceylon where he was a civil servant. They intended to make a little tour of the places round Avignon with him, and after that she would leave them and go on herself to make the first of her newly planned three-monthly visits to Beth to help her at a beautiful old farm in Provence, which she was running for their rich Luxembourg friend Emile Mayrisch. It was really more of a vineyard than a farm, as there was very little livestock; but there was also a large garden with which Beth wanted Ethel's help. This was heart-stopping news for me. My lovely new week-end life was coming to an end. Although Mrs Whitehorn said I must often go up to see her, which I did, what I had felt to be at last the perfect friend I had always wanted would no longer be there. Brightness fell from the air.

Chapter Four

OUT OF BONDAGE
1922-1923

The skies were not uniformly dark, however, for in the few weeks of February before she set off she had dropped occasional hints that there might just be a chance of my joining her and Beth. But she must have spoken of me in very glowing terms, for I soon got a warm letter from Beth herself saying she would be delighted if I would come for the last month of Ethel's stay. My anticipations heightened by Ethel's frequent letters, which were always amusing, I set to work to save. This wasn't easy, for the second-class fare to Toulon was £9 13s and I should obviously need much more than that. How was this to be managed when I only earned £3 a week and had to pay 35 shillings for my board and lodging at Talbot House? But the generous-minded Phil encouraged me by saying that, if we both gave up all the little treats we used to enjoy on our half-days, she was sure I could do it. She characteristically gave no thought to what she would get out of this austere programme. Thus encouraged I managed to save £10, after which I appealed to my parents, who were so pleased I was going to have a holiday, that they at once doubled the sum, and my brother, always generous, added another fiver.

So I felt amply provided when on 1 May I set off to France and took the night train to Toulon, sitting up in my corner and getting grimier and grimier - there were no couchettes in those days. Who can ever forget the thrill of the first glimpse of the south in the early morning sun; the blinding quality of the light, the chalk-white dusty roads, the grey-green olives and the tall black spires of the cypresses? And then, when you get the first glimpse of it, the peacock sea. When we reached Toulon, there, on the platform, was Ethel, almost unrecognizably tanned after those weeks in the open air and the sun. She took me to lunch in a little restaurant along the shore, and then we had an afternoon's wait for the two little local trains that took us to a halt outside Brignoles, where Beth awaited us in a trap drawn by a rather rickety-looking horse called Pepino, which took us through country roads to one where a lane branched off to the Domaine de Franco, the proper name of what was generally referred to as the Bastide. This was an old, sober-looking, not very big two-storey house, standing alone at the foot of a considerable mountain.

But in those already hot days of May the world outside was the chief attraction. On a strip of land beyond the gravelled entrance stood a large stone table where we took our delicious meals in the shade of four huge pollarded plane trees. A narrow canal cut this piece of land off from the main square-walled garden, which was reached by a small stone bridge over the canal. At evening, when the shepherd came down the slope beside the entrance, leading his little flock, the scene had an idyllic quality; and as we ate our supper by lamplight, the harsh yet melodious croaking of the frogs everywhere seemed to me to sum up all the voluptuous pleasures of the south, as it has done ever since, especially when I discovered the beauty of those tiny viridian tree-frogs with their golden eyes, crouching between the main trunks and the branches of the cypresses.

All the working parts of this delightful house were hidden behind it: the farmyard with its specially selected breed of poultry in which Emile Mayrisch took great pride and the rooms for the breeding of the silkworms, a most complicated affair. Caramello, the farmer, and his wife had their quarters there, as had the maid Marichen. Beyond a nut-grove were the vineyards, which produced only a mellow golden wine. One whole field grew superb muscat grapes.

Fortunately Beth, a small, energetic woman, very sunburnt, with short dark hair, brilliant brown eyes, and a passionate, strong-willed nature, took to me at once, saying she had never seen anyone look so happy. But here I must mention the fact that the friend I had hitherto known as Ethel was everywhere called Whity. I had never liked the name of Ethel, both in itself and because I felt it didn't suit her; it was so stiff. At Swanley her fellow students had shortened her surname, as students do, and so it was as Whity that Beth had first known her. As this was easier for all foreigners to pronounce, all her subsequent foreign friends took their cue from Beth, and over the years it was to acquire the individuality it obviously had for all of them, so that I fell into the use of it too whenever we were in France. So after some thought I have decided to refer to her by that name in the French part of this narrative, but as Ethel in the purely English parts.

During the days that followed my arrival we settled to a pleasant routine. All the morning Whity worked hard with Beth in the big garden with its innumerable small beds and plots full of flowers and vegetables, but no green lawns or other such Englishry - not what I would have called a pleasure garden. While they were at work I had wonderful leisure to enjoy the new books that lay everywhere in the living-room and so read my way into the literary world on the fringes of which I was now living. After these mornings we rested in the heat of the afternoon and later strolled along the many little paths beside the river Caramy. Other enjoyments often broke this routine too. A young neighbour of Beth's had a car and took us for drives to those Provençal places with such lovely names as Gonfaron, La Garde Freinet and Grimaud. We took picnics with us and I remember getting a wonderful sense of the ease of life in those past days on one occasion when we were driving along one of the wide avenues that then led out of Hyères, and saw that men were picking the cherries on the trees that bordered it. We called to them and they agreed to fill a huge round open basket we had with us in return for a few bottles of Beth's golden wine and some cigarettes. To eat those huge sun-warmed cherries was paradisal.

Beth's mother was staying at the Bastide at that time. Physically she was quite unlike her daughter, who took after her father, and Whity had compared her to a blue tit, because she was small and exquisite like that elegant bird. Her face was framed in curly white hair and her delicate features were ivory white. She had a keen critical mind and was known in the literary world, especially in that advanced circle where she was a kind of Egeria, as la Petite Dame. So here again there is a name difficulty. Her daughter and her intimate French friends eagerly adopted the name Tit, which she herself liked, so although it sounds slightly absurd in

English ears, I fear I must keep it, only using La Petite Dame for more formal occasions. She was already secretly compiling, unbeknown to him, her records of the conversation of André Gide, the god of them all, which were to be published in four large volumes more than fifty years later, after his death, and in which the name of Whity constantly recurs and mine too sometimes. With her we went one day to St Clair, where she lived with her husband, the painter Théo.

During the long uninterrupted talks that Ethel and I had during that month of May we discovered how widely different were the tastes and interests that had formed our childhood and youth. I learnt that, while I was plunged in fairy tales and myths, she cared nothing for them but was, even at an early age, dazzled by the mystery of the stars. Her parents had given her a tiny telescope, through which she gazed at them out of her nursery window, and so began to have a childish conception of the marvels of the universe and of the smallness and unimportance of man, which surely was rare for one so young. She continued to feel it strongly throughout her life as I know from a letter she wrote me when she was abroad many years later, in which she said 'the thought of my insignificance before the countless and eternal stars has always been my chief source of comfort and exaltation, but to most, I know, it is just despair'.

Another influence which had shaped her was that of a young Sikh, H. S. Malik, whom her father had met and befriended when he was at school in Eastbourne, and who talked to her of Eastern philosophies and beliefs, giving her Tagore to read. My accounts of the Anglo-Catholic faith into which Miss H. had led me, of my confessions, and indeed of Miss H. herself must have seemed almost incomprehensible to her who had been brought up in a typically Protestant household where her gentle, pious father read family prayers each morning to everyone, including the servants. She had rebelled against all that in late adolescence, a rebellion her father accepted. But she listened to me without criticism, comment, or questioning, accepting that if that was what I had chosen, it must be right for me.

On our way home at the end of the month we stopped for two days in Avignon, for Ethel was determined that I should see that cluster of superb cities whose acquaintance she herself had only just made, knowing how they would appeal to my love of the Middle Ages and the classical past: Nîmes, Arles, Uzès, Tarascon, and the Pont du Gard too. We stayed for two or three nights in Paris and had a meal with Gide and Jacques Copeau, the actor, one of the founders of the *Nouvelle Revue Francaise*, whose theatre, Le Vieux Colombier, was part of the whole avant-garde movement. We saw a rehearsal of Gide's *Saül* there, and went with Jean Schlumberger to *Les Frères Karamazov*. It was then that I realized why it was that these leaders of the French literary and artistic world liked Whity so much; for they were accustomed to adulation from their fellow-countrymen, but Whity, with no thought of herself, was entirely natural and at home with them, regarding them as the ordinary human beings they after all were, a treatment to which they responded with equal simplicity, charmed by her wit and gaiety. It was a lesson I was slow to learn.

My return to my dreary job in Camberwell was once again enlivened by Ethel's visits to the library during the two months it remained open. So those remaining months of 1922 could have been a calm and happy time for me if it had not been for the extraordinary behaviour of Miss H. I had introduced Ethel to her before we went to the Bastide and she seemed happy enough about my going and wrote me one or two normal letters while I was there. But on our return, although my feelings for her had in no way changed and I continued to write to her as affectionately as ever, she suddenly began to torment both Ethel and me by a bewildering series of often incomprehensible accusations. The main motives of them were, I think, twofold; the fear of losing me, not so much for myself but for the whole-hearted service I paid her, and the desire to make a personal friend of Ethel, to whom she was clearly greatly attracted. When Ethel did not respond to invitations from her, Miss H. turned against her, accusing her, in her letters to me, of selfishness for thinking only of me. She was obviously in a very unbalanced state, as she was then turning against Father Cary and other former friends in Oxford, where she was no longer at St Hugh's but working privately for a degree.

In September she thought of a plan which would enable her to live in London and win me back to join her there. She heard of a newly-formed housing company, with the grim name of 'The Lady Workers' Homes', who were building flats in Elm Tree Road in St John's Wood. To secure the lease of one of these flats one first had to become a shareholder in the company. I had no wish to live with her but I thought that if I could persuade my parents to let me buy the necessary but quite small number of shares with some money, then in War Loan, which they had been putting aside for me every year since my birth, I should have done my part. Bewildered though they were, and realizing I was being pressurised by Miss H. whom they had never met, but too nice to question me about it, they agreed. By means of similar action by another of her friends the lease was secured, and this friend did agree to share the flat.

But even this did not stop the persecution and the climax was yet to come. I was to get my MA Degree (which at Oxford is something you merely pay for, after a suitable lapse of time) at the end of November. Ethel went down to Oxford with me for this ceremony, and we stayed in rooms together. The day after the ceremony Miss H. invited us both to tea with her and after tea asked me to leave the room, which, though puzzled, I did, whereupon she burst into a tirade against me, reeling off to Ethel the old list of my moral shortcomings: selfishness, jealousy, possessiveness, no thought for others and was therefore a person whom Ethel could not decently know. She then called me back and told me what she had done. Ethel, bewildered and sickened by this performance, left the house and went for a long solitary walk to get it out of her mind, while I remained for a time and then returned to our lodgings, wondering whether Ethel would be there and afraid lest this horrid scene should have had some effect on her. I ought to have known her well enough by then not to doubt. She was waiting for me and as soon as I saw her steadfast loving look I knew that nothing had changed, that she was one 'that looks on tempests and is never shaken'; and that from then onwards her perfect friendship would always understand me, whatever I did, and support me to the end of her life. As indeed it did.

So all that Miss H. had achieved by her efforts to separate us was the breaking of the spell that had so long held me. I was out of bondage at last. But curiously enough Miss H. herself did not seem to have realized this and for the first two months of the next year she continued what Ethel characteristically called her 'soul-drill' of me, by letter. She obviously regarded me as a nearly lost soul; and when I told her that I might soon be going to the Bastide she wrote asking me neither to write nor to go to see her 'until you are a changed person'. And finally 'I do not expect this letter to have any effect on you'. I was only too glad to obey her command that I should not write. But what *was* the meaning of it all? Jealousy, or was she perhaps a religious maniac?

A month after that painful episode in Oxford, I left Camberwell for good, for things had greatly changed. In any case my mother wanted me at home for a while to help her in the house - our dear Alice was still away - and to help entertain my brother, who was then on leave from his job with a cotton broker in Bombay, where the climate had done nothing to improve his irascible temper. I left London.

But Ethel and I weren't downcast at the thought of this separation, for something had happened at the end of the previous August which held out the promise of another idyllic stay at the Bastide in the spring. On returning from her summer holiday with the family, she found an urgent invitation to go and spend a few days at Colpach in Luxembourg, the house of her friends the Mayrischs. While she was hesitating whether to go or not she got a letter from Beth, telling her the reason why they all wanted her. Beth had never made any secret of the fact that she wanted a child, but did not wish to marry, a rather brave decision at that time. Her mother supported her daughter in her wish; and it should be said that the whole question was treated in a sober manner, for there was nothing bohemian or Bloomsburyish about the van Rysselberghes. Whity knew that Beth had a young lover, whom she saw occasionally, but when nothing came of this, the whole question I think faded from her mind. But now that she heard Beth was pregnant, the changes that all that would bring in her great friend's future life deeply disturbed her. The fact that she did not then know the paternity of the child, a great secret which was not to be known for many years, was also upsetting to Whity, who was so close to Beth. So no wonder she was disturbed when she returned home and told me all about it.

The reason why they had all wanted to see Whity at that moment was to ask her if she could run the Bastide for Beth when the time came for her to conceal her condition from the farm people, who would have to be given some convincing reason for her absence and subsequent return with a so-called adopted baby. Whity was the obvious choice to replace Beth as she knew the place, the work and the people, who all liked her. Madame Loup Mayrisch, Emile's wife, generously offered to look after Beth when she had to go away; and I suppose the only person who wasn't entirely pleased was Emile, who had after all bought the Bastide to give Beth a job, and here she was giving up her responsibility for it, at least temporarily. But he had great confidence in Whity and great affection for her too, so all were happy when she accepted.

I don't think that at this time there was any question of my going also, to help Ethel, but by Christmas she was certainly thinking of it, as was I, and the hope of it kept me going during the two difficult months with my brother, who was in a particularly excitable state as he was contemplating marriage to an Irish girl whom he had met on his first voyage to India and kept in touch with when she returned to Ireland. He had endless conversations with me about it, as I was supposed, after my sojourn at Bowden House, to be an authority on such matters as contraception and pregnancy, to which he hoped that his marriage might not immediately lead. I did my poor best, but eventually nature proved cleverer than I! The Irish girl having accepted him, he brought her to Bristol on 1 February and they were married on the 5th at our local church. After their short honeymoon they returned and then stayed at our servantless house for a short time. Eric, none the sweeter-tempered for his new state, often greatly upset my father.

Fortunately they often went away to visit relations in the last weeks of February, so I felt free to go with Ethel to the Bastide at the beginning of March, as Beth and her mother had gladly agreed that I should. When we arrived we found Tit waiting to settle us in. Knowing that I was quite inexperienced in domestic matters, she stayed with us for ten days, helping by letting me order the meals, and giving me excellent advice on how to treat a servant. But Marie, the good little Italian maid they had found, was not only a good cook but so excellent a servant I never had to use this advice.

As soon as we were on our own, we established a routine. Whity of course did all the gardening and 'oversaw' (in so far as there was any need) the more than competent farmer

Caramello, who attended to the vines and the livestock. Beth kept bees too and Whity, who had learnt how to treat them at Swanley, helped with them. Another daily job for her was to climb the row of mulberry trees flanking the garden and strip the branches of their leaves to feed the silkworms whose complicated culture we had watched the year before, and at which Madame Caramello was an expert.

While all this was going on I led what seemed to me the most perfect life, with no responsibility except ordering the meals. So I was free all morning to try and write, concentrating chiefly on a short history of English literature for Whity, and some critical articles which I fear must have been pathetically jejune. I worked at Italian grammar too and had endless time for reading, sometimes reading aloud to Whity. It was just at that time that the first volumes of Proust began to appear and I was living in the ideal circumstances to begin reading them.

This daily routine was broken by some visits from the Mayrischs. Emile came first, bringing his daughter Andrée with him. She was a great friend of Whity's as she had been a student at the School of Economics in 1919 and, like me in later days, spent her week-ends at Chesterford Gardens, where she had become a great favourite with Mrs Whitehorn. The first time he came was partly to see how his farm was getting on in Beth's absence. He came again with Loup at the beginning of May, this time bringing their servants, as they were to stay for a few days at their house, called Malbuisson, in the woods near Bormes-les-Mimosas. Whity and I were invited to stay the night and there for the first time I heard a nightingale, as one sang outside my window all night. The next day Loup drove us to Cannes by the inland route through the Forêt du Dom and the Esterel and back by the coast road to St Clair, dropping us for a short visit to Théo in whose house I had felt so much at home after last year. This first opportunity I had had of a longer acquaintance with Loup Mayrisch was to have an important consequence for me, for when Whity (whom Loup called 'England') told her of my interest in French literature and desire to become more knowledgeable about what was happening in that then lively world of writers, she suggested that I ought to attend one of the famous conferences at Pontigny which, during those inter-war years, were of outstanding intellectual importance. She thought that I might perhaps go in the following year, and as she had great influence with the organizers of it, her recommendation made it virtually certain that I would be accepted, because a small number of younger people was always included. I still remember the deep pleasure that Loup's suggestion gave Whity, who had always vowed that she would do all in her power to help me attain my desire in this matter. Loup kept her word and in the next year, 1924, I duly went to Pontigny, which was to become one of the great events of my life. But more of that later.

A few weeks before that, we had an expedition of a very different kind. On 13 April we had gone to Marseilles to see my brother off to India. He was returning alone because his wife had, in spite of all efforts to the contrary, become pregnant and wanted to stay at home to have her baby. What a strange character Eric was! After those stormy times in Bristol, here he was in his jolliest and most generous mood. He had taken the trouble before leaving London to find out from the Whitehorns that the 13th was Ethel's birthday, so he insisted on standing us lunch at Basso's, the famous fish restaurant on the harbour, and not only that but paying all the expenses of our journey and our night in a hotel, which we had to leave the next morning before actually seeing him off. Over that lunch he told us of a strange incident that had happened at home shortly before he left. My mother had told him one morning at breakfast that, the night before, my father had wakened early and said to her in his ordinary voice (for his speech since his stroke had been slightly blurred) that he had had a 'call from the churches' and that he would soon be leaving her, but wanted to say that he had had a very happy life with her. When later he wakened at his ordinary time and she asked him if he had had a dream or remembered waking earlier, he knew nothing of it. We had to believe this but I don't think either Ethel or I, nor Eric either, saw any kind of premonition in it, or felt disturbed by it.

But all the same it was perhaps a kind of warning, for on 15 May, only a month later, I heard from my mother that my father had had a second seizure and was having treatment. She was so anxious not to spoil my holiday that she still did not think it necessary to send for me; but on the 19th came a wire asking me to return. How vividly I remember the frantic packing and then the mad evening dash over the mountains, in a hired car which had frequently to stop for me to be sick. At Toulon I caught the 9.50 to Paris where next morning I had to change for a train to Boulogne. At Dover I found I had forgotten my passport but the officials seemed to sense my state of mind for they let me through to catch a train to Paddington, where I arrived after midnight, too late for the last train to Bristol, and was allowed by a friendly porter to spend the few remaining hours of the night sleeping on a bench in the waiting room, where he locked me in and duly called me in the morning for the first train to Bristol. When at last I reached home I saw the blinds were drawn, as the custom then was, and knew I was too late.

My mother's wonderfully controlled behaviour, after the long physical strain of nursing was over, helped me through my regrets at not having found my father alive and my first experience of death. It was wonderfully heart-warming too to find our dear faithful Alice waiting for us when we returned from the funeral in Manchester, though I think she can only have stayed for a short time. Ethel's understanding letter from the Bastide, too, saying how much she wished she had known 'that patient, kindly man ... and his devoted generous life' comforted me to think I had so described him to her.

After that she wrote almost daily during her last fortnight at the farm, helping me to feel I was still there by describing all the small events. And before she herself left at our allotted time at the beginning of June she wrote saying she felt that in those three months 'we have made a basis for all time which no misunderstanding should ever be able to shake'. And indeed it never did. On leaving the Bastide she went, as we had both planned to, to see Beth with her baby Catherine, who were at Talloires together with Tit.

On 22 June she came to Bristol to stay with mother and me for a week. As it was beautiful summer weather I spent it showing her all the places I had so often talked to her about. She got on well with my mother too, so much so that she agreed at once when we suggested that, as there was now no longer any reason why we should remain in Bristol, we would sell our house and move to one nearer the Whitehorns in Hampstead. No sooner had we decided this than Ethel went back to London and began consulting agents and inspecting the houses they recommended. It was an exhausting job as she rarely saw anything she felt we would like. Once mother and I went up to look at a few that were just possible, but we disliked them all. However, in the bus on our way back to Paddington mother and I had a glimpse of a wide unmade road, turning off the Finchley Road, with some building going on at the end of it, and both had the instinctive feeling that our house would be there. I wrote to Ethel that night to ask her to go and see it and she had the same feeling. So up mother and I went once again and all three agreed that, only half-built though it was, this was going to be our house. How strange it is that this kind of thing can so often happen! It was a corner house, with a little country lane running up beside the long back garden to a church at the end of it. It had the right number of rooms, the builder was pleasant and seemed reliable. He gave us the plans and said the house would be finished in October. Most satisfactory of all, the price - £1,600, if it can now be believed - was what we could pay. So my mother decided that she would have it and paid the deposit.

On our return to Bristol in August we concentrated on selling our big furniture and carpets, as the plans showed they would be much too large for the slightly smaller rooms of the more cottagey type of the new house. When I remember that my mother was then nearly seventy, it was extraordinary how supple she was about selling so many of the things that had surrounded her all her married life. But she always enjoyed activity.

On 6 October we sold the house for only £50 less than mother had paid for the new one. We went up to London in the last week of that month, stayed a few days with the Whitehorns, and then at last moved into 28 Lyndale Avenue (a number thereafter changed to 15) at the end of October 1923.

For my twenty-seventh birthday that year, Ethel gave me a rich green chrysoprase signet ring with a heraldic-looking frog, which she had drawn, engraved on it, in memory of our two idyllic sojourns in the south. I have worn it day and night ever since then.

Chapter Five

PONTIGNY
1924-1925

The new house had one unusual feature which turned out to be a marvellous refuge for me. This was a very large top room that covered the whole length and breadth of the house, and was therefore the only one on that floor. As the four bedrooms on the floor below were all we needed, my mother suggested that this big room should be a study-library-sitting room for me, where I could work and entertain my friends. As time progressed bookshelves covered all the walls.

I had obeyed Miss H.'s command that I should not write to her again until I had become a Christian, as I had no means of finding out whether I had reached that desired state, but I now wrote her a formal note saying that I should now be living with my mother in London. The realization that I should therefore not be able to live with her seems to have had a calming effect on her and that summer she wrote me several letters that were not only normal but positively helpful, and as soon as we were installed in Lyndale Avenue, she sent back my Oxford furniture, which she had been using ever since I went down.

Perhaps it was the sight of this ideal study that renewed Ethel's hopes that I would one day be a writer, hopes so high that she was distressed lest my need to earn money (when she had no such need for she had a very generous allowance) should make me take some humdrum secretarial post which would leave me with no leisure for anything creative. But there was no need for this fear for my mother still paid for all my clothes and I had a small allowance. I was anxious too to be free to make the most of Ethel's company during the first two months of 1924, for it was to be a year in which I should see little of her.

Her nervous, restless father was beginning to want to go

abroad again and to take her with him; and she for her part was anxious to keep her old promise to go to Beth in March to help her with her garden. So it was arranged that Ethel and her father should leave on 1 March for Hyères, and after a fortnight or so there, Ethel would go to the Bastide. Sadly though I knew I should miss her, I had had an idea after Christmas which excited us both as likely to provide me with the kind of literary work she wanted me to have, and which her presence in the south might help her to procure for me.

There had recently appeared in Paris the first three volumes of a *roman-fleuve* of the kind then in fashion. It was called *Les Thibault* and was by Roger Martin du Gard, a friend of the van Rysselberghes but one whom Whity had not yet met. I suppose it was they who had written to her about the books, which she at once got for me. I don't know whether they were having a popular success or not, but I was immediately so thrilled by them that I was seized with a desire to translate them and felt confident that I could, though knowing nothing of the art of translation, nor even then that it was an art. Ethel shared my enthusiasm and my confidence and went off with high hopes of success. When she had got to the Bastide, 'Uncle Martin' as they all called him, arrived also and there met Whity, whom he obviously took to at once (*la belle et droite Whity* as he called her in a later letter to me). The subject of my wish to translate his books was immediately broached and much discussed, as Beth and her mother shared Whity's view that I could do it. And they both obviously gave him a flattering idea of my powers and personality.

But Uncle Martin, though a delightful, friendly man, was also very cautious, not one to be rushed into anything himself, nor to let me be so rushed without full knowledge of what I was proposing to undertake. So from his hotel in Hyères he wrote me a letter in his elegant handwriting, '*pour faire connaissance*' as he charmingly put it, and to say how pleased he was that I liked his books; but going on to tell me of his plans for the continuation of the work, which would he said take him another twenty years, and perhaps more still. He warned me too that he could not make a contract without the consent of his publishers, Gallimard, who reserved the right to approve the quality of the translation. This letter thrilled me. The thought that, if I got the job, it would provide me with a life's work so fulfilled my hopes and ambitions, and Ethel's for me, that I at once wrote to say that, however long the book, I would like to be his translator. So when he replied, a week later, he suggested that I should translate some specimen passages, which he had chosen to show my ability to deal with varied difficulties. He ended by saying that he did not think *Les Thibault* would be difficult to translate, provided one naturally had a style (as he himself had) that was *'sobre, juste, correct et uni'*, without eye-catching peculiarities. It was in fact because it was written in an unusually lucid and simple style that I felt I could cope with it.

I don't think he was in any particular hurry about this, but I am sure I set to work at once because it was such a pleasant relief to have that kind of work to do in my study as a change from the humdrum life that mother and I lead. Not that this was any longer so humdrum, for we had begun to do a great deal of entertaining. Even Miss H. had written to ask whether we could begin again 'on a different basis', a request I could not well refuse. So she came several times and indeed I continued to see her from time to time for many years. But my heart, so far as she was concerned, was dead. Mother and I were enjoying our life in London too and indulged our passion for the theatre, for it was a season when there were many memorable performances, such as that of Edith Evans in *The Way of the World* at the Lyric, Hammersmith, and *The Immortal Hour* with Gwen Frangcon Davies. And at the music-halls we saw such artists as Grock and Lopokova.

When I was alone and working in my study, Whity's constant letters during the six weeks that she spent at the Bastide, full of descriptions of all the people there, made me feel very much among them too. The atmosphere was obviously very different from the tranquil Eden I had known, for now not only was la Petite Dame there all the time, but Gide too. Among his intimate friends he was always called 'le Bipède' because they felt it expressed his characteristic way of always morally taking two contradictory steps. As he had said in his *Journal* in 1922 *'il ne se passe guere de jour que je ne remette tout en question'*. When Whity heard this name she called him 'Mister Bypeed' and for some reason they all immediately adopted this curious non-word as his permanent nickname. And then of course there was the child Catherine too, just a year old but already with a sense of the ridiculous. Gide was always watching her, and I suppose it was then known among all that company, and by Whity and me too, that he was her father, though the child herself did not know it and, because of the existence of Gide's wife, it was still a complete secret in the French literary world.

Whity saw Gide very clearly and I enjoyed her frank comments. She remarked, for instance, how his appearance varied, so that sometimes, she said, he could look like a degenerate old baboon, and at others really wonderful. This was certainly true, for I also remember how in the 'wonderful' moments, his expression had the calm and noble look of some eastern sage. What added to the baboon aspect was his habit of constantly grunting and snuffling - *'il doit toujours meubler le silence'*, as Catherine said of him later. He spent a lot of time playing the piano, which he did really well, specially Chopin, as he was convinced he alone knew the right way to play him. And finally, as the French habit is, he was always reading aloud to them the book he was then writing, *Les Faux-Monnayeurs*, which he felt the English would prefer to his other work. He read in an extraordinary voice, mouthing and lingering over the words.

As there was obviously little gardening work for Whity to do, and as Beth was so taken up with the child, towards the end of her time she went off on her own for a week-end to stay with some friends at Roquebrune. While she was there she called on the Bussys, who lived in a house called La Souco. She had met them for the first time as long ago as 1919 when Dorothy Bussy, a sister of Lytton Strachey and wife of the painter Simon Bussy, writing to tell Gide she had had a visit from them all, said 'Of all the party, the one to whom I at once and quite unexpectedly took a fancy was Miss Whitehorn. I thought my young compatriot - was there ever anything more English? - most refreshing.' And she went on to describe the charming way in which Whity had told her how she had helped Gide to do some shopping at the Army and Navy when he was in London in 1918.

But apart from such opportunities to see more of our French friends and meet new ones, I have the feeling that she was beginning to feel that these regular visits to Beth in the spring had lost their point, and was glad to get home again and spend the summer with me, enjoying our June holiday with our two mothers at Burpham in Sussex. It was during that summer that I got the exciting news that I had been accepted for the second *dé*cade at Pontigny, between 8 and 18 August.

At that time I knew little more about Pontigny than its name. And as there can now be few people in Europe, even in France, and certainly none in England, who remember that remarkable place and the important part it played in the development of European thought between the wars, perhaps I should say a few words about its origins and the running of it, before telling of my own first visit there. In 1906, when church and state were separated in France and the religious buildings secularized, the great Cistercian Abbey of Pontigny, in the Yonne Department of Burgundy, and all its dependencies were put up for auction. They were bought by a brilliant and erudite man of forty-six, Professor Paul Desjardins, who might have become one of the outstanding writers and critics of France but who chose rather to teach in some of the famous lycées, where he proved an inspired teacher. As he was also an ardent patriot and moralist, he founded a society called, first, *l'Union pour l'Action Morale*, but later *l'Union pour la Vérité*, of which a great many writers and thinkers of the day became members and attended its meetings in the rue Visconti.

But it was the dream of Desjardins to widen the scope of these and make them international. So, having acquired the abbey, he founded in 1910 the first of what became known as the *Entretiens de Pontigny*, which consisted of three ten-day meetings known as *décades*, held every August, each devoted to a different subject - art, literature, religion, education, philosophy, human rights and many more, but not, I think, politics. These continued for four years until the 1914 war put a stop to them, when the abbey became a hospital. The fact that his eldest son Michel was killed in 1918, convinced the professor that it was more than ever necessary to work for understanding between nations and the civilization that France stood for. So the *entretiens* began again in 1922 and continued till 1939, when once again war ended them, this time for good.

It was Desjardins himself who chose the subjects and outlined in short pamphlets the scope he hoped the discussions would take; but he did not lead them himself. Instead he always chose some expert, while he himself, as I was to learn, always sat humbly in the background, occasionally interpolating in a deprecatory way some subtle remark or rare quotation, which made it clear that he was in effect dominating the whole thing. For he was a very strange and complicated man, disclaiming the abilities which would have entitled him to important positions, exaggeratedly courteous to individuals, especially if they were quite simple or unknown, but able with a devastating stroke of irony to wither and humiliate anyone who was self-important or pretentious. At such times his face could assume a frighteningly inhuman, even cruel, expression. Few people, not even André Gide, felt at ease with him.

I learned these last facts while Tit and I were staying with Jean Schlumberger, the writer, who was to lead the *décade* which I was to attend, and who had kindly invited me to stay at his flat on the fifth floor of 78 rue d'Assas though I was still unknown to him. But he was so simple and hospitable that I took to him at once and we became great friends thereafter. He was a dry little man, a Protestant, with strong views, whose writings, either in books or journalism, never made the reputation they deserved, but whom I came to think a better writer than Gide, especially in his novels. During those three days, Gide often came to meals and was so kind and natural with me that I found myself talking easily with him. On the last evening he brought Jacques Copeau, the actor and founder of the Vieux Colombier, to supper.

But the most important visitor from my point of view was Roger Martin du Gard, who turned out to be a delightful person, rather plump, with a distinguished head of thick hair brushed back, humorous and sometimes rather mocking eyes and a mouth always ready to smile. He was of course anxious to make the acquaintance of his would-be translator and seemed very pleased to get the specimen pages I had brought with me. I listened eagerly to all they told me of Desjardins - Gide had some particularly fascinating anecdotes of how humiliating he could be - and altogether, looking back on that period now, I feel amazed to think I should have been so warmly received and treated as one of themselves, not only as a friend of Whity but for my own sake.

In view of all I learnt then I felt relieved to think I should arrive at Pontigny, where Desjardins was on the platform station to greet us, in such illustrious company, and be introduced by them. He then led us to the abbey, which was not far off, up a sandy lane from the main road. At the main entrance Loup Mayrisch and Madame Desjardins were waiting for us. The latter was the warm human heart of the whole enterprise and ran the domestic arrangements splendidly. We saw first the romanesque dining hall. A noble staircase led to the great empty hall above.

The organization of the *décades* was strict in one way but easy in others. The numbers were limited to roughly fifty, of which some thirty-five were eminent men and women, while the remaining fifteen were mostly young men, often *Normaliens*, who had been recommended by someone important, as I had been. For the two main meals, which were extraordinarily good, there was a seating plan, which I imagine was organized by Madame Desjardins: each young person sat between two famous ones, a rather alarming arrangement which proved, owing to the kindly spirit which prevailed, to be very stimulating. In any case these places were changed every three days so that one had a chance to get to know six of the eminent. The *Entretiens* were held in the afternoon, a rather difficult time to keep awake after those good luncheons, either in a drawing room on the ground floor if the weather was cold, or in the garden under the *charmille*, a kind of long tunnel of branching hornbeams, when it was warm enough. The mornings were free for walks, in the course of which many friendships were made, or for reading in the splendid library.

In the evenings we were entertained by the young men with witty intellectual games, charades or even improvised dramas. From what I heard later, the brilliance of those entertainments in 1924 was never to be surpassed.

I cannot pretend to remember anything of the discussion on the subject of our *Entretien*, which was far above my head and, I suspect, above the heads of many of those present who rarely spoke, Martin du Gard and Tit among others. But I do vividly remember several of the people there. I was not the only English member, for there was the distinguished elderly Cambridge classical scholar, Jane Harrison and her protégée Hope Mirrlees, who had written a not very good novel, *The

Counterplot. There were also two Americans, Sandford Griffith, a correspondent of the *Wall Street Journal*, and his tall and radiant wife Kate. I quickly made friends with a nice young Frenchman, Jacques Heurgon. I confided to him my wish to collect a library of the French classics and he later obtained them for me in that excellent little scholarly edition Jouaust, which I still have. It was not a very international gathering that year, the most outstanding foreigner being the German critic Ernst Robert Curtius, who was much sought after and popular.

Among the French contingent our friends of the *Nouvelle Revue Française* were of course the most important, but there were also Charles du Bos, who looked rather like a mandarin and spoke beautiful English in a ponderously accurate way, and André Maurois, who had just become well known. Gide's interventions were always delivered in that curious, hesitant, self-contradicting manner of his which la Petite Dame so brilliantly reproduced in her four volumes of his conversations.

I returned to London after one more night in the rue d'Assas, but Ethel was then on holiday with her family, so I could not pour out all my impressions to her as I was bursting to do. But in a letter she told me she had heard from Beth that I had been much appreciated at Pontigny, particularly by Gide. If I was greatly elated by this I was to be brought down to earth again very soon afterwards by the continuation of the translation story during which, over a period of six months, I passed from the height of contentment, through bewilderment, to the deepest disappointment. As I think that would-be translators often have this kind of experience, though perhaps in a less extreme form, it may touch many sympathetic chords if I tell my story here.

Unbeknownst to me, Uncle Martin must have shown my extracts at Pontigny to both André Maurois and Charles du Bos, and asked their opinion of my work. But whether or not they were too occupied there to study it with close attention to the French text, if indeed they had it there, they both unanimously pronounced my version 'very good'. Martin, as I'll now call him for short, was so pleased to hear their verdict that on 25 September he wrote me a most enthusiastic letter, telling me of it, saying how much he had hoped for this after our meeting in the rue d'Assas, giving me his full consent and asking me, if I still felt able to face the task, to begin looking for an English publisher, as he knew his own publisher and friend, Gaston Gallimard, would have no objections.

But a month later came a very different letter from Martin. He was, as I said, a very cautious and conscientious man, and he must suddenly have thought that, as he himself knew no word of English, the opinion of two of his compatriots, however bilingual, was not enough, and that he ought to seek the opinion of an English friend. This he did, apparently quite forgetting that he had given me a firm agreement. Who this English friend was, he never told me. He merely sent me a long quotation from his letter. I must quote the relevant parts of it in the French in which it presumably was written, as it was thus that Martin understood it.

It said that *'elle ne sait pas ce que c'est qu'une phrase anglaise. Elle se contente le plus souvent d'aligner les mots dans l'ordre du texte français, ce qui fait tantôt un charabia inintelligible pour un véritable anglais, et tantôt un effet de grotesque*; then, perhaps blaming himself for his own harshness, he surprisingly ended by saying he thought that, with a little more effort *'une personne sachant le français aussi bien que celle-ci pourrait faire une traduction convenable'*. It was no wonder that Martin felt as perplexed and bewildered by this letter as I did, for he went on to say that he intended to consult someone else, to suggest that I on my side should do the same, and that we should think calmly about it.

My state of mind on reading that criticism may well be imagined. I could not fail to see that it was outrageously exaggerated, for I felt sure that my English, even if too literal and stiff, could not possibly justify such a shattering condemnation. It took me a fortnight to reply to him, telling him that the criticism had caused me *'une espèce de vertige mental'* and that I had sent the letter on to Tit. In the meantime I had also consulted an English friend of mine (I don't remember who this was) who was a good judge, severe but reasonable. She had praised my translation of the conversations, of which the books were full, but agreed that the descriptive passages were a shade too literal, though she was sure that I could easily improve them with a little more work. As for la Petite Dame, she came gallantly to my defence, pointing out to Martin the exaggeration of the critical letter, speaking of my general level of culture and saying that he had heard on all sides I had a good English style. She sent me a copy of her letter and I had one from Beth too, who also felt I could easily improve on my first draft and cheered me by excitingly suggesting another visit from me in the spring. But there was nothing I could do about it until I heard from Martin again, and this I did not do until February, when I got a letter telling me he had been putting off from day to day the very bad news that he now must give me. He had sent my translated extracts to a dozen people, English and American, and all had judged them severely for the same reason: too literal. He told me he had done his best to defend me, because he felt so sure we could work harmoniously together. But he finally had to relinquish me when the American firm of Liveright offered Gallimard very advantageous terms for the whole work; but though they had as yet no translator of their own to propose, they refused my version of these short extracts. He only hoped that I would not be too hurt. Looking back on it all now, I think they were probably right to a great extent, as to my over-literalness, but too harsh in not giving me the chance to improve my work. In any case I never saw the version that was finally published, if indeed it ever was.

I filled in those months of waiting by doing some secretarial work for a Dr John Rees, to whom I had been introduced by Dr Crichton Miller. And in fact I went on working for him until May, as Ethel had left in February, just before I got my bad news, for her annual tour of Italy with her father, after which she went for her routine visit to Beth where she found both Martin du Gard and Gide staying. The former did not stay long, though she saw he was genuinely sad at the end of the translation story, but Gide remained and, as usual, she found him amusing and original company, as he insisted on trying to speak his very bad English with her. His inability to speak our tongue, in the literature of which he was so widely read, while at the same time being able to translate *Hamlet*, never failed to astonish us. He had just sold *Les Faux-Monnayeurs* so well that he bought Beth a car and of course took it for granted that Whity would teach her to drive. This idle life once again made her feel she had no essential reason for being there and no special friend of her own to talk to, so she longed for the visit which Beth had invited me for in May, and for which I was equally eager. I stayed for two weeks and we had a week in Paris on the way home where we saw the Pitoeffs in *Saint Joan*.

Back in England, after taking our mothers for their June holiday, I returned to Dr Rees and worked for him again for two months, warning him that I would once again be off to Pontigny in August.

I was much looking forward to my second visit there, where I now felt at home. And as my account of it made Whity want to come too Loup got an invitation for her as well and we went off happily for the first *décade* of the *entretiens*. The subject was *Se Raconter Soi-même*, under two aspects: I *L'Autobiographie dans la Fiction*, and II *La Fiction dans l'Autobiographie*. In other words, the introductory pamphlet asked: *'Est-il possible au romancier de n'être aucunement historien de soi-même'* and *'Est-il possible à l'historien de soi-même de n'être aucunement romancier?'* This of course was a subject with a wide range of interest even for those who were neither novelists nor autobiographers, and the discussions between these two types of writers and the critics were vastly amusing. I remember Martin du Gard's round-eyed astonishment when some eminent critic blandly asserted what his method of working indicated. He had never had any such intentions, he declared, and his basic inspiration was entirely different. Most of the other novelists agreed with him. I remember too how Hope Mirrlees, astonished by the imputations of some inner mystery to her, declared in her blunt English accent, *'Moi, je n'ai pas de vie intérieure!'* - a remark that staggered the French.

Whity as usual, got on well with the foreign members of the conference, who this year were more interesting than they had been the year before, particularly the Italians and the Russians, all of whom became lifelong friends of ours. Among the former was a charming young man, Guglielmo degli Alberti, who spoke perfect English, having been brought up by an English governess who taught him all our nursery rhymes, and with a sense of humour that exactly fitted our own. He had been there the year before,

But he seemed to me so brilliant that I had been tongue-tied with him until Whity's easy fun released me and I joined in too. The Russians were old Tatiana Lvovna, Tolstoy's favourite daughter, and her own daughter Tanya, who both now lived in poverty in Paris. Loup Mayrisch was particularly generous to them, for they were very poor. I cannot remember whether it was then or on some later occasion that Prince Mirsky was there, a rather enigmatic though pleasant man.

The evening entertainments were less brilliant intellectually than the year before, but Whity with her gifts for acting and mimicry scored a particular success one evening in a charade by coming in dressed in a motley collection of clothes she had managed to collect, as she always did, and gave a masterly impression of a nervous English spinster, guide book in hand, going round a picture gallery. After gazing at the very ordinary pictures on the walls, she suddenly stopped short before a group of harmless cupids on the marble mantelpiece and managed by her half-shocked, half-fascinated gaze to give the impression that it was an obscene sculpture to which, after quick looks around the room to see if other 'tourists' were looking, she kept returning for another furtive and excited glance. After that the French and Italians were quick to see what a gifted mimic she was and she became a great favourite.

I think the experience of being a person very much in her own right, must have encouraged and strengthened her greatly to strike out on her own, as she had now decided to do. We had that summer had many talks about what she might do and where she might go, and as I had told her much of the charms of Geneva and the possibility of jobs there, she thought she would try her luck there, where I could introduce her to friends.

So on 30 September, just three weeks after we returned from Pontigny, she left. Her going could not but have been a wrench for both of us. But what helped her to feel happier about leaving me was not only that I had work for Dr Rees immediately I returned, but that my mother and I had had the blessed news that our dear old Alice, whose mother had just died, would be returning to us in November, so there would be less domestic work for me to do.

Chapter Six

THE STUDENT WORLD IN GENEVA
1926-1929

When I wrote to my friends in Geneva about Ethel, I remember feeling doubtful whether they would take to her, as I realized they all belonged to different worlds and would have nothing in common. Those doubts were justified. The Felkins - Elliott was now on the League of Nations - duly asked her to lunch but took no further notice of her. And although Alice Cathrall offered her a room as a paying guest in her sumptuous flat high up in the old quarter she did not attempt to get to know her or indeed see anything of her. Her first enquiries about possible jobs produced nothing, and she found that the University courses she had hoped to join, where she might perhaps meet other students, did not start till the end of October. So for the first two or three months she was often desperately lonely, wandering about the town and eating in cheap cafés, so it needed all her fortitude to remain.

Then suddenly things changed, very much for the better. In the rue St Leger, a wide and noble street, overlooking the Promenade des Bastions, she discovered the International Students Union. The rent of this large building was paid by a rather visionary lady called Miss Storey. But the whole enterprise was American-financed and was the brain-child of a typical idea-mad American woman called Mrs Hadden, who had complete control. The Director of the Institute was a young woman called Polly Duggan, half American, half Irish.

Polly at first told Ethel she had no paid jobs to give her, but willingly accepted her offer to work voluntarily both in the office and the club. In the former, Ethel quickly revealed a gift for administration and orderly office organization that she could previously hardly have known she possessed. As

67

for the club, she had already proved in those far-off days in Camberwell that she had the knack of getting on with young people of all kinds, both ruly and unruly. This much bigger and often difficult international crowd in Geneva therefore presented no problems to her and she was soon both popular and respected by even the wildest among them.

When Polly saw what a treasure she had found, she at once offered her a full-time job at the Swiss equivalent of £5 a week (two pounds more than I with my University degree had ever earned!). But she laid down two conditions: that Ethel should stay at least six months and possibly into the busy summer season, and should work long hours, half in the office and half in the club. These were rather daunting, as she had hoped to get home for Christmas, whether she had found work or not; but the job was too good to refuse and so she accepted. Moreoever, now that she was in funds, she was able to leave Alice's flat and take a room in an unusually good pension, owned and run by a kind-hearted Swiss woman called Madame Tschiffeli.

Except for a few Asiatic officials on the league Ethel never got to know more than one or two of the other foreigners working there. But she found real friends among some members of the very reserved old Genevese families who took no notice of the Anglo-Saxons working in the proliferation of societies that sprawled over Geneva in those days. (One wit had even pretended there was a *Société pour répandre l'emploi du subjonctif parmi les classes pauvres!*) Her entry into the first of these Genevese strongholds came through Raymonde de Candolle, who worked voluntarily in the club in the evenings and who, appreciating Ethel's fun, invited her home to meet her mother, Madame Augustin de Candolle, an aristocratic old lady with a great sense of humour, who lived in their beautiful early-nineteenth-century house, Le Vallon, set in a park full of sloping paths and many trees on the fringe of the town. Ethel soon became a favourite not only with the mother, but with one of her sons, Roger, then a young man at Oxford, good-looking and very gifted musically, who was later to become a lifelong friend to us both, as was his mother.

An equally great Genevese friend was Madame Bedot. She was a delightful character: a convinced atheist with a mocking humour, but always ready to laugh at herself too.

She had a most beautiful seventeenth-century house at Satigny, about twenty minutes by train from Geneva, where Ethel was always welcome.

I, meanwhile, was continuing my own life as before, although it was beginning to broaden a little. My part-time work for Dr Rees was still the basis of it, but though I never came to believe in the efficacy of the work he and Crichton Miller did, I found it of absorbing human interest the more I got to know about it, so much so that I continued to work with them off and on for another year. They, on their side, must have found me an efficient secretary for they made full use of me. In April of that year, when I went to Bowden House to replace the secretary, I found I had to work for three doctors!

My social circle was growing wider too, for I saw something of one or two of the people I had met at Pontigny, Prince Mirsky for one. Then there were the two Americans, Kate and Sandford Griffith, whose acquaintance I had made there as long ago as 1924. I discovered that they lived quite near to us and during that year I saw much of them. They were a striking looking couple, obviously denizens of the new world (the first I think that I had ever met) and I remember how they had stood out as refreshingly different from all Europeans at Pontigny. I still do not know who had sponsored their presence there. She was a very tall beautiful woman, with brilliant laughing eyes, always wearing bright clothes of brilliant patterned silks. Her husband, shorter than his wife, gave an impression of great toughness and vigour, with a quick mind and much humour who, to my surprise, spoke beautiful French, full of colloquialisms.

When I met them again in London I found that he was the representative of an American firm called Dillon Reid. But in his spare time he was trying to write a book on some German banker. When he realized what a useful secretary I was, he asked me to help him by going every evening and at weekends too, to help him with his book, which I would then type on the following day. This seemed to me a very pleasant way of adding to the part-time work that I was also doing for Dr Rees, and increasing my salary too, for Sandy was a generous employer; so I accepted, and began the work in January 1926. Unfortunately this agreeable situation only lasted two months, for at the end of February he was recalled to New York and it was uncertain for a time whether they would return. Such comings and goings were, I was to find, typical of them.

Ethel at last came on leave from Geneva at the beginning of March. She arrived in good spirits, having enjoyed the previous weeks for several reasons. Best of all, she had seen Beth on her way through Paris, when they stayed together and met some of our other French friends too, Uncle Martin among them. When she got to London her chief joy, of course, was the renewal of our daily meetings and the chance to visit our friends in the country together.

Her leave passed all too quickly, but before she left I had time to tell her of an idea I had had which greatly excited me. Among the French books I had recently picked up was one in a cheap series of classics called *Lettres complètes d'Abélard et d'Héloïse*, translated by Octave Gréard. They were merely legendary names to me. I didn't even know from what language the letters were translated, and since I omitted to read the preface, as my way was, I remained ignorant of any literature about them. I plunged straight into the text of Abélard's first letter, which gives the few bald facts of his love story, and then went on to the two subsequent love letters of Héloïse to him. These filled me with such admiration for her, and astonishment at the nobility and modernity of her conduct, that I felt a kind of indignation that she was always mentioned as a secondary character to Abélard, whereas she was obviously the greater human being. She deserved a book in which she should be the protagonist, I thought, and I felt that I was perhaps the person to do it. But how? Two years earlier André Maurois had brought out his *Ariel, La Vie de Shelley*, which made the *biographie romancée* fashionable. I seized on it as a model. All one needed, I felt, was enough sympathy and imagination to invent the feelings she must have had during her love-affair and its tragic aftermath. And I was foolish enough to think I had that imagination.

When I told Ethel that I thought I had at last found a subject that inspired me with the desire to write as she had always hoped I would, she was thrilled and immediately thought what a splendid opportunity I would have to begin the book when I visited her in Geneva for a holiday in May, as we had planned I should. That month in Geneva was one of the most serenely happy times I had ever had, a mixture of perfect companionship and hours of solitude in a town I came to love. Dear Madame Tschiffeli had given up a fine big room with comfortable divan beds in opposite corners of it, and there we were awakened every morning by a smiling Swiss maid with trays of coffee, those chubby little Swiss rolls with butter and the famous black cherry jam.

Ethel's office hours varied, so when she was free in the mornings we got up late, talking and reading in bed or wandering contentedly about those charming residential roads whose gardens were filled with flowers. When Ethel went to work, I dutifully retired into the little writing room adjoining our bedroom that kind Madame Tschiffeli had provided for me when Ethel told her what I hoped to do. But once there I found, as so many writers do, what a labour it is to begin; I also had faint stirrings of feeling that perhaps I was not on the right track. Still, I kept on for at least a short time each day. Then the craving to go out and explore the town in the leisurely way I loved came over me, and I would wander slowly along all the steep and narrow streets of the old city, or I would sit in the Jardin Anglais, admiring the great plume of water that was sometimes turned on, or cross the Pont du Mont Blanc to the little swan-surrounded island with Rousseau's statue on it. Geneva never lost its charm for me. But wherever I was, I always managed to get back to the rue St Leger in time to meet Ethel when I knew her office hours ended and walk back to our pension with her.

There were the week-ends too, when Ethel was free from Friday evening until Sunday lunch-time, and we made the most of the four of them in May. Sometimes she would take me to make the acquaintance of her Genevese friends, all of whom quickly became my friends too. A favourite week-end expedition took us, like most foreigners in Geneva, by funicular up the Salevè, the protecting mountain that loom behind the town. But we left to our last week-end a visit, recommended by Elliott, to Bellay, the birthplace of Brillat Savarin, where wonderful meals were still served at the Hotel Pernollet, kept by a descendant of Brillat Savarin's cook, and where we had a memorable lunch.

It was a glorious end to a perfect holiday in which we were utterly happy all the time, with endless fun, laughter and teasing; inventing absurd names for each other and talking our nonsense language. Someone, I don't know who, once said that the essentials of true friendship are stimulus and repose and we gave each other both in full measure. In the letter she wrote to me after I had left, she said she felt we had taken another step towards the perfection of love we imagined we had reached before and that she was convinced we had something deeper and finer than the vast majority ever dream of.

June was a very full month for Ethel, with endless typing of monthly reports, answering queries from newly arriving students and finding rooms for them, which all meant putting in very long hours. Then, just at the moment when they were all hard at work preparing for the busy summer season, they heard from the redoubtable Mrs Hadden that she was arriving on 1 July with a complete new staff, but hoped, absurdly, that they would all work together! Polly and Ethel of course decided they would have to resign and spent the rest of that month in a wretched state of frustration and indecision. The generous Miss Storey supported their resignation and paid for Ethel to attend various student conferences in Yugoslavia and several other eastern European countries. But though she was grateful for this, she felt keenly the blow of having to resign from the club. 'I feel more disappointed by the wreck of this job than I thought possible', she wrote to me, 'I become nothing again.' She was upset not only for herself, but for me too because, as always, she had been hoping that if things went on as well as they were doing, she might possibly bring me somehow into her work. A year later, that wish of hers for me was to be gratified.

As this chapter is so largely concerned with the student world, and I have dropped that dark hint about the gratifying of Ethel's wish that something good for me should come from her work in it, I think it is better at this point to forsake the chronological narrative I have pursued so far, and look ahead to those agreeable summer-schools in Geneva that were really to some extent a development of the International Club.

Although I never knew exactly what their origin was, I feel pretty sure they were the outcome of the close friendship between Polly Duggan and Ivison Macadam, who, at that time, was both a minor official at Chatham House, the Institute of International Affairs, and the head, I think, of the Confédération International des Etudiants (the CIE) which was an important body. The idea of the summer-school was connected with the series of lectures which Professor Zimmern gave every year in Geneva and which American undergraduates of international affairs were encouraged to attend, as they counted as a part of their university courses. Macadam suggested that Polly and Ethel should run the summer-schools, and both agreed.

But at the last minute, in early July 1927, Polly turned up at the Whitehorn's house in Hampstead to announce definitely that she was not going to participate. Ethel had already had some vague intimations of this and had sounded me as to whether I could and would take Polly's place; an idea that I jumped at as a change from my rather dreary work in Dr Rees's office that would enable me to be with Ethel again in a town I liked so much. The dates of the summer-school were from mid-July to the end of August, and the place where it was to be held was, in term-time, a school for children called Le Collège de la Grande Boissière, more familiarly known as the Institut Widemann from the name of its headmaster. (It is now the Ecole Internationale.) It was an ideal building for the summer-school, set well back from the main road in which it stood, and comprising a large block of several storeys with excellently equipped bedrooms for the students on the upper floors and comfortable sitting rooms below, while at right angles to it was a pleasant ground-floor dining room. Beyond these buildings the ground sloped away in a wild garden with magnificent trees. I had a little office at the end of the long drive which led to the college.

That first year we had mostly English and American students, though there were a few Czechs and Dutch too. They were an extremely nice lot and we all got on well together from the start. We explained to each group when they had settled in that they were quite free to go about by themselves, and that there were no rules - we merely expected them to behave well and to be on time for the excellent meals that were provided, (the Widemanns saw to this so we had no domestic duties). The gates would always be open so they could return in the evenings when they liked but we hoped that they would do so quietly. They all took this to heart and responded as we hoped they would. We also allotted their rooms to them, regardless of sex, not putting the boys and girls in different quarters. The only person who complained about this was a middle-aged woman - what would now be called a mature student - who, when she found we would not alter our arrangement, threatened to leave, and did.

Ethel and I divided the work between us. I did the financial and paper work in my little office, such as collecting from each student the price of the tickets we charged for the various outings that it was Ethel's job to arrange to those delightful places near Geneva, for after all they were having a holiday as well as attending lectures, and when the whole party wanted to go we joined them and went too. We had a delicate-looking Scot called Thomson (an official in the British Universities League of Nations Society, BULNS) to help Ethel with the practical arrangements like the hiring of charabancs. (By a strange coincidence, we met this young man again at a dinner party fifty years later, and Ethel, who had a good memory for faces, remembered his. One can imagine his astonishment when she asked him if he had been in Geneva in 1927. He had completely forgotten this experience, but her question quickly brought it back to his memory. He had become a distinguished medical journalist. Rather disappointingly, he didn't remember either of us!)

Outstanding among the students in that first year were two delightful American girls from Vassar, one of whom, Elizabeth Ramsay (now Klagsbrunn) became, and remained ever after not only our good friend, but an expert, widely known in Europe as well as in America, on the placenta. We had a lot of social engagements; I with the Felkins, who gave dinner parties for their house guests, one of whom was Lowes Dickinson, and Ethel with her Eastern friends in the League, as well as with our Genevese friends. Ethel was particularly delighted when Margery Perham, to whom I had introduced her some years before, and for whose work and person she had a special admiration, turned up for a holiday at Talloires and then went on to Geneva to study what was then called 'British native policy and the League of Nations Mandates System'. The summer-school ended in the first days of September when Ethel left to go to Beth at St Clair for a much-needed rest. I returned home.

Soon after I got back to London, Ivison Macadam asked me to dinner and was apparently so pleased with my account of the summer-school that he determined to repeat the experiment in the following year; and to make sure that Ethel and I would run it again, he got her to sign a contract for it when they happened to meet in Geneva in February 1928. That meeting with Macadam was to lead, more than ten years later, to a most important change in my life and work; a change in fact that determined the remainder of my working days, for he was one who did not forget his first impressions, which must in my case have been favourable. So, by bringing me within the orbit of her student interest, Ethel did indeed fulfil her wish that good might come of it for me.

The third and last of our summer-schools took place during the usual summer months of 1929. It was certainly the best, but why it was the last I do not know. More and more, these summer-schools had come to seem holiday and social occasions, as in fact anyone who could pay the fees was free to come. Once again, some students came for what was now the third time and we had a wider spread of nationalities because of those who turned up under their own steam, as well as the usual groups. All seemed to have a sense of humour and all got on well together, teasing each other and generally enjoying themselves. They were all pleased to be in Geneva, which at that time was an exciting place because so many famous figures were known to be in the town, whom they might see at any moment. One night at dinner, a rather unsophisticated English girl came to sit beside me and told me what a pleasant afternoon she had had, because such a nice old man had sat beside her on a bench in the Jardin Anglais, and talked to her most interestingly. When he got up to go, he said good-bye and added 'My name is Einstein.' When I asked her what she replied, she said 'Oh! I said, mine's Simpson.' I asked her whether she thought that was an adequate recognition. Light suddenly broke upon her and she gasped 'Do you mean he was EINSTEIN?'

There were a few other groups staying in the College at that time, among whom was a Russian, Nicolas Zernov, who, during the meal-times, kept his very blue eyes fixed on me from several tables away. Afterwards he came up and asked if I could spare him 'two or three hours' in my office. I managed to find one hour in which I discovered that his main aim was to convert me to the Orthodox Church of which he was a devout member. Although I resisted this attempt, I enjoyed his mind and conversation, and later he became a most faithful and lifelong friend for whom I did one of my more unusual jobs.

On our slow journey home we paid a memorable visit to Pernand Vergelesses. We went by train to Dijon where Pascal Copeau met us and took us to where his father Jacques, the founder of the Vieux Colombier theatre in Paris, had retired to set up his school of acting with the help of his daughter Maiène. She later became an actress herself, and remembered Whity from those long-ago days at St Clair, when she was one of the children who called her the Commander and loved her because she played with them. Maiène showed us over the school's workshop, out of which was to come, many years later, the Compagnie des Quinze, which visited London, and a member of which was Michel St Denis who, after the war, became head of the Old Vic Theatre School. Maiène and Pascal drove us all over that wonderful region whose names are a combination of poetry, history and unforgettable drafts of heavenly wine: Beaune, Corton, Volnay, Pommard and so many more. It was a fitting end to that so-happy summer in Geneva.

In that otherwise cheerful summer of 1929, a dark shadow fell momentarily across the normal brightness of my domestic life. It was just thirty years since our dear faithful Alice had first come to us, one of the greatest strokes of luck in my life. She had been the playmate and comfort of my brother and myself in our childhood and indeed kept the whole household together. When she returned to my mother and me in London after the death of her own mother, she became the rock on which I based all those absences which made up my life, knowing how she would cherish my mother, who always wholly relied on her. At the beginning of 1929, robust creature though we had always thought her, Alice began to suffer with terrible headaches. We sent her to the woman doctor we had then, a brusque person, obviously impatient, in those pre-National Health days, at having to deal with someone's maid. So after the scantiest examination, she declared there was nothing at all the matter with her, it was merely my mother who was making too much fuss of her. Not satisfied with this, we demanded a second opinion, which she of course could not refuse, and so we were given a letter to a surgeon at the Royal Free Hospital, which was then somewhere in the City.

I went with Alice and when we arrived and were sitting among the out-patients, I spotted a charming medical student called Blaguigna Illitch, a Yugoslav who had been at our summer-school the year before. This was a great stroke of luck for she at once came up and, knowing the ropes, helped us to get quickly to the surgeon, where I was allowed in too. He immediately X-rayed Alice and I can still remember the stern voice in which he asked 'Who is this woman's doctor? She must be written to at once!' from which I gathered it was something very serious. And so it was, for she was admitted to the hospital a week later and operated on immediately. I do not of course know the technical details of her illness, but it must have been grim, for although I called regularly I was not allowed to see her for many days and then only briefly. I often wonder what it was that the surgeon wrote to the woman doctor! When at last Alice was restored to health and sent back to us, she was soon strong enough to go to her native village, Porlock Weir, for her month's annual holiday where the sea air completed her cure while my mother went to Folkestone for hers. So I was free that summer to go again to Geneva for the third and last of those summer-schools.

Chapter Seven

FOREIGN FIELDS
1926-1929

Now to go back to 1926. When that happy month of May was over, I returned to London and worked again for Dr Rees for another four months. But when I told him that I should want to go abroad again in October, I think he felt he had had enough of my constant absences and must get a more permanent secretary; so by the end of September we parted company, though I think on the best of terms.

Ethel on the other hand, as I have said, when her job came to an end, attended various student conferences in Europe, then in September went, with Beth this time, to Pontigny once again where that year she told me there was an even more brilliant gathering than the year before.

Guglielmo degli Alberti was there again and now became a great friend, thereafter drawing both of us into the intimate circle of his own Italian friends, especially Umberto Morra, an associate of Berenson's and much later to become Italian Cultural Attaché in London, and Alexander d'Entrèves. I wonder if Professor Desjardins ever realized how well his foundation of Pontigny was fulfilling his hopes of binding the intellectuals of Europe together.

When the *Entretiens* of that year were over, Whity drove Beth back to the Bastide, then in its autumn lusciousness of grapes and figs and pears, with the frogs still voluptuously croaking. I arrived early in October in time to enjoy all this. I stayed for three weeks, revelling in that calm, pastoral life, with occasional trips to Bormes, where we saw Emile, the owner of the Bastide. But, generous though he was, I think he was getting disappointed with Beth's increasingly casual running of it, now that she had Catherine on her hands, and began to think of selling it, which would mean that Beth would have to find somewhere else to live.

At the beginning of November, Whity and I left for that visit to Italy, my first, which she had promised to go on with me, to show me at least some of the places she had seen with her father the year before. My resources were limited but I had calculated I could manage the northern cities: Florence, Siena, San Gimignano, Venice, Padua and Verona. It was a lovely leisurely visit and I revelled in every moment of it.

When our money began to run out, we headed for Milan and our train home, spending our last night, as we thought, in the cheapest hotel we could find. But in the morning Ethel found a letter from her mother, to say that Roger, coming on leave, had been put off his ship in Naples with malaria but would pay all our expenses if we could go and visit him. So we quickly found a Naples-bound train, feeling madly excited that we were going to see a part of Italy we hadn't had time to anticipate. We found a pleasant pensione and, on calling at Roger's hospital, found him slightly better and quite prepared for us to enjoy ourselves sight-seeing.

Staying at our pensione, were two old American ladies, who spent their days going nowhere. We began to talk to them of all the interesting places to see round Naples and, having roused their curiosity, we found through the kind proprietor that we could hire a car that would hold six people; ourselves, the two ladies, the chauffeur and a guide, who took us to all the places we wanted to see. Whenever we got to one of these sights our old ladies remained firmly in their seats, saying that we could tell them all about it.

As soon as Roger was discharged from hospital we went with him to Rome; we drove round the city the next day, seeing it for the first time bathed in the golden powdered air of a late autumn afternoon, and put him at night on his first-class train while we hung about for some hours for our slow, stopping one which crept slowly along, until after several changes, we reached London thirty-six hours later.

During my absence in the autumn, I had heard from mother that the Griffiths had returned from the States. So, early in 1927 I began working again for Sandy at their house, in the evenings and occasional weekends. Their spontaneous way of life cast a spell over me under which I lived and worked for several years. I of course introduced them to Ethel, who felt their friendly charm as much as I did, and I was happy that, for once, I had friends to give her who had given me so many. But she didn't stay long for she had had an invitation from Loup Mayrisch to stay at their house Colpach, in Luxembourg, at any time she chose, and to take me with her. As she had always wanted to show me that country and the many friends she had made there immediately after the 1914 war, she thought this would be an ideal moment to introduce me to another 'foreign field'. And I of course eagerly joined her there.

It was a great experience for me to find myself in that beautiful house about which Whity had told me so much. It was a large house. The grounds were spacious and included a formal garden over which a beautiful Pomona by Maillol presided. But what impressed me most was a huge bronze statue by Bourdelle, which one came upon in a clearing of the dark fir woods that surrounded the house. This was called 'The Dying Centaur' and showed the huge horse with his front legs still upright but the hind quarters already sinking in death, while the man's body was upright too, though his head sagged sideways over his shoulder. It was about fifteen feet high. Inside the house, all was comfort and beauty.

But it was the company that fascinated me most, both those who were staying and those who came to the excellent meals (at one of which I tasted wild boar for the first time). They were gay and warm and friendly people and I found them more human and a shade more earthy than the French. But the outstanding personality among them all was Emile Mayrisch himself, the head of the great Arbed steelworks, whom they all called 'Le Patron' and whom I had briefly met several times at the Bastide. Whity had told me much about him, for she knew his quality and venerated him for his wisdom and authority. A big, burly, bearded man, he sat at the head of his table, with a large black box, a kind of hearing aid, on the table beside him, for he was almost totally deaf. One had to shout into this to make him hear, which intimidated most of the guests, including me of course. But not so Whity; she sat beside him and there I saw another instance of her humour and her unself-conscious awareness of the other person, for she would lovingly tease him and shout outrageous nonsense into the box in her always amusing French, which made him beam with delight at thus being noticed and brought into the conversation. No wonder he was devotedly fond of her, as she was to discover a little later. Whity and I stayed there for ten days.

After those happy days in Luxembourg, we both returned to London where I was once again taken up with the Griffiths, not only working for him but trying to help Kate too. She begged me to help fill her days by giving her lessons in world history, of which she was woefully ignorant, having been to a so-called progressive school in America where she learned nothing. She came to our house for these and I spent a lot of time preparing outline talks, covering enormous stretches of time in each lesson. I didn't begin further back than Greece, but when we got to Rome and I was explaining why the dates changed from BC to AD she startled me by remarking, 'How neat of Christ to have been born at the year one!' What a poor teacher I was!

I fear that life cannot have been very gay for Ethel that summer as I was then working in Sandy's office and so had less chance of doing things with her. She knew too that a great many changes were taking place in the lives of our French friends, which would alter that old pattern of regular visits she used to follow so happily and this made her think more seriously than ever of her own future, and regret the collapse of the Geneva job. Beth's father, Théo the painter, had died in the previous December. His death solved the question of a home for Beth after the Bastide was sold, for she immediately decided to turn his studio, splendidly situated on rising ground above his former house beside the road at St Clair, into a new home for herself, and sell the old house. La Petite Dame at the same time found an ideal flat for herself in a new block just being built in the rue Vaneau in Paris. Adjoining hers there would be another flat, exactly what Gide needed, for it consisted of one huge room big enough to hold his vast library, with two other small rooms, one a sparsely furnished bedroom. He hated possessions, except his books, and took it for granted that he would have all his meals in Tit's flat with which his was joined by a corridor. Beyond his, through a connecting door, there was another studio flat for any friend who wanted a lodging. The whole floor seemed expressly designed for them and soon became known as the Vaneau, where Whity and I were invariably welcomed, and which became a fascinating centre of French literary life.

After this comparatively uneventful summer came the first of those summer schools in Geneva described in the last chapter. When it ended, I returned to my work in the City with Sandy which became rather a wearing experience, because his office was so badly run that we often quarrelled, and I gradually began to discover what a disorganized, not to say rather shifty, man he was. Ethel was not altogether happy at my being involved in it, though he still, in our social meetings, retained a certain attraction for both of us. At the end of the year he went to the States, whether voluntarily or on recall for some reason I do not know.

After that year's summer-school was over, Ethel went on to stay with Beth at St Clair, where she saw the new house, already well advanced. It was to be called 'Le Pin' because of the huge umbrella pine on its terrace. She found not only Beth but Catherine in a good mood, and indeed, it almost seemed as if the child, now nearly five years old, was aware of Whity for the first time, and fell in love with her, saying one day in one of her unexpected poetic phrases 'I love Whity more than the sky, because she has a lovely face'. On the whole, however, I don't think it was a very happy visit for Whity because at St Clair there would be no garden for her to cultivate.

If the year (1928) that had just ended had not been very eventful, it was followed by one almost too full of movements and events, one of them tragic. Sandy had returned from the States, telling me he was now to live and run the Dillon Reid office in Paris, which he knew well. And by way of keeping my services, he offered me a retaining fee of two pounds a week, the condition being that I should do for him any odd jobs that he wanted doing in London, such as selling their house in Golders Green, and be ready to go to Paris at a moment's notice to work as his secretary, when of course all my expenses would be paid. All this sounded rather exciting and as if it would give me responsibility as well as experience, so I accepted in spite of my doubts about him. As he was eager to move as soon as he could, Kate went flat-hunting in Paris and soon found one.

In February Whity went again to stay with Beth and while she was there Emile Mayrisch turned up alone at his house at Bormes and Whity had talks with him there. During these he told her how deeply he loved and esteemed her. He was most anxious to do something for her, for I think he must have seen how rather lost in life she was feeling now she had no gardening for Beth and had lost her Geneva job. He said too that he wanted to lavish things on her and spoil her in some way. Whity was, of course, quite overcome at learning all this, admiring and venerating him as she did as someone far above her. But all was left vague for the moment and he returned to Luxembourg and she to England.

In retrospect, what a happy thing it was that she should have had that short time alone with him at Bormes. For on 6 March she learned that he had been killed in a road accident in Luxembourg. It was Pierre Lansel, a Swiss doctor in London we both knew and who knew all our Luxembourg friends, who had the telegram about it and told Whity. She rang me at the office and asked me to go to her. I found her greatly shocked, but outwardly calm. I took her home for the night, but the next day she was in a quandary whether she should go to the funeral or not, fearing to be in the way, and yet wanting to be there. Pierre Lansel settled the question, saying, rightly, that her presence would comfort them all and she would be no burden, as she was always ready to fit in anywhere. So off she went.

The day after the funeral, I had to go to Paris, according to my agreement. So I was there when I received Whity's letter sent me the day after the funeral, telling me what a tremendous ceremony it had been, more imposing even than those on the death of one of their rulers. The Grand Duke had headed the procession of 20,000 people which followed the bier, all the shops and factories were closed, there were eight lorries full of flowers and even the prisoners of Luxembourg had sent a telegram of condolence, for he had been a universal benefactor, much beloved by everyone. He was buried in the garden at Colpach, in the presence of his friends, many of whom had come from France and elsewhere. It was not difficult to imagine her feelings, remembering the recent past and thinking of the friend she had lost. Whity begged me to return to London as soon as I could, which of course I did, comforting her as best I might. In any case, she was never one to brood over her sorrows or indulge in vain regrets, for she had great strength of character; but her grief and sense of loss lasted a long time. She understood too that I had my job to do and it turned out that I had to make several trips to Paris that summer.

In spite of the sad loss of Emile, Ethel was quite enjoying her summer, largely because Beth had reversed the usual order of things and came with her mother and Catherine to spend the summer in England, sometimes in London but chiefly at Alfriston, where I joined them in the intervals of my times in Paris. Our life in London that year was also enriched by the friendship of the philosopher, Cecil Delisle Burns, whom we had met through Margery Perham in Geneva and who had a beautiful house in Keats Grove, Hampstead, where he held regular Sunday tea-parties at which one always met interesting people from a variety of worlds. A thin, ascetic-looking man with bushy hair, he had a wide range of interests, was easy to talk to, and loved nothing better than entertaining friends.

Ethel had another 'foreign field' in prospect then, for Roger had written to ask her to go and stay with him for six months in Ceylon, where he was a Civil Servant, and at that time, the Mayor of Kandy. She accepted, especially as the coming winter held out no other prospects for her and he had generously offered to pay her fare. It was fixed that she would go in late September as soon as possible after our second summer-school ended, so we hurried back to London for Ethel to make her preparations and pay farewell visits to her friends. I can't remember feeling any particular pangs at the thought of the long separation ahead of us, for Beth had invited me to spend the autumn with her, thinking perhaps that being together we should less miss the friend we both loved best, and should be able to share her news when letters at last began to arrive. It was the first time I saw Le Pin and I found it an enchanting house, both to look at and to stay in. It had a huge living-room, looking over the wide terrace where stood the great umbrella-pine after which the house was named, and then on down to the beatiful bay below. Out of the living room there opened a charming small circular room with a desk in it, which Beth gave me to be my own refuge and to write in.

For I had decided that now the time had come for me to return to that long-neglected project of writing *Héloïse*, which for some reason I had put aside after my first sketchy attempts. Yet I persisted in my idea of a *biographie romancée*, though still harbouring doubts as to whether this was the right way to do it. However that may be, I kept on with my romantic version until I had virtually come to the end of my book, except for a little polishing. Apart from this so-called work, the other great pleasure of that time was the chance to indulge in uninterrupted reading, especially sitting round the fire in the big room in the evenings, for it was a rather chilly autumn. I had no other leisure occupation or pastimes. I neither sewed nor knitted, nor sketched, not being adroit with my hands as Whity was. And I didn't really enjoy cards. And of course it was a daily pleasure to go for walks in that heavenly country.

But the most thrilling pleasure for us all was when the Indian mail at last began to arrive in November, when Catherine would run into the room shouting excitedly, 'Whity letter! Whity letter!', sometimes a joint one, sometimes one each, and we all laughed foolishly with the happiness of reading Whity's vivid and always amusing account of her exploration of the ancient wonders of the island, which she managed to see, thanks to a man in the Australian Department of External Affairs who shared her interest in them. She loved riding too and Roger had managed to get her a horse, so she was able to go out alone on it in the early mornings.

After those lovely autumn months, I returned to London on 20 December in a mood of great elation. But that quickly changed to a sort of panic when on the 22nd I heard from Margery Perham in the vaguest way that someone called Helen was working on a book about Héloïse too. I immediately started making enquiries and found out, I think from Cecil Delisle Burns, that my rival was Helen Waddell, who was only just beginning to work on her *Peter Abelard*, which did not in fact come out until 1933. Curiously enough, knowing what a scholar she was gave me a kind of comfort, for I thought there might still be room for my romantic version. So I calmed down and in January, still undaunted, I finished polishing the last few pages of my *Héloïse* and sent it to Barbara Gwyer, then Principal of St Hugh's and a great friend of Margery Perham's, to ask her to be kind enough to give me her opinion of the book and, if she approved it, to send it to her brother, Sir Maurice, at that time one of the two heads of the firm then called Faber and Gwyer. Although I don't remember hearing from her, she apparently thought well enough of it to send it on, but the firm turned it down. I was, of course, disappointed that they had, but years later, when I had made an entirely different thing of it, I was glad.

Whity sailed for home on 29 March, reaching Marseilles on 6 April, where Beth met her and drove her to St Clair. There she found a houseful of her French and Luxembourg friends, all excited to see her again and finding her, as Beth told me later, at the peak of her beauty and powers. After a riotous fortnight, when she was as ever full of inventive games and fun she left for Paris, where I was impatiently awaiting her. She had most characteristically sent me a cheque for ten pounds to help me get there, and we had a perfect week of endless talks, staying at our favourite hotel Cayré, and seeing all our Paris friends.

In the talks we then exchanged, she told me of the two serious proposals of marriage she had received in Ceylon, and how she had unhesitatingly refused both, because of her unwavering sense of the contrast between the values and interests of those utterly conventional men and their fellows, kindly and decent though they all were, and those of the friends she loved at home, especially me, on whom her heart was fixed, as mine was on her. Having turned them down, she enjoyed their company, for she had often suffered, especially during that year in Geneva, from her lack of the company of men friends. That she had acted in this way made us both realize, although we may not have spoken of it at the time, that this was how it would always be for both of us, since for neither was marriage ever an ideal. We had both already had, and were to have again, attractions and affairs of varying intensity, both emotional and physical, with other people. But when this happened we always told each other, knowing the understanding both could rely on that these passing passions, however absorbing they might be momentarily, especially in my case, and in spite of occasional flickers of jealousy, chiefly on my side I think, could not possibly endanger our irreplaceable and overwhelming love for each other. So it had always been in the past, and so in the future it was always to prove.

When we returned from Paris, she slipped happily into her old routine, very glad to see again her mother, for whom her long absence must have been very hard to bear. She took her for many country drives that summer, on some of which I accompanied them. In June, she and I went to Oxford to spend a week seeing Margery Perham, who had just been awarded by the Rhodes Trust her first travelling fellowship, an unheard-of honour for a woman at that time. She set off later that summer on an enormous tour that was to last from October 1929 to March 1930, during which we kept in touch with her through the very full diaries she sent to six of her friends, and which, entitled *African Apprenticeship* together with her account of a second tour in 1929-30, *East African Journey*, were published for the first time over forty years later.

Chapter Eight

MORE TRAVEL, CHANGES AND POLITICS
1930-1934

The Christmas dinner of 1929 was the last that my mother and I were to enjoy in that hospitable house in Chesterford Gardens that had been like home to me throughout the 1920s. Looking back on those years they seem an era of carefree lightheartedness, not only for Ethel and me but for our foreign friends too, an era when everything went as we wanted it to, and we had little sense of responsibility for anything or anybody. But with the beginning of the 1930s occasional shadows began to fall across the once cloudless sky, and the French as well as ourselves, began to feel a growing sense of responsibility. Various changes occurred in both Ethel's and Beth's lives. It was a decade in which Ethel's and my paths often diverged; although nothing ever loosened the bonds that held us. And finally it was a decade in which I began to think of my book on Héloïse in more serious terms and to discover, at last, after so much wasted time, how I ought to do it.

Outwardly my circumstances were not changed, and I continued to live at home throughout the decade. But at first I had not even those semblances of a secretarial job that had filled my time before. In January Sandy had come to London to tell me he was definitely leaving Paris for New York and asking me to look after Kate until she could join him. Six months later he wrote from New York saying he had given up business and become a stockbroker, was doing very well and had acquired a beautiful house on Long Island which he hoped I would visit. But I felt that sounded phoney, and I think Kate too was a bit afraid of what lay before her.

Ethel was equally unemployed at the beginning of that year, finding her own life dull and frustrating. But we continued to spend our time happily seeing friends and enjoying the London winter season. That was the year of the great Italian art exhibition at Burlington House, which we visited continually. Among the theatre attractions there was John Gielgud in *Hamlet*, and on the lighter side Noel Coward's *Bittersweet*, most memorable and nostalgic of all his musicals.

What rescued Ethel at last from that not very eventful time was an invitation from Beth to go and spend two months at Le Pin. She set off at the beginning of May and found herself in very different company from that in her former visits to Le Bastide. For one thing, staying at the Mayrischs' house at Bormes was their daughter Andrée, a young woman in her late twenties. Andrée was brilliantly intelligent and amusing, not beautiful but with thick-lashed blue-green eyes. She had recently married Pierre Viénot, a very remarkable young man who, when only seventeen, had managed to get into the French army in the 1914 war, in which he was badly wounded. Later he shared Emile Mayrisch's conviction that peace between France and Germany was essential for the future of Europe. He was therefore a frequent visitor at Colpach where he married Andrée. Whity thought him the perfect husband for her friend Andrée and herself became a devoted friend and admirer of his, as she was to show much later in life.

Meanwhile they both joined in all the expeditions that Beth arranged for her household at Le Pin, Catherine still retained her former interest in Whity, whose gaiety and fun obviously puzzled her in a grown-up. La Petite Dame was there, but for once Gide was not. They were however expecting Jean Schlumberger for a short visit at the end of June. He had just published a long novel called *Saint Saturnin*, which had been a great success, and made all 'the friends', as we called them, think more highly of this modest writer than they previously had. Dorothy Bussy was going to translate it.

That August Whity, Beth and I had decided to go to Pontigny. The subject of the *décade* that year was 'Y a-t-il trois psychologies: celle de l'enfant—celle du primitif—celle de l'anormal—ou bien est-ce en tous trois la même?' I have quoted this to show how much in its infancy the science of psychology was in those days. Outstanding among the company that year were the Italians. Edoardo Ruffini, his

89

beautiful wife Giorgia and cousin Nina, all became lifelong friends of ours. When the *décade* ended Beth begged Whity to drive her to Luxembourg, where she wanted to see one of her girlhood friends. So I returned home alone, and as things turned out it was a good thing I did.

For soon after I got back Mrs Whitehorn told me that her husband, who had seemed perfectly well before we left, was now mortally ill with cancer of the liver, and she did not know how to get at Ethel whom she wanted to come home quickly. I had no precise knowledge of where Ethel was at that moment, but I knew what to do and here I must pay tribute to our Post Office, whose efficiency in those days was a matter of national pride. I merely rang the right department, and told the official who answered what little I knew of Whity's whereabouts. He quickly went to work and the next morning rang back to say he had traced her and put me through. I had the luck to find Whity in and to be able to tell her the sad news. She came home the next day and so was in time to help nurse her cheerful father through the three weeks that his illness lasted, before he died a dignified and uncomplaining death.

Thereafter changes came quickly. The house at Chesterford Gardens was obviously too big and expensive for the family now, so it was sold, and in January Ethel and her mother moved into a smaller one in Briardale Gardens, leading out of the Finchley Road almost opposite Lyndale Avenue, so that Ethel and I now had the joy of living nearer to each other than ever before; We greatly enjoyed that winter of 1931, seeing more and more of the Delisle Burns, at whose house there were always new people to meet; there were also regular Sunday evening chamber-music concerts in the St John's Wood house of some of Margaret Burns's relations, the Howards.

In addition to such things I had had a very pleasant task to perform that winter, for at Pontigny la Petite Dame had told us she wanted to take Beth, Whity and me for a tour of Greece. As she had no idea what she wanted to see, apart from Athens, she asked me to do the planning. There were of course no such things as package tours in those days, and in any case she wanted to do it in great comfort and had no time-limit. I therefore had a free hand, which delighted me. During that winter I began to read such books of travel in

Greece as I could find and had the luck to come across one called *Hellas Revisited*, by McNeile Dixon. I wrote to him praising his book, and asking him how I could get hold of the dragoman, Constantine Bizanis, who had arranged what sounded to me the ideal tour. He answered me at once, telling me how to proceed. I immediately wrote to Bizanis, who sent me a full and detailed programme and it was arranged that we should go for six weeks in April and May.

It is not my intention to write a detailed account of that unforgettable journey, but as few people can enjoy anything like it nowadays, I must record some of its more memorable moments. We went of course by sea from Marseilles. The journey took three days. When our ship reached Piraeus there stood awaiting us a dignified man with the carved face of an ancient Roman, and a large Lincoln car.

We spent the whole of the first week in Athens, which gave us time to visit the Acropolis and the National Museum many times, as well as having a day on Aegina, where we discovered Bizanis's skill as a cook! For while we were seeing the temple he retired behind a bush, whence arose most savoury smells, so that when the exploring was over we sat comfortably down on fallen columns and had a lovely hot lunch. In that first week too we took ship to Crete, where Cnossos was the only palace then excavated.

On returning to Athens we spent a night in Corinth and then set out across the plain of Argos for Mycenae. But on the way there I developed a sore throat and a high fever, and was so ill that, after a wretched night in the sordid hotel called the Belle Hélène, where the one waiter was a local youth with a squint and a limp, named Agamemnon, Bizanis seemed doubtful whether we ought to continue with our journey. But I refused to give up and so next day we went on to Epidaurus. After seeing the theatre, where my throat was so bad I could hardly speak, we went into the temple of Aesculapius, the god of health. And it was on coming out of that that Bizanis suddenly said, as though it was something that anyone might expect, 'The god has cured Miss McLeod'. Indeed he had, for my fever had suddenly dropped, my voice was normal and I felt myself again. It seemed a miracle to all of us, and we went happily on through Arcadia to Sparta with enough time to linger at Olympia, which I think moved us more than any place so far, so redolent it seemed of the ancient games there.

The last memorable part of our tour was on our journey to Skyros, where Beth wanted to see the grave of Rupert Brooke, who had been a great friend of hers before and during her Swanley days. To get there we had to cross from the mainland to Chalkis on Euboea whence we reached a little port and boarded a small wooden ship. We landed on the coast nearest to the grave and climbed up to that solitary, willow-shaded tomb, where Bizanis discreetly left us alone.

We returned to Marseilles on 2 May and on the 6th Whity left with Tit, returning home quickly because Beth had invited her for yet another holiday in June. But I stayed on with Beth for another two or three weeks. I had no other holiday in prospect that year. So I felt I must make the most of this one, and thus had accepted an invitation to Geneva where I had not been for two years. I had one of my happiest visits, seeing all my old Swiss friends, as well of course as my English hosts and their League friends.

Soon after I got back to London, Ethel set off again at the end of June for a very special holiday, to which Beth this time had not invited me, well knowing it would not be the kind of thing I should enjoy. They were to camp for ten days on the Ile du Levant. They were joined by a tall, elegant, good-looking young man called Pierre Herbart whom Gide had introduced to Beth and whom she obviously found extremely seductive, though Whity had some doubts about him. But he fitted in very well and enjoyed it all as they did.

Whity stayed on with Beth till the beginning of August so it was only in mid-August that I saw her again and she was able to tell me, what Beth had only told her before she left St Clair, that she had fallen so deeply in love with Pierre and he with her that all her old theories counted for nothing and she was going to marry him as soon as possible. It can be imagined what a shock the speed and secrecy of all this was for Whity, for she realized instinctively, even after that short acquaintance, the type of man he was. But there was no time for reflection, for Pierre, who described himself as a journalist, had immediately to go off to the Far East on some sort of mission; so they were married on 14 September and Beth, already pregnant, though I think she did not then know it, remained behind to begin altering Le Pin, so lately perfected, to suit his wishes. Ethel returned to England.

If our paths had diverged often in 1931, they did so more still in 1932. And as once again Ethel had the most interesting time in that year, from the point of view of our foreign friends and their political and personal preoccupations, I will recount our two lives separately this year, instead of intertwining the events of them as I have previously done, and begin with hers. Towards the end of January 1932 she set off for Luxembourg where she had many more friends than I had met. They all gave her a warm welcome and she was as usual happy there; but this time there was a shadow over their usually cheerful lives, for her friends were a prey to gloomy feelings about the situation between France and Germany. Feelings were apparently running so high that our friends thought war was inevitable. If I had shown her before she left a letter of New Year greetings which I had received from Roger Martin du Gard she might have been prepared to find such apprehension in Luxembourg, for he had written of *'ce sinistre gouffre vers lequel nous poussent les sombres pronostics des gens bien renseignés. Car le monde s'écroule autour de nous, ce n'est que trop certain'* and he went on to say *'la société capitaliste ... est bien coupable ... on ne trouve pas d'arguments pour la défendre'*. I don't remember that there was so much apprehension in England at that time, although left-wing circles were certainly beginning to turn communist.

She got another glimpse of this feeling on her journey south when, in passing through Paris, Gide had given her a splendid lunch at Prunier's. Their talk was partly about communism which she was surprised to hear him, who had always seemed to lack interest in anything except literature, say occupied seven out of every ten of his thoughts. (But no doubt she was wrong, for in his *Journal* of that day he wrote *'De coeur, de tempérament, de pensée, j'ai toujours été communiste. Mais j'avais peur de ma propre pensée, et, dans mes écrits, m'efforçais plus de la cacher que de la dire'*).

But he talked about Pierre too, and as it was he who had introduced him to Beth, thinking he might be a possible husband, Whity was surprised to hear him say that Pierre was not only a homosexual (though not intimate with Gide in that way), but that he also took drugs. This naturally strengthened her own instinctive distrust of him which she had felt from the first meeting. So her visit when she at last got to St Clair was not exactly a peaceful one, for the house was full of masons tearing down what had so recently been put up and altering the disposition of the rooms. When they heard that Pierre was expected back on 4 March, knowing that he would not want to see her there, Whity at once left with Tit for Paris. There a much happier life awaited her, for Gide, hearing they were coming, at once suggested that all three should go and spend six days with Roger Martin du Gard and his wife in their beautiful rose-brick seventeenth-century house, Le Tertre, at Bellême in Normandy. It was a wonderfully happy visit. Whity listened absorbed to the endless conversations between those two good friends, about every topic that presented itself but chiefly about communism, which both felt was theoretically the ideal system of government, though neither at that moment seemed to think of its application in Soviet Russia. They would often turn to her to ask what was being thought in England where, in spite of many with strong left-wing views, I don't think such passionate opinions were then held.

Back in Paris Whity stayed for another week with Tit, when Gide insisted on taking Whity to plays and films he wanted her to see. At the Vaneau she met other writers too, some of whom knew Pierre Herbart and described him to her as an arrogant, self-willed and sometimes violent man, which she felt boded ill for Beth's marriage with him. But they tried to defend him on the score of his youth, for he was after all fifteen years younger than Beth. The cult of heroism and adventure was in the air at that time, and the personification of it was André Malraux, who had won recent acclaim for his novel *La Condition Humaine*, but was then under a cloud for his illegal appropriation of some statues he had discovered while flying over a lost part of Africa. Pierre had some of Malraux' characteristics, but not his undoubted gifts. Whity, incidentally, had just met Malraux, with his nervous ticks and too rapid talk, and when writing to ask me if I'd ever met him she said 'A shadier piece of work I've rarely seen'. How sound her instinctive judgement always was!

Thinking back to that time it was remarkable that she, who after all was no intellectual, was so much at home with all those advanced writers, who all thought so highly of her and obviously valued her for her character as well as her charm. And she, for her part, took it all so simply and naturally, which again was part of that charm. Her head was so little turned by it that, on returning home, she cheerfully decided to take up private gardening, by way of filling her days and earning a little money. And needless to say, I was happy to have her with me once again and to hear of the happenings in France following her visit. At the end of April Beth's baby, a boy, was born, but lived only a few days. On 11 May Beth wrote to say that she was going to sell Le Pin on which so much time and money had been spent as Pierre didn't like it.

Towards the end of the summer Ethel, having listened to all that theorising about communism, but having no strong views of her own, thought she would like to go and see for herself how it worked in Soviet Russia, which none of her French friends then seemed to think about. One day while she was making plans we met Prince Mirsky in town for drinks and heard that he too was going back to Russia. On 17 September Ethel sailed from Hay's Wharf for Leningrad on one of the Intourist tours then being arranged. Whether Mirsky went with them or separately I don't know, but I rather think not. The voyage took five days. After a few days in Leningrad they went by train to Moscow for a week, then back to Leningrad. I remember that on those journeys Ethel told me they were all herded into wooden compartments and Russians crowded in from the corridors to stare at them. She asked their interpreter to tell them that in our country only cattle travelled as they were doing. 'But how could it be different?' was the reply. She returned to England in October. But Mirsky was never seen or heard of again.

If 1932 had been a rich and happy time for Ethel, it was an important one for me too, though in a less spectacular way. I began by fulfilling a promise I had made my Russian friend Nicolas Zernov, whom I had met in Geneva in 1927. This was that I would correct the English of the thesis he had written for his Ph D degree at Oxford, a job which the university authorized in the case of a foreigner. Although unfamiliar with his subject matter, which had something to do with the history of the Russian church, I was able to grasp the essence of what he had to say, but saw too that it was badly expressed in faulty English and very repetitive. So as he gave me a free hand I set to work to re-write it, cutting out repetitive passages and even a few details that seemed to me unimportant, and correcting the English while keeping the thoughts he was expressing. It had to be ready by early May, which meant working ten hours a day towards the end. He was very pleased with what I had done, presented the thesis in May and got his doctorate in June, with high praise for the originality of his ideas and his excellent English. And I got the £20 fee the university paid!

I daresay that job gave me the assurance I needed for the next and more important literary task I had in mind, which was really the beginning of my serious labours on *Héloïse*. I had always hoped to use Scott Moncrieff's translation for those parts of Héloïse's and Abélard's letters that I intended to quote. But the more closely I read it the more I felt that, knowing Héloïse as I felt I did, there were a few turns of phrase that I would have put differently. So I thought it behoved me to check his translation with the original Latin. I knew enough Latin myself to do that, though it was rather rusty, not having been used since the days of the first exam at Oxford. Our friend Cecil Delisle Burns helped me by borrowing for me the Latin text of the letters from a specialist library called Dr Williams' Library, which allowed its members to keep books as long as they wanted.

I set to work immediately on the laborious checking of Scott Moncrieff against the original and occasionally making small alterations. But in doing so it occurred to me that this was a very second-hand and piecemeal proceeding and that I owed it to my book to make my own translation of the many passages I wanted. Although the medieval Latin was comparatively simple, translation, as I had reason to know, always presents difficulties of choice; and I soon became so absorbed in the task that I never slackened the pace, even on holiday.

In addition to borrowing the Latin text for me, Cecil was to do me a still greater service. He and his family had recently left Keats Grove and moved to a bigger house at Turner Close, in the Hampstead Garden Suburb. There they gave more tea-parties than ever. And it was there that, one day in March 1933, I met Helen Waddell, whose novel *Peter Abélard* had just come out. This was a momentous meeting for me. For one thing I was greatly relieved to find that the book I had been told she was working on in 1930 was not a serious study of the whole life of Héloïse, as I had feared it might be, but a novel with the early love-story as its main theme, and nothing of the later life of Héloïse.

So I didn't feel daunted, but instantly decided that I must throw away all that I had done, and instead try to produce a full and sober study of Héloïse based on all the evidence I could find and continuing to the end of her life. Helen Waddell was so easy and friendly that I told her of my ambition to do this, and she encouraged me, obviously seeing that I was a novice and no rival in the field that she had made her own.

So it was with renewed hope that, almost immediately after meeting her, I went at last to the British Museum Reading Room and pulled out the volume of the huge catalogue in which everything concerning the famous pair was listed. It was an enormous list covering the whole field, from contemporary chronicles and histories, all the editions of the letters from the early sixteenth century on and the absurd paraphrases of them, and all the books the story had inspired right up to the present day, in addition of course to all Abélard's works. I knew that I should have to search through them all, in case I came across some treasure, but rather surprisingly, instead of daunting me, this filled me with the thrill of research, which ever since then I have felt to be the most enthralling pursuit in the world. Since I had had no training in such scholarly work, I had to find my own way, especially through the ancient chronicles and histories, some in Latin, on which I began to work straight away. I knew I should not be able to get very far that summer, for there was something else I must do before I finally settled to the years of work that it would take. But it was enough to feel that I was on the right track at last, and that I had put my first poor effort behind me.

That something else that took me away from my present absorbing interest was an entirely new world. Ever since the Griffiths had left Europe Kate had been sending me pressing invitations to go and stay with them, promising to show me all the wonders of New York. But her reply to one I sent her on our return from Greece was filled with an almost deeper nostalgia for the old world she had only had time to glimpse and a longing for me as in some way the personification of it in the days when we had been together. Although she protested that Sandy was doing well and that they were happy together, I was aware of a growing loneliness in her letters and an inability to cope with life. All this made me determined to go and see her now, as it might be a long time before I had another chance. Both Ethel and my mother, and friends like the Burns, were in favour of my going, so I sailed in the Berengaria at the end of September 1933.

Two surprises awaited me on the day I landed. The first was a painful shock, for there awaiting me was not the tall, upright beauty with the conquering air that I remembered, but a drably dressed, slightly bent figure, the brim of her slouched hat partly covering a lined face in which the bones stood out. She brightened a little at the sight of me and drove me to the beautiful flat of her elegant father and his second wife, overlooking Central Park; and there I had my second surprise: the staggering beauty of New York as I looked down on the green of the Park, getting more and more vivid as the dusk deepened and little lamps came out all over it. Then as the turquoise sky deepened to dark blue, suddenly the massed sky-scrapers at the west end turned all at once into towers of dazzling diamonds. It was time to go, crossing the bridge from Manhattan to Long Island, where I found the quiet old house where I was to spend the next three months. It stood outside Huntingdon on the edge of the wide waters of the Sound, so that one only had to run from the garden to the sandy shore, where it was warm enough to bathe at all times of the day right up to the beginning of November.

During my first weeks Kate drove me through New England and parts of Massachusetts to visit her friends and relatives. But the more I saw of them the more I was struck by the fact that none of them seemed to be aware of the profound change in her, any more than Sandy was when we returned to Huntingdon and he frequently came out from New York, where he was obviously living a separate life, to see something of me while I was there. He looked older and harder and was often harsh with Kate, who wilted under his sometimes cruel treatment, but he could not or would not see that she was mentally ill, as I could see she was when we were alone together and her state of despair became obvious.

'As I knew no one in all that vast continent professionally qualified to help her, I had to rely on myself. So I thought the best thing would be first to try and re-awaken her old interest in her appearance, reminding her how she had conquered everyone she met both in London and in Paris. She responded quickly to that and immediately went out and ordered fine new clothes. The next thing was to stimulate her interest in all that was going on around her in the New York world of the theatre, music and the arts, by reminding her that she had promised if I came to show me the pleasures of the city. And as there seemed to be no shortage of money we then began regular visits to the city, sometimes even staying overnight in comfortable hotels, so that we led a hectic life for several weeks, going to plays, concerts and films and having meals out, at which Sandy often joined us, sometimes bringing interesting people with him. But more than all these ephemeral pleasures I loved the Metropolitan Museum, where we spent many hours. And because I couldn't have enough of such galleries, Kate took me, by a luxurious overnight boat, to Boston for a few days, so that I could visit the wonderful Isabella Stewart Gardner Museum, and the Fogg Art Museum at Harvard.

She had hoped I would stay with her for six months, but I felt I must get home by Christmas, to begin work on *Héloïse* in the New Year. But she was now, so it seemed to me, so much her old self again that together we made plans, and she herself suggested all sorts of things she wanted to do after I left, such as visiting Mexico on horseback. So it was with hope renewed for her that I took a passage home, again on the Berengaria. Kate wrote to my mother to tell her all she felt I had done for her. I found a note from her in my cabin, signed 'From Katie, reborn'. So it was with a heart at peace and full of hope for her that I got home in time for the Christmas festivities. A few letters from Kate in January told me that she and Sandy were now on good terms with each other. Throughout the rest of that year I heard nothing from her, but she was not a regular letter-writer so I did not worry. But the following Christmas I heard from Beth, who knew Kate's sister Tan, that Kate had shot herself for what sounded like a trifling reason. So all I had given her was a brief respite from a fate whose end had perhaps been in her from the beginning.

Chapter Nine

Héloïse
1934-1938

It was now seven years since, as I related in chapter six, my casual reading of the two immortal love-letters of Héloïse in a French translation had filled me with such admiration for her that I conceived the idea of a book of which she should be the main character. But my curious blindness as to the way to treat my theme lasted until I had done my worst; and it was not until 1933 that the scales fell from my eyes and I realized that the only way to do full justice to my still burning admiration of Héloïse was to go to all the possible sources.

So it was with a renewed sense of mission that I went to the British Museum Reading Room early in January 1934. What I wanted to do was to read everything I could about her: contemporary documents and chronicles and later literature too. I wanted to visit the places in France where she had lived and then to write a biography that would, I hoped, represent her truly in all the nobility of her mind and actions from childhood to old age. But since the book I at last wrote on the basis of all this study is now out of print, and many readers may never have heard of her, it may be useful if I here give the briefest possible outline of her story.

She was born nearly nine hundred years ago, in 1101, and brought up in childhood at a convent in Argenteuil. There she received an education such as few women of her time were given, especially in Latin so that she was able to express in it the deepest feelings of her heart.

When she left the convent, at the age of about seventeen, and went to live with her one relative, her uncle Canon Fulbert, in his house in the cloister of Notre Dame, the rumour of her amazing learning quickly spread throughout Paris and caught the ear of Abailard (as his name was originally spelt), a brilliant and handsome man nearly twenty years her senior, who was the most famous teacher and lecturer of his time, as a result of which he had many rivals and enemies. Hitherto he had been so absorbed in his work that he had had nothing to do with women; but now, hearing of this wonderfully learned girl, he felt a sudden desire to conquer her. To facilitate this he asked Fulbert to let him lodge in his house, offering in return to teach the niece of whom Fulbert was justly proud, so much so that he at once agreed, telling Abailard that he might be with her at any hour of the day or night that he could spare. As soon as he saw her, Abailard felt such an uncontrollable desire for her that it was not long before he evoked an answering desire in her, young, innocent and passionate as she was, full of pride at being his pupil and dazzled by his proximity.

Not surprisingly, after a few months of blissful love-making, the scholars began to notice a change in their master and all Paris heard of the reason for it, Fulbert was the last to do so. His discovery filled Abailard with shame, but not so Héloïse, as her desire had now grown into a deep love in which she gloried. She exulted even more when she found she was with child and as Fulbert had driven Abailard from the house, she wrote to tell him of it. Abailard then took her, in the habit of a nun, to his birthplace, Le Pallet in remote Brittany, and there she remained with his sister, until her son Astrolabe was born, and Abailard came to fetch her back to Paris, leaving the child behind.

It was on their journey that Abailard tried to persuade Héloïse that only by marrying her could he appease the wrath of Fulbert. It was then that Héloïse showed not only the selflessness of her love, but the clear-sighted originality of her mind. For she saw that marriage would be a bar to any future preferment for Abailard in the ecclesiastical world. She told him too that she would rather be his harlot than the wife of the Emperor Augustus. But nothing could persuade him to change his mind and, as always, she gave in to him. Fulbert promised that the marriage should be kept secret and it took place in great privacy, whereupon Fulbert at once broke his promise and divulged it. But Héloïse, true to her word, stoutly denied it, whereupon Fulbert began to ill-treat her so violently that Abailard took her back to Argenteuil, where she adopted the habit of a novice. The news of this made Fulbert fear that Abailard meant to break his marriage vows and, now beside himself with rage and the desire for revenge, he hired some assassins, who broke into Abailard's house at night and there brutally castrated him.

At the news Héloïse hastened to his side to comfort him. But the man she found was, perhaps understandably thinking only of his own agony and how it would change his future. He at once told her that he had decided to become a monk at St Denis. What was worse he insisted that she should take the veil at Argenteuil before he went to his monastery, even though he knew she had no vocation for the religious life and this would mean cutting her off from the world for ever. This revelation that he did not trust her love to keep her safe from any other marriage hurt her bitterly and made her feel that he had never really loved her as she loved him. But she made no protest and, returning at once to Argenteuil, she went through the ceremony, protesting that she was doing it of her own accord, as a penalty for what her love had brought on her husband.

During the ten years that she spent at Argenteuil she received no word of comfort or help from Abailard. But though he did not write, Abailard at St Denis could not have failed to hear that his abbot, the famous Suger, was plotting to turn the nuns out of Argenteuil on some trumped-up charge in order to annex their building. Realizing that Héloïse would have nowhere else to go, Abailard at last wrote to her, inviting her to go with a few of her chosen companions to a little oratory which some of his scholars had built on a piece of land beside a small river not far from Nogent-sur-Seine. He loved the place and called it the Paraclet, the Comforter. In 1125 or 1126 Abailard had accepted the abbacy of the abbey of St Gildas on the wild western rocky shores of Brittany, and left his beloved oratory untenanted. So his offer to give it to Héloïse was a godsend to them both. As soon as she and her nuns arrived there, Abailard left St Gildas to go and install them. And so at last they met again, she still a young woman not yet thirty, for ever in love with this man now nearly fifty who, neither by a look nor a personal word alone with her, showed that he remembered what once she had been to him. The life that she and her little community settled down to live there was one of extreme hardship and poverty until gradually the neighbouring noble families, hearing who she was and admiring her uncomplaining dignity, began to help them with food, money and land. And for a few years Abailard came from time to time to see how they were faring, but was careful never to see Héloïse alone. Then suddenly his visits ceased and he sent no word of explanation.

The reason was that the monks of St Gildas, a corrupt brutal set of men, hated their abbot and sought by all means to harm him, and tried to poison him; so he had to spend all his time safeguarding himself. To help his loneliness he wrote an immensely long account of his life, in the supposed form of a letter to a friend but rather, one would imagine, to leave the world an account of his life in case the monks deprived him of it. This document is our main source of information about his life; and by some means unknown it came into the hands of Héloïse, as perhaps he meant it should. In it he wrote fully and vividly of the dangers that at present threatened his life, but only described briefly the events of his love-affair with her.

The fears for his life with which this document filled her, and the memories of their past love which it aroused in her, broke down at last the heroic silence which she had managed to maintain for so many years and she wrote him the two ardent love-letters that are among the greatest of their kind in the literature of the world and that no one who has read them can ever forget. In his reply, Abailard makes no reference to her charges, which he does not deny, but begs her to try and put those thoughts out of her mind. He ends with a beautiful prayer for her community to say for his safety, which at least made her feel how much he still relied on her.

It is doubtful whether she ever saw him again in life, for soon after this exchange of correspondence, he returned to Paris and there wrote some of his most important works. But his enemies at once seized on them and began persecuting him again. At that, Abailard, worn out with the unending persecution, set out for Rome to appeal to the Pope himself. But he was now a very sick man and he got no further than the great Abbey of Cluny whose abbot, Peter the Venerable, a wise, humane and kindly man, was an old friend of his and had admired Héloïse since her youth. He successfully appealed to the Pope on Abailard's behalf and let him spend his last years in peaceful meditation, during which he wrote a most moving *Confession of Faith*, and sent it to Héloïse.

Soon afterwards he died, aged sixty-three. Peter sent the news of his death to Héloïse in a most compassionate letter that showed how well he had understood what Abailard had meant to her. He then secretly removed the body from the monastery where Abailard had died and took it to the Paraclete so that she might bury it in the crypt there, as Abailard had asked, with what feelings one can only imagine, no doubt leaving her heart there with him.

Héloïse was still only forty and was to live for another twenty-one years. But during those years, which few who write about her ever mention, she continued to justify Abailard's confidence in her and put his rules to good use by founding no less than six daughter-houses in different parts of France, in an Order of the Paraclete, showing outstanding powers of administration and taking care to have all her deeds ratified by a succession of popes. Women flocked to serve under her benevolent rule, as one of her contemporary admirers wrote. Yet in spite of this universal reputation for the perfection of her behaviour as a great and blameless abbess, the memory of what she and Abailard had once meant to each other seems to have lingered in the popular memory, so that when at last she died, on 16 May in either 1163 or 1164, the Chronicle of St Martin of Tours relates that when Abailard's tomb was opened that she might be buried with him, his skeleton raised its arms to receive her and clasped them fast about her, for, says the Chronicle, 'she was in very truth his lover'.

To make of this outline a fully documented book, incorporating all the research that it entailed, chiefly at the British Museum and the Bodleian, as well as visits to the Bibliothèque Nationale and the Archives Nationales in Paris, translating the texts and slowly writing my new version as I went along, meant such unremitting work that by the autumn of 1935, after nearly two years of it, I felt I needed a break. Fortunately in early October my friends Elliott and Joyce Felkin asked me to pay them a visit in Geneva. I stayed with them until the end of the month and then Beth, hearing I was in Geneva, invited me to go and see her new house at Cabris, an enchanting hill village above Grasse. She invited Whity too, and as Pierre was in Paris, we three had a happy, carefree holiday, exploring the beautiful surrounding country, still unknown to us, and staying in her new house on the hillside above the village, looking over the uninhabited valley below to a range of mountains behind which lay the sea. We left at the end of November and spent a few days at the Vaneau with La Petite Dame and Gide, who was always coming along the passage to join us at meals and entertaining us with his invariably unexpected and amusing conversation and reading us bits of the fantastic letters he received.

But in spite of all these breaks I never for a moment forgot Héloïse and one day while we were in Paris Whity and I went by train to Nogent-sur-Seine and took a taxi to the site of the Paraclete where a much more recent foundation had replaced Héloïse's abbey, of which nothing now remains except a shallow underground cave, now much fallen in, where once there stood the crypt in which she had buried the dead body of Abailard. It needed much imagination to conjure up that scene, where Whity was almost as much moved as I; for during those last two years, except for a few absences of her own, she had been constantly near me, following my progress on my book with unfailing interest and encouragement.

Immediately we got back to London I returned to my work with renewed zest and strength for the last six months which it was to take before I went in June 1936 to St Hugh's to tell Miss Gwyer that I had now nearly finished this new version and to ask her if she would again recommend it to Fabers. I did not actually finish until March 1937, and I doubt if I should have finished it even then if Ethel, seeing how exhausted I was, had not once again come to my rescue, by suggesting that in late January 1937 we should both accept Loup Mayrisch's invitation to us to go to Luxembourg for a brief visit. Ethel too was in great need of a change for her mother, to whom she was so devoted, had died suddenly in October. Her death saddened us all, and I was particularly grieved that she had not lived to see the publication of the book that she had always believed I would one day write.

I remember still what a bitterly cold month it was and how I enjoyed the warmth and comfort of beautiful Colpach, which seemed more luxurious than ever when one gazed out at the coloured peacocks strutting over the thick snow in the garden beside the frozen lake, or came in from a visit to the Dying Centaur under its weight of snow in the dark encircling woods. Many of our old friends came to see us and I felt as if I had been transported to some enchanted place which, if I had known it, I was never to see again. I only had ten days to enjoy it before returning to London on 1 February to finish my work. Now began the search for a publisher when Ethel drove me with my precious parcel to Fabers in March. I was curiously confident that, because of Miss Gwyer's recommendation, they would accept it. But to my dismay, after a two months' wait, back it came, rejected. Having recovered from this shock, I then sent it to Macmillans. They were to take even longer and in fact by the end of August I still had not heard. During those months of hope deferred I never relaxed my efforts to find a job, applying for anything I saw advertised and begging all my friends to let me know if they heard of anything. But even glowing testimonials from Miss Gwyer never got me anything, so by the end of the summer, I was so downhearted that once again Ethel felt that only a holiday would cheer me.

This time we decided to break away from our usual haunts and go to Vienna, which neither of us had ever seen. We had a gloriously happy fortnight in that beautiful city at the beginning of September. On our way home we stayed for a few days at the Vaneau after which Ethel returned to London and I went once again to Pontigny with la Petite Dame, Gide and Martin du Gard. Although I didn't know it, this was to be the last of my visits there, for the days of those conferences were coming to an end. It was also important for another reason. At the suggestion of Ethel and other friends I had taken a copy of my manuscript with me. Our literary friends were not interested in that sort of book, but it got an enthusiastic reception from one of the main leaders of the discussions that year, an Austrian called Ernst Kris, who was the keeper of the Sculpture and Ancient Art Department of the Kunsthistorisches Museum in Vienna. For some reason he conceived a high opinion of my abilities and was astonished to learn that I had no position of any kind in England. This astonishment increased when he read my manuscript and was so impressed by its scholarliness that he could not understand why Fabers had rejected it. His amazement grew when, while I was at Pontigny, mother sent me on another letter of rejection, this time from Macmillans. This made Kris, who had very recently begun to practice psycho-analysis and become a great friend of Freud, think that perhaps a course of treatment would change these depressing aspects of my life. But, even if I had been tempted by this suggestion, of course my financial position put it out of the question.

As soon as I got back to London, I sent the manuscript to the Oxford University Press. This august body took very little time to turn it down. Still undaunted, I sent it to Rupert Hart-Davis, then a director of Jonathan Cape. This time I got it back more quickly still - only three weeks - praised as usual but rejected though 'with some reluctance'. I felt I was getting on! But four refusals in a year were certainly enough, and as it was now Christmas I decided to take a rest.

But not a long one, for in January 1938 I sent it to the Cambridge University Press, who laid it before the Syndics. They sent it, as the Cambridge custom was, to a reader at Oxford, Professor F. Powicke, Professor of Medieval History. Although he praised it as 'nearer the truth and more stark in its judgment than anything on Héloïse in English, saying he had read it with 'sympathy and indeed excitement', he quickly spotted that it was not written by a trained historian. He therefore recommended the Syndics not to turn it down, but to suggest that I should re-write it and present it again after two years more study, when he would gladly help me in any way he could. The Syndics duly sent his letter on to me, and though I realized that it would have increased the importance of the book if I had added more of the history of the time, I still felt that it would not have altered my judgement of the qualities of Héloïse as a human being. Apart from all of which I was of course in no position to spend two more years of study on the book, as I explained to Professor Powicke, whom I met and thanked for his well-meant advice. He fully understood and wished me luck with the book as it stood. After this meeting, feeling I had reached the end of the road, I put the manuscript away and tried to forget it by resuming my search for a job.

In that I at last had a stroke of luck, for at the end of April I got work that entirely suited me. The job was to help with the final editing and checking of the footnotes of Lord Hailey's enormous *African Survey*, which he was too ill to do himself. So a team of some six or eight men and women had been engaged to do it, and we worked in the attics of Chatham

House. All the members of the team were intelligent and jolly people who got on well together and I found it very life-enhancing to work for the second time with a group. There was much conversation and I presume I must have told them of my disappointments with the publishers, for one day a member of the team called Margaret Lambert told me she had a friend called Norah Walford who worked at Chatto and Windus and offered to send it to her. Although I had no hope I said she could if she liked, so I gave it to her, and Norah at once showed it to Ian Parsons.

Ethel was so delighted I had got a job I was enjoying that she felt free to leave me and accept an invitation from Beth to spend June and part of July at Cabris. On the perfect summer evening of St John's Day, when they were sitting on the upper terrace, watching the traditional bonfires blazing out on the hillside across the valley, the frogs in the new little swimming pool began to croak and they both instantly thought of me and wished that I was there too. Whity wrote and told me too that when she heard the first cicida her thoughts went straight back to the supreme happiness of our days at the Bastide. I don't think she was ever entirely happy when I was not sharing a pleasure with her - 'the colour and light seems to go out of things when you are not here', she wrote once 'and I miss your bursting fun and zest'. So now she suggested that we should have a week's holiday together at our favourite Bay Tree Hotel at Burford in early August.

I jumped at the idea of that, feeling I had earned a week's leave, so off we went for a week in which there was abundance of light and colour, for the weather was flawless and the fields were full of yellow flowers and inspired her to make four exquisite watercolours; and there was not only fun and zest but excitement too, for one day when we came down to breakfast, there was the familiar parcel lying on my plate. My heart sank and I threw it to the ground, feeling that if I opened it our enchanted week would be spoilt. But Ethel encouraged me at least to open it and there at last was the kind of letter I had so long hoped for, from Ian Parsons saying they all thought the book admirable, would like to publish it and offered me a generous contract. He was only returning the manuscript, hoping I might make one or two small cuts. Of course we rushed to telegraph the news to all my patient well-wishers; and the next day showers of those gold envelopes that the Post Office used in those days for greetings telegrams poured into the hotel. The nicest one came from our dear old Alice who, as a sailor's daughter, said she had danced a hornpipe with delight.

Back in London I went at once to sign the contract and learn of the work that awaited me, for they wanted the book to be ready to show at the beginning of November at the Sunday Times Book Fair, which was then the main annual shop-window for new books. I don't think I have ever worked harder than I did in the next two months, for after all I had then two jobs. The main work on *African Survey* had to be finished by the end of September as had also the cutting of the text and the notes on my own book, which meant all day and late evening work. And then of course came proof-correcting and indexing. It seems incredible nowadays to think of printers working at such lightning speed, not to speak of binders. And apart from all that technical work, Ian Parsons found time to get for me linen in the exact shade of purple I felt was appropriate for Héloïse.

After all this combined frantic effort, the bulky *African Survey* (1700 pages long) appeared on 7 November, followed by the elegant *Héloïse* on the 8th. She was given a prominent place at the Fair and began to sell at once. And I sent twenty copies to the friends who had waited for her so long. Good reviews began to come in almost at once. Reviews continued to appear throughout the first months of 1939.

That year, too, to my surprise the book had a wider appeal than I had anticipated, for one day at the beginning of May I received a letter from a Frenchwoman called Lolette d'Ardenne de Tizac, a friend of Rebecca West, saying she would like to translate the book and had suggested it to Gallimard, the most famous of all French publishers, who had accepted it. She had already translated the first twenty pages, which she sent to me to see if I liked the way she had done it, which I did. The next day Ian Parsons wrote to tell me he had received from Gallimard their proposed agreement which he had signed and returned. On the 16th Gaston Gallimard himself wrote to me to say that, if I too agreed with all this, he would ask Mademoiselle de Tizac to try and finish the work by October.

Thereafter, Lolette and I worked very hard, for I felt I must check her work, especially on the notes, which were the basis of the whole book. Together we finished it by January 1940. I met her briefly when I happened to be in Paris in February during the phoney war (of which more later) but she hadn't then received the proofs. When she did get them I don't know, for when France fell in the following June all correspondence between our two countries of course ceased.

During those five years when I concentrated mainly on my work, various events and changes had taken place in Ethel's life and those of some of our friends. Apart from these things, she was much taken up with a commitment which was very characteristic of her, as it called on all those powers of devoted dedication to a younger and, she felt, gifted person, which were deeply engrained in her nature and from which I had myself so richly benefited.

While I was in America, at one of those Sunday musical evenings we used to go to with our friends the Delisle Burns, Ethel had noticed a slim, dark-haired and dark-eyed young violinist called Eda Kersey, whose quality she at once perceived. She sought her out in the interval, when Eda was standing alone and looking lost, and soon found out that she was shy, self-taught and had few friends to help her. So Ethel decided to try and do so, first driving her about to such small country engagements as she had, and even taking her for a short country holiday with her mother, while I was immersed in my work. All this at first gave me a few flickers of jealousy, I must admit, but not for long, when I saw how much the young woman was blossoming and getting more confidence under Ethel's kindness and interest; so much so that, within a year or two, she was playing at Promenade Concerts which, in those days, took place at the Queen's Hall (burnt down in the war), doing much work for the BBC, and playing with well-known pianists like Kentner, and giving recitals at the Wigmore Hall. When I had time to get to know her better she became one of our close circle of friends.

In the autumn of 1934 there were no more musical parties, for the Delisle Burns had gone in the late summer to America to stay with friends, and there Cecil fell so seriously ill with tuberculosis that Margaret wrote to tell me they would never be able to live in London again and asked me to try and sell their house in Turner Close and find a flat where their two sons, Ben and Dom, could live with their old nurse as housekeeper. I was already dealing with all Cecil's correspondence and affairs and I managed all this easily enough. By the next spring Cecil had improved enough to be brought home, so Margaret asked Ethel and me to try and find a house in the country where they could live. We therefore spent occasional days driving round Kent and Sussex visiting house agents and looking at the houses available until we finally found a suitable one at Hawkhurst which they eventually took. I mustn't forget to mention here that Margaret by no means took for granted all the secretarial and practical work I had done for them, and knowing my need to earn money she rewarded me generously.

All these things and my own work concentrated my thoughts very much on domestic affairs during 1934 and 1935. But by 1936 both Ethel and I were becoming aware of the increasing signs of political unrest in a wider world, and for us this began with Soviet Russia, because Beth had gone there in January of that year to live for six months, following Pierre, and being joined later by Gide, who at last went to see for himself whether communism was as perfect in practice as he had dreamt it in theory. He was of course made much of, and fêted lavishly, as they realized what a propagandist he might be for them in France. But Gide was not taken in by what he saw, and when he returned to Paris he said to la Petite Dame *'le communism n'est plus la-bas. Il n'y a plus que Staline'*.

Before I say more about the increasing feeling of unrest, I must mention a curious little incident that took place in July, when Beth came back from Russia and stayed with Ethel. Ethel took us both for a little tour in the Cotswolds, and among other places to Fairford, where there was a fair in progress. A gaudy caravan announced the presence of a gypsy fortune-teller called Britannia. She was a striking-looking old woman with a brown, leathery, wrinkled face and the brightest blue eyes I had ever seen. It was difficult to persuade her to take us all together, but she did. She had not much to say to Beth or me but when Ethel's turn came, the gypsy began by warning her 'Don't be too kind to that old brother of yours!' Ethel of course hadn't mentioned Roger who had, in fact, come home on retirement from the Ceylon Civil Service the month before. So we wondered what on earth she could have meant. But Mrs Whitehorn suddenly died, and, as the family was broken up, it seemed natural that

Ethel should live with her bachelor brother, although they had nothing in common and he was the last person she would have chosen to live with. So that was what the gypsy had meant.

Going back to the world situation, 1936 as we all remember was also the year of the Spanish civil war, and our first realization of Nazi participation in it. Ever since 1933 there had appeared occasional short pieces in the English newspapers about camps for Jews in Germany, but I don't think much notice was taken of them. When I went to Pontigny in 1937, the subject for discussion that year, '*Vocation sociale de l'art dans les époques de trouble mental et de désespoir*', seemed another sign of the general unrest; and the presence there of Ernst Kris, who was after all a prominent Jew from Vienna, tended to turn the thoughts of the other participants very much to Austria. In 1938 Roger Martin du Gard, who had taken a great liking to Kris, visited him in Vienna in the course of a European tour he made after winning the Nobel prize for literature. He was there at the time of the *Anschluss* in March, and realized what danger threatened Kris and his family. On his return to Paris, Martin du Gard began to write to me, as he knew that Kris had become very much a friend of mine too, urgently asking me to use British influence to get Kris and his family out before it was too late. In the end it was, I think, combined British, French and American influences which succeeded in May in getting not only Kris but Freud and several other analysts to London, where Kris and his family joined the increasing group of our friends, which by then also included Ernst Gombrich, already working at the Warburg Institute, and his charming wife Ilse, whose presence consoled us to some extent for the fact that we were soon to be cut off from all our other foreign friends.

Kris had terrible tales to tell us of what was happening to the Jews in Austria, so it was not surprising if throughout 1938 all thinking people in England were beginning to feel the menace in the air. Even I, far less politically prescient than Ethel (who had seen warning signs ever since Hitler left the League of Nations in 1933), was aware of it for I certainly felt when I was correcting my proofs while Neville Chamberlain was flying to Munich, that it seemed impossible to believe that the world in which one reads books would be in existence in the following week.

Redland High School

The Abbey of Pontigny

Abbaye de PONTIGNY — Le Prieuré

The Priory at Pontigny

Enid at five

Ethel at five

Ethel in 1932

Ethel in 1922

Ethel in Africa in 1951

Ethel in retirement

La Petite Dame

Loup Mayrisch

Beth

André Gide

Roger Martin du Gard

Jean Schlumberger

1 bis rue de Martignac: a corner of the salon

And yet I went on correcting those proofs, just as all those working with me went on with their jobs too. For it is a strange universal truth that all human beings, if they are to preserve their sanity, must continue to lead their ordinary daily lives up to the last minute, however useless and unnecessary they perceive them to be.

Chapter Ten

THE MINISTRY OF INFORMATION
1939-1945

Although 1939 was to bring about a momentous change in my life, a change that led me along a definite, slowly mounting path for the next twenty years, during the first two months of it I continued with my part-time work on the *African Survey*. This dwindled to nothing by the end of February, but before I left Chatham House, Ivison Macadam, who was now the Secretary of the Royal Institute of International Affairs, asked me to go and see him. It may be remembered that I had met him once ten years before, at the time when he had something to do with those summer-schools in Geneva which Ethel had asked me to run with her. So once again it was through her that I was to be offered a job such as I had never imagined I could do. For he told me he had been asked to find someone who could organize some secret work in preparation for what would be an important part of a Ministry of Information in the event of war. It would be done at a house in Chesham Place which belonged to Chatham House but was still empty. A group of experts, already chosen, would come there in their spare time to write reports on propaganda in the countries on which they were specialists. My job would be to furnish the offices with the necessary equipment, by means of access to the Ministry of Works through a private line, to engage secretarial staff to work for the experts, and arrange a daily tea-time meeting when they could discuss their problems with each other. I should have Michael Balfour to help me with the experts.

I protested that I had never organized anything in my life, had been a secretary but had never had one, nor even dictated a letter. But he was absolutely certain that I could do it, said it would only take three months and took me along to see Chesham Place. He gave me a few days to think it over; but of course my mother and Ethel were delighted I had been offered it. Ethel, with more prescience than I, had been working since January with the Women's Farm and Garden Union, interviewing women for a possible Land Army.

The experts were to begin arriving five days later so I had no time to lose. I soon found that the secret telephone number I had been given worked wonders, and when I had calculated the number of desks, chairs, typewriters and filing cabinets I should need, I rang up for them and everything arrived that same afternoon in plain vans. I had asked for a very large dining-table too, and chairs to go with it for the tea-parties, and very handsome furniture, just returned from our Embassy in Vienna, was sent. Macadam had told me I could spend up to £400 for a carpet for the main room out of Chesham House funds, and buy a large tea-set too, which I much enjoyed doing. Next I engaged from a typewriting bureau three or four shorthand typists, and was fortunate enough to find an experienced Canadian girl whom I felt sure could organize their duties for me. I am certain they all immediately saw what a novice I myself was, but none of them ever took advantage of my ignorance of secretarial practice, which I did not attempt to conceal. All obeyed me from the start and were discreet and loyal and we had much laughter together. I may say at this point that throughout my subsequent career I never had any but perfect secretaries.

When the experts began to arrive they complied at once with my request that they should telephone each morning to let me know when they would come in and would want a secretary, and the system worked well from the start. There were not a great number in that first group, who were dealing chiefly with America, the Dominions and the colonies, and one or two with the Middle East, and I noticed that more and more of them came for the tea-parties, where I was helped by our housekeeper. As we all got to know each other, the discussions became more and more relaxed and interesting, and such was their zeal that their reports, with which Michael Balfour helped them, were finished well within the three months' time-limit, to Macadam's gratification. He then told me that a second and much bigger group would begin work in larger quarters at the beginning of June, and said he hoped I would manage that too.

As this promised to be a much heavier task, and it didn't

look as though I should have any holiday that year, Ethel and I seized the opportunity of the Easter break, which fell just then, to go to France, where she wanted to show me the great Abbey of Royaumont, built by St Louis, where she had worked for a time as an ambulance driver when it was used as the Scottish Women's Hospital during the First World War. I was thrilled to see that splendid place, and she was happy to find her old haunts quite unchanged in that peaceful countryside, with primulas and purple anemones still growing in the marshes and frogs singing in the reeds. We returned refreshed, I to Belgrave Square and she to Tothill Street, where the Government, which had now taken over the Land Army work, had housed it in the WVS headquarters.

Number 38 Belgrave Square was a very much larger house than the one at Chesham Place and so I needed to order a great deal more furniture and also engage several more secretaries. We also had the help of Con O'Neill, who had just returned from our Embassy in Berlin and was seconded to us from the Foreign Office. There were also some senior civil servants, obviously ear-marked for the future Ministry, as was I too, for in August I received a letter from the Civil Service Commission, saying the Treasury wished me to hold myself at their disposal for some unspecified post. The greater number of the experts were dons from Oxford and Cambridge, but there were also some diplomats, some notable journalists and men of affairs among them.

Before I leave this period there are two typical things worth mentioning. One day a telegram for one of our members was handed in to me, addressed simply to him at the Ministry of Information. At the top of the envelope the Post Office had written 'Not known - ask the German Embassy'. When I rang the Knightsbridge Post Office to tell them there was no such Ministry and to ask why they had applied to the Germans, they innocently replied 'Oh, we always do, because they always know'. So much for our secrecy. Wherever this Ministry would be, when and if it existed, I felt sure it would occupy still bigger quarters and I therefore thought it might be useful if I filled the large cellars and underground kitchens at Belgrave Square with as much office furniture as they would hold. So once again I telephoned my secret number and once again the equipment came without question and was stored away. So when on

2 September I was told that we must all proceed to the Senate House of London University, which was to be the site of the Ministry of Information, and asked how many vans I should need to bring all the equipment with me, the number was considerable. I waited for them to arrive and went with them myself, to be greeted on arrival with cries of surprise and delight from the lower-grade civil servants whose job it was to see to the furnishing of the war-time ministries. As there were several of these - the Ministry of Economic Warfare and others - there was not nearly enough office furniture to go round and they could hardly contain their gratitude at the sight of this unexpected bonus.

Inside the building the wildest confusion reigned. Only the civil servants seemed to know what they were doing, while few of the hoards of amateurs like myself knew what posts, if any, they would be given. Since little has been written or is known of that strange war-time growth, the Ministry of Information, it may be useful if I give a very brief outline of the shape it took, some of the personages who filled it, and the work they did. In the upper rooms of the Senate House there dwelt, one after the other, the swift early succession of Ministers, from the little (legal) Lord Macmillan, John Reith, Duff Cooper to Brendan Bracken, who remained to the end. Under them, as Directors General and such, there were constantly changing starry figures like Walter Monckton, Harold Nicolson, Kenneth Clark and Cyril Radcliffe, who was the best and longest-lasting of these. (I give no titles, not remembering who got what when.) On the spacious ground floor of that building were the Press and Censorship quarters, where the journalists hung about all day.

Separated from all this by a wide corridor was a large building where in smaller offices the main daily work was done. Here was the Home Division, whose job it was to put the nation on its guard against a possible enemy. Here too were the Overseas Publicity Divisions: European, American, Latin American, Empire, Far East and Middle East, acting as channels of information between their countries and England. Near them were the Publications, Photographs and Films Divisions, producing material on different aspects of the war. There were starry figures among them, too, but of a more fixed and less shooting variety than the brighter lights above us; journalists and writers like H. V. Hodson, Cecil Day Lewis, Graham Greene and Laurie Lee, and film magnates like Sidney Bernstein.

As soon as I had grasped all this, I knew it was the European Division I wanted to join, and in that the French Section, which was the biggest, presumably because France was our main ally. So I sought out Leigh Ashton of the V and A who surprisingly was the first, fleeting, head of the Division, and asked for a post in the French Section, telling him what I knew of France. To my relief he agreed at once and gave me a post as Assistant Specialist. This meant I was second in command to the Head of it, who was one of our Belgrave Square specialists, Ronald Balfour, a Fellow of King's, Cambridge. He was a kindly but retiring and timid young scholar, without the slightest idea how to do the ordinary work of a civil servant. Fortunately we were soon joined by Dorothy Pickles, with her unrivalled knowledge of French politics and politicians, and her beautiful French, much better than Ronald's or mine. I got an excellent secretary too, Eileen Reynolds, who had been with Ifor Evans and Mary Glasgow, who were the Intelligence Division. They were sorry to lose her, but she wanted to join us, because she had a real love of France and remained with the Section until the end of the war.

As there was very little work to do at first and I chiefly handled it, it was thought a good idea to send Balfour to Paris, to explain to our Embassy there who we were and what we were supposed to be doing. As he really did not know and had an unfortunately jerky voice and manner, he made a very poor impression. This must have been reported and accordingly Michael Wright, our liaison with the Foreign Office, who was aware that I was really doing the work, suggested that after Christmas I might visit the Embassy, to try and restore our image. So at the end of January I was provided with a questionnaire and went for a week. I was warmly received by the Minister, Oliver Harvey, who invited me to take part in the daily staff meetings. I made the acquaintance of many other people too, journalists and such, so it was a very busy week and I had time to see only two of our old friends. But I met the translator of *Héloïse* too.

In spite of these comings and goings, there was still no sign of the war in Europe, so in March Ethel and I were able to go to Cabris for a fortnight's perfect, light-hearted holiday. Beth, Tit, Catherine and Pierre were all there and we spent our days driving about that beautiful countryside; when we went to Nice to see the Bussys, we brought Gide back with us. It seemed quite impossible to believe that we were seeing them all for the last time for many years. On our last night Loup Mayrisch, with her daughter Andrée Viénot arrived. Loup looked a nervous wreck, and that was the last we ever saw of her.

On my return to the office I found that there was a new head of the European Division, Ivone Kirkpatrick, a foxy-faced, cold-eyed man from the Foreign Office, who obviously had the greatest contempt for all of us. As the period of the phoney war was at last coming to an end, with the German invasion of Denmark and Norway in early April, Kirkpatrick needed no telling that Balfour must be replaced. As all our letters of appointment said that we could be sacked without cause given, the poor man was dismissed. It was humiliatingly done, he told me, but I had the impression that his main feeling was one of relief.

It took some time to find a replacement and in the interval I had to cope with two difficult situations. The atmosphere was now getting very tense. Hitler had pounced on Belgium, Holland and Luxembourg on 10 May, so on the 14th, when the German armies were heading for France, it was decided that the Queen would speak on the radio to the women of France, to try and hearten them and stiffen their morale. The speech was to be prepared in the French Section, so Kirkpatrick told me to ask three or four journalists to come to our office and tell them the sort of thing we wanted them to write. One can imagine the strain of it, even for experienced journalists, in our general office. But Kirkpatrick could not curb his impatience and marched into their room with a stop-watch, saying 'I give you three minutes!' I can't remember how it all ended, but somehow the speech was written, translated and given. But obviously it was all too late.

The second difficult situation came two or three weeks later. As the German army was advancing steadily through northern France, one day André Maurois, who was a liaison officer with the British army, burst into my office and, almost hysterical with fear, launched into a tirade whose theme was that we had let the French down by not sending enough divisions. I suppose the ghastly situation at Dunkirk had unnerved him. Why he had come to me I don't know, except that I had known him for many years. I tried to calm him by giving him the stock answers which of course I knew, but his denunciations got more and more fierce until I began to feel that I was myself responsible! So I suggested that he should seek higher authority elsewhere in the building. I was sorry for the poor man who, as a prominent Jew, had much cause for personal as well as national terror.

I suppose it was because I had had to deal with all this that I was that month promoted to the rank of Specialist and given an increased salary. But all the same it was a relief when I heard that a new Head of Section had been found. I felt less relieved when I learnt that it was to be Raymond Mortimer, whom I knew and liked but felt was hardly the man for the job. When he arrived I took him the day's files to deal with their correspondence. But when I returned an hour later he said he couldn't possibly answer such silly letters and had decided that the time had come for speech rather than writing, so he was off to the BBC to see if there was anything he could do there, and I was again alone in charge. In the general confusion I got no instructions and was beginning to wonder, after France fell and General de Gaulle arrived in London and made his famous speech, whether there would any longer be a need for a French Section. But very soon afterward there arrived from France Oliver Harvey and several of his staff and he was immediately made Head of the French Section, while several others were given posts under him. He seemed very pleased to have me there as an old hand who knew my way round the Ministry.

Now that France was lost it became clear that England would be Hitler's next objective, and I think this gave us the sense that at last we were in the war and must adapt our lives accordingly. For one thing rationing started, not yet in its severest form but enough to make housekeeping rather more difficult for households like mine with only old people to do the shopping, or single people with work like Eda. She was getting more and more engagements in provincial towns. So to ease her domestic problem, Ethel, who had completed her job for the Land Army, and was working for the WVS driving East-end children to the country took her to live in

Roger's flat with her, as he was in the north in some Government administrative post. Having Eda there made it easier for Ethel to drive her to some evening engagements in London. Then occasional daylight bombing started. Our friends the Burns moved from Sussex, too near the coast in case of invasion, to Dorking. And finally Kris, as a marked Viennese Jew, fearing for his wife and children if the Germans succeeded in invading England finally decided that the time had come for him to leave England. He had been offered a job in America, trying to persuade the States to come into the war. He wrote me many rather desperate letters about it, and he never thereafter ceased to feel guilty at leaving the land he loved, which seemed to him a kind of betrayal.

When the daylight bombing of the summer changed to massive night-raids in August there was much widespread fear, especially before we had any anti-aircraft guns to defend us. My mother, in fact, both then and thereafter, remained extraordinarily brave and cool, as did Alice, although the shattering noise of the bombs jerked her arthritic limbs cruelly. I remember one night when the din overhead was infernal, I crept into my mother's bedroom to see if she was afraid, and found her standing in the middle of the room with a stick in her hand, looking very warlike. When I asked her if she was scared by the noise 'Oh *that!*' she said scornfully, 'No, but I'm sure there's a mouse in the room. Listen'. I tried and sure enough I could hear a faint rustling in the waste-paper basket. It jumped out at that moment and scuttled round the room. 'There it is' she cried and went for it with her stick, actually killing it with a well-aimed blow, after which she went peacefully back to bed.

After such disturbed nights as these, it was a great relief for me when morning came and I could go once more to work among my cheerful companions in a solid building. I was not only secure but happy in that building where I now had work to do that I enjoyed and that brought me into contact with many people, both French and English. After de Gaulle was established at Carlton Gardens, many French people escaped to join him in what was not a government, as he was not a head of state, but a kind of shadow government, comprising an information service with civil, military and naval departments. These began issuing publications concerning the achievements of the Free French Forces, and one of my jobs was to have regular meetings with the staff producing them as I had control of the paper they needed and they had to come to the Ministry for photographs to illustrate them.

But of course, being French, they were not all of one mind, and a particular problem was caused by a small group which wanted to bring out a high-grade intellectual monthly review called *La France Libre*. This little group was headed by André Labarthe, who was anti-Gaullist, as was also his second-in-command, Raymond Aron, who after the war became, and still is, one of the foremost French writers and philosophers. A friend of theirs, the Baroness Moura Budberg, persuaded Hamish Hamilton to publish it for them, but they needed finance. Accordingly they approached the Ministry, which agreed to purchase large numbers to send to any countries abroad where there was a considerable French population. It was one of my jobs first to find out through our Representatives in those countries how many they thought they could sell, and secondly to scrutinize the editorials for any anti-Gaullist material. The copy was brought to me every month by Moura, who gradually became and remained a good friend.

Still another task which fell to me was arranging with the chief members of the Oxford University Press all the details of their publication of English versions of de Gaulle's books - another enlargement of pleasant English acquaintance for me. I also had something to do with the French versions of the Ministry's own publications of our war effort. And occasionally those who were employed on making French versions of the sub-titles of independently-produced feature films which the Ministry was going to use came to me for advice and help, as when, on one occasion the translator was foxed by the phrase 'Take your thirty pieces of silver and go!' Obviously not familiar with the Biblical origins of the words, she thought that pieces of silver must mean shillings and should therefore be translated as francs, but was worried what rate of exchange would now be appropriate.

All these things constituted the major part of my work throughout 1941 and 1942, during which years the Section itself kept changing, losing Oliver Harvey, who returned to the Foreign Office. Guy Hamilton, who had been in the press office in our Embassy in Paris, took on the work on the French versions of the newsreels. At one moment the senior staff dwindled so much that only he and I were left and he was consequently made Head of the Section. But he proved not to have the necessary quality of leadership and preferred to confine himself to his film work on the French newsreels, and on social contacts with the senior French, leaving everything else to me. I thus had so much to do that my health began to suffer and an unhappy situation developed. Early in 1943 a new Director of the European Division was appointed, a diplomat called Oswald Scott. He quickly saw that something must be done and decided to send Hamilton to Algiers as a sort of liaison office between us and the many Gaullist Frenchmen who had gone there after the liberation of North Africa in November 1942. So once again I found myself in charge and in fact the only senior official in the Section.

It was not easy to find new staff at that stage of the war, but with Oswald's help we got Timothy Eden, Anthony's older brother, who was amused at the idea of working under a woman, or indeed working at all, but soon got into the way of it. Betty Askwith also joined us, but the third member I found for myself, as he was a friend already working in a different part of the Ministry. This was David Fullerton, once of the Oxford University Press, who would, I thought be just the person to take on the French publications side I had previously handled and who was keen to do so. I had to argue with Mr Woodburn, the friendly Establishment Officer, to get him to agree to this transfer and in the course of our talk he made a very revealing remark. 'I see what's the matter with you, Miss McLeod. You believe in putting a round peg in a round hole. Now in the civil service we think it better to put a square peg in a round hole.' But he saw that this was sometimes a painful process and took time, so as it was urgent he agreed. Two excellent secretaries completed the happy team we now became and in June they finally made me Head of the Section, a rare appointment for a woman at that time. And when Oswald went on leave in August, he appointed me his deputy for the whole Division.

While I had been taken up with all this, Ethel also had had a regular job since April 1941. Anthony Steel, a Fellow of Christ's, Cambridge, who had been one of the experts at

Belgrave Square and remained a good friend of mine thereafter, had never found the right job for himself in the Ministry; so in October 1940 he had joined the British Council as their Regional Representative for London and the South West, under Nancy Parkinson, the Head of their Home Division. But it was a big job and he soon found that he would need an assistant, especially for one rather boring aspect of his work. I had introduced him to Ethel and they at once took to each other, as her wit matched his. He therefore asked her if she would like the job, and as her WVS work had come to an end, she agreed and was appointed on 1 April.

The work proved very boring, for it meant she had responsibility for the Gibraltarians, whom the British government had misguidedly brought to England, fearing they might be in danger if the war got as far as Spain, and lodged them in scruffy private hotels all over London, where they were very miserable. They could not speak English, they hated the climate and feared the bombs, and Ethel's job was to visit them constantly, inventing occupations for them and finding some means of educating the children. This work told on her spirits and left her too much time to brood on the gloomy events of the war. Taking Eda to her concerts in the evening was a relief but an emotional strain too, as were also her frequent week-end visits to the Burns at Dorking to try and help Margaret, who had no let-up from nursing Cecil, whose health was deteriorating so rapidly that he died in January 1942.

But though she had to continue with her work throughout 1942, she did have one very cheering piece of news on 22 April 1943, and that was the arrival in London of her old friend Pierre Viénot, whom she had first met at St Clair in 1930 at the time of his marriage to Andrée Mayrisch. It had been a great shock to her when in July 1940 she heard that he had been arrested by Pétain because he had insisted on joining the army. For the next three years he was kept partly in house arrest, but also spent months in prison under Laval. How he had managed to get to England she did of course not know; but as a good many distinguished Frenchmen were coming to England at that time, it seems probable that his escape was managed by SOE (Secret Operations Executive) with the help of the Resistance. De Gaulle, who was still in London at that time, and who thought highly of him, decided to make him his Chargé d'Affaires when he himself went with him *Comité National* to Algiers, which he did on 30 May 1943.

One can imagine Pierre's pleasure on arriving in London at finding his old friend Whity, and what it meant for her to see again one of the French friends cut off from her by three years of war. As he knew little if any English he had months of hard work before him. But to help him with his official work he had a close friend, Olivier Wormser, who had himself escaped from France in the summer of 1940, when he was in the French navy, and by a very roundabout route managed to reach London in June 1941. He joined the Free French navy and was at sea with them for a year until he returned to London in 1942 and joined the naval section at Carlton Gardens. As he knew how ill Pierre was (and had been since he was wounded in the First World War) he asked Whity to take him sometimes to some quiet country hotel for the week-end where he could rest. She was of course delighted to do this and in the following September, the first occasion when he could get away, they went to the Leicester Arms at Penshurst for the first of several visits.

But in the autumn of 1943 I too had great need of help. During those four years of war, with their dreary daily existence, both my mother's and Alice's spirits had kept up wonderfully. As for Alice, neither age nor pain dimmed the interest she had always taken in sporting events, especially horse-racing, when she studied form carefully, placed her bets by telephone and was nearly always lucky. She played such games as whist most skilfully too and as long as she could drag herself to any local whist-drive, off she went, nearly always bringing home extraordinary prizes in the way of fruit or chocolate, which she would give to my mother. *Her* spirits, on the other hand were kept up by the passionate interest she took in the war news and also in my doings in the Ministry, especially in the events of 1943, so much so that the moment I got home each night, generally in a state of exhaustion, she would expect such a detailed account of it all that I fear I often got irritated and we quarrelled. Every night too she feared for my safety on my journey, as bombing still continued. So Ethel suggested that it might be better if I got a room in town for the week nights and only went home for the week-ends. I feared that this idea might upset my mother, with whom I had lived so long, but to my relief and surprise she at once accepted this plan, thinking I would be spared the journeys and she the anxiety. Ethel, whose work took her round London every day, quickly found me a room in Clarges Street, which I moved into in late September.

I have never been sufficiently grateful to Ethel for persuading me to make that move when I did, for it was such a pleasure to get back to my own room and bed at the week-ends not feeling exhausted, and my mother gave me such a joyous welcome that I felt I had never been happier with her. But, alas, there were to be only six such week-ends before, on returning to the room late on the 9 November, I found a message asking me to go home at once as my mother was ill. It was a nightmare journey and when I got there I found that my mother had died an hour earlier. It had been a quick and merciful death. Alice had been sitting at her bedside for a chat before going to bed, when my mother said 'Oh Alice!'; lay back on her pillow and was gone. Not knowing my telephone number Alice had rung Ethel, who came round at once, sent me the message and stayed to help Alice till I came. She spent the night with me to try and comfort me for the shock and help me through the formalities of the following days, which had to be brutally rushed, so overcharged were the undertakers in those death-ridden days.

When those were over I had to get back to work and leave Alice to bear the silence after her long years of my mother's daily company. But she had a brave spirit and to help her, agonizingly arthritic as she was, she had the services of a most kindly old sailor called Mr Ginn, whom I had found cutting a neighbour's hedge some months before and who came instantly, at my request, to help with the shopping and clean the house. And I of course hurried home every evening and spent long week-ends with Alice, when together we carried out the melancholy task of sorting my mother's possessions, which took us five months. But after that I decided that I could no longer leave Alice alone, for we had heard in the Ministry that another and even more formidable bomber - the terrifying pilotless V 1s - were being prepared by the Germans. So in April 1944 a niece came to take her to her home village of Porlock Weir, where her sister-in-law had a room for her. It must have been a sad journey for her after our parting on Paddington platform.

It was strange to be alone in my house at last, though Mr Ginn still came to shop and clean and, knowing my complete ignorance of cooking, would leave me little notes like 'How to make a nice, rice pudding'. Rather than sit there alone in the evenings, I joined the fire-watchers and wandered around the roads when there was an alert. The thought of this increased Ethel's anxiety for me and she would telephone each night when the 'all clear' sounded to know if I was still there. But she couldn't come and live with me, for she felt her duty to Eda and to Pierre was paramount and she must be always at hand to help if either of them needed her.

After a month of this we both felt we needed a change, so on 2 May we went to The Bay Tree at Burford for a fortnight's holiday. The weather was perfect and the world seemed as happy and uneventful as it had always been there. But on our last night, 5 June, we heard the steady drone of aeroplanes and gliders flying in the direction of France from the nearby airfields, and guessed that D Day had at last come. The morning news confirming this filled everyone with elation; and although we had been told that we must remain where we were when that long-awaited morning came, we felt we must disobey and return to London, as we both had pressing work to do, arranging a series of Anglo-French parties, to the second of which, on the 16th, Pierre had promised to come.

But unbeknown to us Churchill had suddenly decided that the 16th would be the day when de Gaulle should cross to Normandy for a brief visit, taking Pierre Viénot and some others with him. They were to go to Bayeux and would have time to see a few surrounding places and meet as many of their compatriots as possible. One can imagine what a historic and moving occasion that must have been, both for all those French people who saw at last the man who had kept France in the war and for those like Viénot, a sick man whose health was steadily worsening, to have this chance to set foot once more on the soil of their beloved country. Miraculously he returned in time to come to the Anglo-French party we were giving just as it was ending, his face jubilant with joy as he told us where he had been. And fortunately Ethel was there to greet him, for this was to be the last time she would see the friend she had tried so devotedly to help.

On the same day when she returned home she found Eda suffering from a pain in her back which their local doctor had diagnosed as indigestion! But as it worsened over the next fortnight, Ethel decided to take her up to Ilkley, where she had a great admirer, Arthur Gott, who was a brilliant doctor and also a keen musician. He at once diagnosed an inoperable cancer of the liver, which a specialist and an X-ray confirmed. With wonderful courage Ethel at once wrote to tell me this shattering news, adding that she was also going to tell Eda, who had said she wanted to know; and saying 'I am sure she will have the nobility and firmness to hear what I believe is bound to come.' In her next letter, with no thought for the sorrow it would bring her, she said 'Now we know she must leave us, I do pray for her that it is to be soon.' Her prayer was granted, for Eda died on the night of 13 July. I got the message at my office next morning, and caught the night train to Ilkley. I found Ethel stunned but calm, as were the Gotts, with whom we spent the week-end after the cremation, returning to London together on the 17th.

As Ethel told me that even throughout those sad days she had never ceased to worry about my solitariness, I suggested to her that, rather than return to the flat with its empty room, she should come and live with me. She gladly accepted and we had three peaceful nights in my house. But on the fourth, at three in the morning the telephone rang. It was our Swiss doctor friend, Pierre Lansel, to tell Ethel that his patient Viénot had just died of a massive heart attack. He knew we could do nothing but he wanted Ethel to know. She had half expected it and so, tired as we were, we managed to get back to sleep. But four hours later, with the most shattering roar I had ever heard, a V 1 fell on the other side of the road, demolishing houses there but killing no one, while the blast from it blew all my doors and windows in obliterating some interior walls and part of the roof. I realized what had happened when I heard Ethel's amused voice saying 'I thought you promised me a room to myself' and saw that there was a huge hole in the wall that separated us, where the bricks had fallen on to her bed, just missing her head. Friends and assistants were not long in coming to our rescue, among them the so-called heavy-rescue men who at top speed piled all the contents of my no-longer habitable house into vans and drove them away to be stored in an empty but sound house in the neighbourhood. So my plan to give Ethel comfort and companionship in my house came to nothing, Fate decided otherwise and we both went to Roger's flat, where I had Eda's room, which I was to occupy for three years.

A week later, feeling that my household goods were as vulnerable in that empty house as they had been in mine, I accepted the kind offer of a grocer in Sawbridgeworth, of which one of my colleagues had told me, to store my stuff in a large granary behind his shop; and those heavy-rescue men came again and took it there. A week later still Ethel and I, taking our faithful Mr Ginn with us to make a day's outing for him, drove down to see it. To my astonishment I found it had all had to be carried up a narrow ladder, grand piano and all, and lay in a jumble: books, china, glass higgledy-piggledy. But as far as I could tell, it was all there down to the last crumb, quite literally, for we spied the two breakfast trays we had prepared, their contents, bread, butter and marmalade thickly coated with black dust.

That was the last service Ethel was able to do for me after those six tragic weeks, for when I returned to my office at the beginning of August she had to go to Northern Ireland, where the Government had sent the Gibraltarians when the V 1 attacks started, installing them in Nissen huts for the autumn and winter where they were more miserable than ever. There could hardly have been a crueller job for her than being with those wretched people, lonely and heavy-hearted as she was herself as she gradually realized her loss of the young violinist, whose gift and personality she had cherished so devotedly for the last ten years and for whom she arranged a beautiful memorial service on 22 September at St Martin's. But she struggled valiantly to overcome her grief and had one piece of luck to help her, when she met a cheerful and affectionate woman, Eileen Olsen, the wife of a Norwegian sea-captain then abroad; she became quickly aware of Ethel's state and insisted that she should leave her impersonal hotel and share her snug little cottage, where she could cosset her a bit. She also lent her a big old car, without which Ethel could hardly have reached some of the outlying places she had to visit; and the beauty of the countryside she was thus able to see gradually brought her peace of mind and acceptance.

But she had to continue with her grim task and what made the contrast between her life and mine crueller still was that at that time mine was full of excitement. In September Oswald Scott had issued a circular to every relevant organization he could think of in London, telling them of the increased standing in Anglo-French affairs he had given me, and this may have had something to do with the fact that, after the Ministry had received and entertained at the end of October an important delegation of French journalists, among them Gerard Bauër of the *Figaro* and Jacques Debû-Bridel, our Minister, Brendan Bracken, received from the newly formed French Ministry of Information in Paris an invitation for me to go to France as their guest for a fortnight. I think I was the only civilian to receive such a privilege as early as that. Ever since Paris had been liberated in August Ethel and I had had the feeling that we were at last nearly in touch with our friends again. But now the thought that I should actually be going to see them all again thrilled her for me. As usual she was not envious, only a shade wistful that she could not see them too.

Although the invitation had come in November, it was not until 6 December that I was able to fly to Paris in a RAF Transport Command plane, wrapped up to the nines in fur coat and boots as I had been warned that there was no heating anywhere in France. An official from the French Ministry of Information met me and installed me in a comfortable hotel, after discovering that the one where I was first booked had only paper sheets, like many others in Paris. He said they had no programme for my fortnight, but would arrange anything I wanted to do. He put a car and chauffeur at my disposal in Paris and then tactfully left me to my own devices.

I of course spent all my first days visiting our friends at the Vaneau and others who had returned to their icy Paris flats, though many were still in the warmer south where life was easier. To all the friends I saw I distributed the little packets we had saved from our rations - things like tea, soap, cigarettes and chocolate - having painfully to tell them they could only have one thing each; I vividly remember Jean Schlumberger's long hesitation over the choice between cigarettes and soap; the soap won. Of the many meetings I thus had the one I remember most was that with Andrée Viénot, who had installed a tent with an oil stove in it in the middle of her big, cold drawing room. We crept inside it and sat on the floor while I gave her the details of the death of her husband. Only one official event had been arranged for me in Paris, and that was a reception which *Les Editions de Minuit*, which had published that remarkable series of clandestine booklets by most of the French intellectuals, had arranged, and where I met large numbers of them: such well-known names as Aragon, Eluard, Mauriac, Vercors. I doubt if any of them knew what the French Section of the MOI had done, but the warmth of their gratitude to England was obvious and sincere. And it was there that I heard it confirmed that the French translation of my *Héloïse* had appeared in 1941 and been on sale on every bookstall in France, which greatly surprised me; perhaps this was before the Germans had begun to ban all foreign books.

After Paris I had said it would give me much satisfaction to go to Strasbourg and see the Rhine. So they sent me with two or three accompanying Free French officers and, after one night in Strasbourg, I was driven to a forward post where I could actually see the enemy encamped on the further bank. On returning to Paris from that expedition I asked if I could go to Normandy, and return by the route that Leclerc's liberating army had taken.

My final request was to be shown a torture chamber, so that I might have personal evidence to disprove those who were already beginning to say in England that the stories of such were all anti-German propaganda. So they took me to Issy-les-Moulineaux where I entered a huge low-ceilinged windowless room, into which people were pushed through holes near the roof, and where the asbestos walls and ash floor were made furnace hot; and I saw the imprint of agonized hands on the walls until the victims were finally tied to posts and shot, posts to which blood-stained rags still clung.

It was 23 December before I returned to England. Ethel met me, but I only had time to give her news of all our friends before we parted again, I to go and see my family at Tunbridge Wells, and she to Ilkley to see the Gotts who she was sure would be thinking of Eda that Christmas, as was she.

Even before I left for that visit to Paris there were signs that the Ministry was beginning to break up, or be changed into something else. People were leaving, thinking of their future careers. Early in February, fifteen of us (fourteen men and myself) received letters from the Treasury to say that Cyril Radcliffe had recommended us for permanent employment in the Civil Service because of our 'outstanding ability'. As this was highly flattering I felt I must go, as requested, for an interview with the Civil Service Commission, which turned out to be a large and imposing body of men. They asked what branch of the Home Civil Service I would choose and when I said none, I wanted only the Foreign Service, this threw them into a quandary, because at that time women were not accepted in the Foreign Office, although the future possibility of it was then being discussed. But even then, they said, my seniority, as they delicately put it, would present difficulties, owing to my lack of training in their ways.

It all sounded so uncertain that I put them out of their embarrassment by telling them I had received an offer of a post from the British Council, and of course they instantly begged me to take it. It was true that over the past months I had, through Anthony Steel, met several senior members of the Council over lunch and they had definitely said they would like me to join them. So I now told Richard Seymour, who was then Deputy Secretary General of it, that I would be open to the offer of the post of Head of their French Section and he immediately wrote to Mr Woodburn to ask when I could be released. He replied that I could be on 6 October, so I agreed to join the Council on 1 November.

As there was hardly any office work during the intervening eight months, I had plenty of time for my personal affairs, and also to enjoy the crowded cultural events, both French and English, that made up for the poverty of the preceding years. The chief of my personal affairs was Alice, whom I was longing to see again. As Ethel's work, like mine, was virtually over except for a last month's visit to the departing Gibraltarians, she was able to go with me to Porlock Weir no fewer than three times, in February, July and September, when we were able to take Alice for drives to see the favourite haunts of her youth. We enjoyed other week-ends in the country too, and I particularly remember one when we stayed at The Chequers at Pulborough in April and on a morning walk heard some of our aeroplanes flying over and, on looking up, noted that they were flying south-west instead of the usual south-east. We instantly guessed that they must be going to the Bordeaux area, in a corner of which pockets of German troops were still holding out. We were right and it was good to know that, after they were bombed out, the whole of France was at last liberated. To return to my personal matters, in June Ethel went with me to Sawbridgeworth to arrange for the return of my household goods, which arrived a week later. She helped me too with all the cleaning and dusting and beating that had to be done before the carpets and furniture could be reinstalled in my house, where the local authorities had made the war damage good in a rough-and-ready fashion. I then let the house at the beginning of July.

As for the cultural explosion, as it might well be called, representatives of every side of artistic and intellectual life poured out of France that year like people released from prison, as indeed they were. Musicians like Ginette Neveu, the gifted violinist so soon to be tragically killed in an air-crash, Poulenc and Bernac gave concerts. We saw films by Cocteau and Malraux. There was a visit by the Comédie Française which the British Council helped to sponsor. There were lectures by Duhamel and Vercors, whose clandestine little book, *Le Silence de la Mer* had found its way out of France two years earlier and so poignantly summed up what the German occupation meant. There was a light-hearted exhibition, *Le Théâtre de la Mode*, which charmed us in our shabby rationed-material clothes. But the biggest cultural impact was made, I think, by the visits of many French writers, to whose work Cyril Connolly had given publicity in special numbers of *Horizon* which were eagerly read; for it was a period when most English writers were markedly francophil. He gave a party too for Aragon, at which I remember one comic incident. For when Connolly asked him to read one or two of the exquisite lyrics he had been writing, Aragon launched instead into an immensely long and dull epic so that our attention began to wander until at last Philip Toynbee, when he saw him turning yet another page, broke out 'Oh no, *really!*' On a humbler level the French Embassy also brought over professional women, mostly teachers, who went to provincial audiences, telling them what life had been like under the occupation.

Ethel also had contact with visitors from Europe, mainly the Netherlands but also France, when in August she was asked to be hostess to a group of teachers for whom the Ministry of Education had organized a course at Dulwich, where they could meet their English opposite numbers, and describe their experiences. One of the places she took them to was the BBC, where they were moved to tears when they saw the room whence were emitted those nightly messages which kept their faith and hope alive during the war years. Her warm care obviously meant much to them, and when at last her turn to go to Paris came, she found that the French ones had organized a surprise party for her. She had a fortnight too with the friends she had waited so patiently to see, staying at the Vaneau and seeing them all, even Gide, who had been still in Tunis when I was there.

I had left the Ministry before she went, after working for a few days at the Central Office of Information, installed in a block of flats off Baker Street. The contrast with the Ministry made me realize how happy I had been during my years there, and how sad I was that they had come to an end. That sadness was increased when I learnt that it was shared by some of the civil servants, for with their formal letter of release, Mr Woodburn and his charming assistant Barbara Atkins sent me a touching message of farewell. Even the Deputy Director General, Sir Eric Bamford, a senior Treasury official who had been seconded to the Ministry for the war and was one of the kindliest men I ever met, wrote me a letter of good wishes for the future, saying it was against his better judgement that they had let me go. But I felt in my bones that it was time for me to depart and that one of the happiest periods of my life was over.

Ethel had returned from her Paris visit on 31 October, and so was able the next day to drive me to the British Council, in different parts of which our working lives were to lie for several years to come.

Chapter Eleven

The British Council
1945-1953

Apart from a general idea of the work of its Home Division, which I had gleaned from Ethel, I knew nothing of the British Council except that it was an organization that had been founded in 1934 to undertake cultural propaganda for Great Britain in the rest of the world, as the French and Germans were already doing for their countries. The mere idea of this was to earn it a hostile reception from the popular press whose contemptuous attacks began early and never relaxed. It had done a certain amount of work in Latin America and the Middle East just before and during the war, and had also established institutes and small libraries in a few neutral European countries, but had naturally been unable to do anything in the enemy-occupied countries. However, with the coming of peace in May 1945 a European Division had been formed in its headquarters at 3 Hanover Street, where Ethel dropped me before going on to her own office in Brook Street.

The head of this European Division was Kenneth Johnstone whom I then met for the first time. He had been seconded by the Foreign Office to work part-time for the Council since its earliest days, and then, after a varied wartime experience, had returned to work there full time, at first with no particular title. He was a man of wide learning in the history, literature and sometimes the language of several East European Countries, and of France too, for that matter. He was gentle, courteous and witty and proved a most considerate and pleasant chief during the many years I worked under him.

Apart from Charles de Winton, who had worked in Portugal since 1938, I found I was the only Regional Officer, as we were called, who had any knowledge of the country for which he was responsible. As a newcomer, rather older than most of the others, and with a reputation for knowing much about the country for our work in which I had been recruited, I was therefore in a slightly different position from the others. But they all gave me a warm welcome, and although I was to enjoy many advantages which they did not, and was in fact throughout my years there very generously treated by the Council, my colleagues never showed the slightest jealousy of me.

The first of these advantages was that Kenneth proposed that I should go to Paris as soon as possible, to run myself in as it were, by making the acquaintance of the staff there. As early as 1939 the Council had leased a small property at 78 Champs Elysées. In August 1944 the Council had established an office there. There were already specialist British Council officers dealing with education, music, science and the fine arts, and a librarian beginning to build up a small library.

By way of preparing for this visit I thought it would be as well if I were to know something of the workings of the Divisions concerned with these matters in the Council's London offices. To their great astonishment therefore I called on the heads of them all, and particularly on the men dealing with finance. I had been told that one of the duties of overseas Representatives was to make a budget for the cost of their operations for the following financial year, and as this was a matter of which I understood nothing, I asked for explanations about it. The Division concerned said that this was the first time that any Regional Officer had ever been to consult them on their mysteries and as a result we remained on excellent terms thereafter.

So I was well briefed when I left for Paris at the end of November. During my fortnight there I not only got to know our staff and learnt what they were doing, but saw something of the Embassy staff too, particularly Peter Tennant, whom I had first met in my Belgrave Square days and who had just been appointed Press Attaché and as such would be working with our people. I also had time to meet those of my wartime Free French contacts who now had official posts and to tell them of my new one, as well as many of the writers who had visited London during the past twelve months. Finally, and best of all, I spent such leisure hours as I had with Ethel's and my old French friends, all of whom were now back in Paris.

It had been a full and exciting fortnight and I returned to London well pleased with my new job.

Ethel meanwhile had been making strides with hers, which had begun at about the same time as mine. Foreign students in general had been a preoccupation with the Council since the earliest days. They had formed a Students Committee to help those who came to England to find jobs in British firms, and others who wanted to learn English, but not at first any who wanted to go to British universities. So when in 1939 the Council began to get organized they added a Students Department to look after them in general, and recruited Miss Nancy Parkinson to run it, as she had had similar experience when working with the National Union of Students. She now began to organize area offices of the Council in big cities throughout the United Kingdom, which were to make up the Home Division of which she became head.

When the war ended she decided that the time had come to set up a Student Welfare Department, and as Ethel's work with the Gibraltarians had come to an end she asked her to organize and run it. This was a job for which Ethel was ideally suited, involving as it did both her power of administration and her ability to get on with students of every nationality, which she had shown in Geneva twenty years before. So she set to work at once to organize a Department covering such diverse activities as the meeting and lodging of students, their introduction to our way of life and planning for their instruction in it, a centre where full use could be made of their leisure hours as well as travel for their vacations. Nancy approved the plan as it stood and it was to retain the same form in future.

That Christmas Beth came over on 22 December for a fortnight's visit, her first for over six years, as did the Bussys, who came to their London flat in Gordon Square then too. There we met many francophil English writers and the month of January 1946 saw the beginning of the stimulating social life I was thenceforward to lead. Part of this was due to the re-establishment in London of the French Embassy and Institute. The Ambassador, René Massigli, gathered round him an exceptionally friendly staff, two of whom, Louis Roché, the Minister, and Michel Fontaine, I saw constantly, both at the Embassy and in private meetings. The Cultural

Counsellor, René Varin, was a man full of ideas for exhibitions, always consulting me in his arrangements.

Another Embassy in whose social life Ethel also was included was the Italian one, where the Ambassador was Count Carandini, whom she had known in Rome, while the Cultural Attaché was our old friend since the Pontigny days, Edoardo Ruffini (Dado to his friends). Neither of these was a career diplomat, but had been given these posts because they were among the few Italian intellectuals who had refused to take the fascist oath during the war. Another link with our happy Italian relations was Dado's cousin Nina, who wrote in January saying how much she would like to translate my *Héloïse*. I of course was delighted, and the British Council came to my rescue because a department there was handling all the complicated negotiations between English and overseas publishers. Nina had found a good one, Rizzoli, so she began to work at once. But even so, with the usual delays, it was to be five years before the Italian version appeared. To complete the presence in England of our old Italian friends, Alexander d'Entrèves became the Professor of Italian at Oxford.

All that social life with the French in London enlivened my office work in France which was then at its most intense. The Council had planned to work there on a most lavish scale, with provincial offices under Regional Directors in Lille, Nancy, Lyons and Toulouse and they had already chosen the men for Lyons and Toulouse. At my suggestion they also appointed to the Toulouse office an elderly ex-judge called Stuart Gilbert, a considerable French scholar who was to become well-known as the translator of Malraux, and who helped to launch me on the translating career I was later to have. But the main choice the Council had made before I arrived was that of the Representative for France, a Welshman called David Howell, an ex-captain from the educational side of the Navy. He was a good administrator and spoke French, but was not particularly cultured in any way. I worked with him in the London office before he left for France and I soon saw that he was not a man who liked working with a woman in posts as important as his own. I therefore think it was a mistake on the part of the Council when they sent me with him to France, thinking it would help him if I introduced him to the many important French officials whom I already knew, such as Louis Joxe, the director of the Relations Culturelles and Julien Cain the administrator of the Bibliothèque Nationale and a great many others. But though I did my best to put him forward and stress his importance, I could see he felt jealous and irritated that I already knew them well. We got on better when we set off on a tour of the provinces, since I did not know many of the professors of English in the universities, nor even our own consuls, so that we were able to exchange our views of the impressions they made on us in easy equal conversation as we drove along in a car that was always breaking down because of the poor quality of the petrol.

That tour brought me two great personal joys. As we were driving through Provence I suddenly realized that we were passing quite close to the Bastide, where Ethel and I had been so happy in 1922 and 1923, so the chauffeur drove us up to the empty house to let me revive my memories of it. The other was when we were in Nice and I took the evening off and drove up to Cabris to spend it with Beth, happy to find the village quite unchanged. It was dark when I left and I was surprised when our chauffeur, an ignorant fellow, on reaching the coast at Cannes, turned to the right. When I pointed out to him that he was going in the wrong direction, as Nice lay to the east of Cannes, he replied *'en principe oui'* but continued as before until I forced him to obey my instructions.

Back in London I found that much had been happening to Ethel too. As more and more students were arriving she had been given more staff and much larger premises, a house on the south side of Grosvenor Square, where there was room not only for offices but for the large centre where she was planning to hold evening and weekend entertainments. She was beginning to interest the local people in the students too, such as the Mayor and Council of Lambeth, who gave a reception for them.

Greatly though we were both enjoying our work, it was exhausting too. But except for a week in June when we went to Porlock Weir to see Alice, we had to wait for our main summer leave until September. For Ethel had been asked to spend the first three weeks of August at Dulwich taking part in the second of those summer-schools for European teachers of English, which her presence the year before had helped to make such a success and this year evoked even warmer affection and esteem. I had a family event to celebrate at the end of August too, when Ethel and I went to Tunbridge Wells for the wedding of my niece Pat, who had been a Wren during the war and was marrying a clever and pleasant young medical consultant.

But at last September came and for this, our first real holiday since before the war, we decided to go to that part of France, the Dordogne, previously unknown to us and to most English people, I rather think, which Cyril Connolly's book *The Unquiet Grave* had given us a longing to explore. The year before I had met in Paris an attractive woman called Maggy de Lostende who had invited me to spend a few days with her sister, who lived in a charming old *prieuré* in the village of Montaigne, where his tower still stood - a building that immediately fired my imagination. She said Ethel would be welcome too so we first spent three magical days visiting that extraordinary tower were Montaigne wrote his essays, in a room on the narrow beams of whose ceiling he had had his favourite quotations painted, to inspire him as he wrote. Time seemed to have stood still there; for the unhurried pastoral life of the village was still attuned to the pace of the huge honey-coloured oxen. We then proceeded to Beynac, on the banks of the great river, where Beth joined us, and whence we explored that romantic countryside. And of course we saw Les Eyzies too and best of all, the amazing, recently discovered, cave at Lascaux, so soon afterwards, alas, to be permanently closed. But Ethel was eager to see Cabris again, with all that countryside she remembered so well, so she and Beth left me and I was collected by the amiable Stuart Gilbert from Toulouse, who had a car and who, while cynically professing not the slightest interest in them himself, drove me to see all the other places in the region - Brantôme, Bourdeille, Souillac, Sarlat and Fénélon that I craved to see. I left him at Toulouse and went by train to Paris, where Ethel joined me at the Vaneau, bringing a huge basket of muscat grapes and figs from Beth for my fiftieth birthday on the 20 September, which we celebrated with all our old French friends around us. It was as though the golden world had really come again.

Back in London in October I found that Kenneth had been organizing his Division, making of it two groups, South Europe and North-West Europe. Alethea Hayter was to be Director of South Europe, as Charles de Winton had now gone to Rome as Representative; North-West Europe, of which I was to be the Director, comprised nine countries: France of course and then Switzerland, Belgium, the Netherlands, Luxembourg, Denmark, Sweden, Norway and Finland. Although I had been recruited only for France I realized that now things were going smoothly there I must accept this extension. I had a good assistant, Angus Macnaghten, to help me. This of course meant a considerable increase in my work. I had to read the files to find out what we were doing in those countries, for all the correspondence with which I now had to deal, with the help of my excellent secretary Sheila Gray. But the most enjoyable part of the new work was that I had to go and visit my new countries to get to know the staff and meet the principal people in the university and social worlds with whom they dealt. There was a more delicate side to my missions too, although I don't remember being expressly charged with it. The Representatives in most of them were schoolmasters, who were generally not cultivated men, accustomed to dealing with foreigners or organizing an office. The Council vaguely felt this and wanted to know my opinion of them. I fear that I found four or five of them not up to the standard I knew we needed and when I came home I said this. As they had been appointed only on contract for two years they gradually disappeared and were replaced by better qualified men. These tours which I had to make covered the years 1947 to 1951 and I much enjoyed them as they gave me a chance to do some sightseeing in countries that I did not know.

Another part of the work was to get in contact with the Cultural Attachés of my countries who were being appointed to help them with any problems they had. The best of these, after Varin, was Dr Jane de Iongh, who was a well-known historical biographer in the Netherlands. Yet another aspect of the work was that the Foreign Office had drawn up Cultural Conventions between Great Britain and several of my countries, appointing Mixed Commissions consisting of professors and officials concerned with cultural matters who should meet in alternate years in England and the other country. I sat on two of these, the French and the Dutch ones, and much enjoyed the meetings where in addition to discussing our mutual problems there was much entertaining, each country doing its best to entertain the members at lunches and dinners. I particularly remember one such meeting at Aix-en-Provence.

But in spite of this increase in my work, and in Ethel's too, as more and more students arrived, we had ample time for our own private lives. They began with a very sad event in that bitter winter of 1947 when the streets of London were under lumpy frozen snow and the government had to reimpose the black-out. At the beginning of February our dear friend Loup Mayrisch died after years of suffering. Ethel went to her funeral at Colpach and there met a great number of her old French and Luxembourg friends, to so many of whom Loup had been a great benefactor and to whom I also owed much. When April came we both began to think we needed a change of habitation. My tenants had left Lyndale Avenue and we both felt we wanted to return there. This meant that we must try to get a housekeeper: no easy task then. Luck attended us and it was not long before we found one, a charming woman called Elsie Gadd. She was a good cook, most intelligent, with a slightly mocking sense of humour. She agreed to the wages we offered and said she didn't mind being alone all day if she could have a cat. So she joined us at the house in April 1947 and was delighted when Ethel's friend Eileen Olsen turned up one evening with a tiny fluffy golden kitten with huge golden eyes, so small that he still wobled as he walked. He became the prop and stay of Elsie's life. We called him Honey.

When I see what that house is like now I feel what a shabby looking place it must have been in those days. Yet I was happy to be there again and for Ethel the move was a major event. All her life she had lived in other people's houses, either as a daughter, a guest or a lodger, and now at last this was one of her own as we shared everything. To crown all, there was the garden where she could do exactly what she liked. She set to work at once on it, buying plants and even trees, especially the willow, then only about six feet tall, which now tops the church at the end of the garden. The presence of Elsie and Honey gave us both the sense of being a family and made it easier for Ethel not to miss me when I was on my Council tours.

Almost immediately friends came to see us and our new home. The only one who couldn't, alas, was Loup Mayrisch. The first to come were the Ruffinis, who were returning to Italy. They were followed by Elena Carandini, as she and Nicolo were both leaving the London Embassy so we lost our Italian connection here. Next came la Petite Dame for what turned out to be the first of eight annual visits. In 1949 Catherine and her recently married husband Jean Lambert came because they wanted to see the ceremony when an honorary doctorate was conferred on André Gide. It was while she was with us that to my surprise and pleasure I was made a *Chevalier de la Légion* d'Honneur in recognition of the work I had done for France during the war. In 1949 we had a very different kind of visitor, my dear old Alice who we thought might benefit by a course of treatment at the Charterhouse Clinic. She was thrilled to see the house again and the garden she had made but I fear the treatment did little good. Two pleasant aspects of that visit which I remember were the wonderful way that Elsie looked after her, having previously said she would not be able to live up to her. The other was when Julien Cain, the great administrator of the Bibliothèque Nationale, who happened to be in London and was having tea with us, went out and sat with Alice in the garden and talked to her. She answered quite simply and it was extraordinary too see how two such splendid people in different walks of life so easily got on together.

To return to the work side of our lives, while I was enjoying the increase in my duties, a very different treatment was being meted out to Ethel. She had steadily carried out the plan for her Department which Nancy had approved; she had a staff of eight loyal people and more and more students kept arriving, the majority of them Africans. The whole thing was so successful that in 1948 Ethel was given the MBE and in the next year the Colonial Office asked the Council to take care of the students that they brought over, as they had no means of looking after their welfare. Nancy, who had not paid much attention to the Department, never once attending any event, saw in this a chance to diminish

Ethel's popularity, which I fear she had been looking for. She told Ethel that the Department would now be too big for her to run, so she was going to demote her to the position of Deputy-Director, responsible only for the welfare work, and appoint over her a man who had always been an overseas Representative not connected with the students in any way. He would now be the Director and administrator. This was a humiliating shock to Ethel who could not see how these functions could be separated, but she could do nothing but accept and when the new man arrived in 1950 she loyally strove to initiate him in all branches of the work.

Perhaps it was to help Ethel with the welfare side of her work that she was sent in January 1951 on a three months' tour of Nigeria and the Gold Coast where she had a very arduous programme to fulfil and thoroughly enjoyed it. At the same time I was sent on one of my most prolonged tours to five or six of my countries and though I sent her an airmail letter from each one none of them arrived so she had no news of me all the time she was away. What did arrive was a telegram which I sent her in February to tell her of André Gide's death. A secretary in the office where she happened to be opened it and handed it to her saying: 'Someone you know is dead.' Never one to panic, I think she instinctively guessed that it couldn't be me in spite of getting no letters. All the same it was frightening.

On her return she found that no one took any notice of the report she wrote and also that the office was now so administered that there was no work for her to do except to find lodgings for the students, all of whom of course crowded round her, especially those whose parents she had seen. So at first she filled in her time with looking for what was called private hospitality as much as she could, but for the rest of that year she led a miserable office life, with nothing to do. In the following March Nancy sent for her saying that she knew she was unhappy where she was and intended to offer her the post of Resident Warden of a hostel for women African students in Kensington. Ethel at last protested saying that she couldn't possibly take the resident job since she lived with me, as Nancy well knew. So Nancy said she would try to get the authorities to make it a non-resident job - obviously quite an impossible thing - and again kept Ethel hanging about waiting for the decision which took six months to reach. So finally in September 1952 Ethel gave in her resignation able to bear it no longer. This was accepted but the Controller of Establishments, who knew as all the main authorities did, how she had been treated, asked her to defer the announcement of her resignation till March, the end of the financial year, which meant they could go on paying her till then although she was free to leave at once.

I had taken some of my leave before that when I went with my old friend Elliott Felkin on an Italian tour which we had arranged a long time previously, and I think it may have been my letters describing this that finally drove Ethel to resign as it made her want to see some of the places I was visiting. She did in fact go straight to stay with our Italian friends for two months, a holiday which did much to console her for the treatment she had received. One strange event happened when she was in Rome, when she was taken to a cocktail party, I think by the Ruffinis. She knew no one there but there was a fortune-teller and for fun Ethel consulted her. Although there was no possibility that she could have heard of Ethel before, she looked in her crystal ball, or whatever it was, and said 'There is a woman in London who is your enemy.' After Italy she stayed for a while with our French friends and then returned to London for Christmas, her old self again. In the following February she went to Jamaica to stay with our friends Dom and Ann Burns - he was now a brilliant architect and was building a university there. On her way home, she stayed with one of her old students in Bermuda and saw many others of them who could not believe that she was no longer Director of the Department she had created. On her return to London in March 1953 the whole band of students gave her a wonderful party and a booklet in which they expressed their gratitude for all she had done for them and signed their message with a huge list of their signatures. Nancy had not authorized this and one of Ethel's colleagues there told her that when she heard of it she was furious. The only explanation I can think of for the contrast between the ways in which Ethel and I were treated must lie in the different characters of our two controllers. Kenneth Johnstone was human, just and kindly and Nancy was ambitious, ruthless and obsessively jealous of any other woman's popularity.

It may also be that I was more forceful and full of energy,

and much readier to protest than Ethel; for everything favoured me. In 1951 a commitee was formed in the Council to review the staff and decide whether we were all in the right alphabetical grades which was the system the Council used. The Chairman was Grade A. Both Ethel and Alethea were Grade E, which I had been also, but now I was made Grade D and at the same time Deputy Controller of our whole Division on trial promotion. This lasted for two years until in 1953 Kenneth became Assistant Director-General and I was made Controller of the European Division in his place.

Apart from this brief outline of my own Council career there were many pleasant happenings during those years, in some of which Ethel happily shared. In December 1950 we had both gone for a brief visit to Paris to see the first night at the Théâtre Francais of André Gide's play *Les caves du Vatican*. It was a brilliant occasion socially, but a sad one too, for the play was too long and poor André Gide, though now old and ill sat up half the night shortening it with the help of Beth's husband Pierre. We were glad to be with them at that time as it was the last time we were to see Gide who, as I said, died in 1951. I don't think I went to see the office then as Captain Howell had come to the end of his four years, and his successor Harvey Wood was much occupied with moving our Council library from its unsuitable premises in the Champs Elysées to a charming old-fashioned little building in the rue de Chanaleilles which his Jewish friend Bernard Chayette, who was longing to get the whole of our Champs Elysées premises had arranged for us by way of an exchange.

In 1951, while Ethel was in Africa, I was in Denmark where I broke my right wrist and was sympathetically cared for by the lively and witty Representative H. S. Keyes (always of course known as Roger). Painful though it was, when I returned home I determined to fulfil a dream I had long had and that was to turn our two ground floor rooms into one. Ethel knew I intended to do this and helped me choose the colour scheme before she left. I thought it would be easier for both of us if it was done while she was away, so I sat for many cold evenings and weekends typing work that I was then beginning. I had already done a few small things for John Lehmann but now, at the request of Roger Senhouse, who had persuaded Secker and Warburg to bring out translations of the whole of Colette's work, I began on one or two of these.

By the time Ethel got home at the end of March the room was finished, the walls freshly painted, and the new carpet and curtains in place. She was thrilled to see it all and to get back to the garden where, that summer, we gave the first of our garden parties.

In November of that same year I had to go to Paris to help set up in the Bibliothèque Nationale a splendid exhibition called *A Thousand Years of British Books* on which a group of bibliophiles had been working for many months previously in the Council's London premises. Ruth Atkinson was their secretary and she and I helped to set it up in Paris. Ethel came over with her friend Eileen Olsen to see it, although she characteristically did not attend the opening day which was a big social occasion. T. S. Eliot opened it and there was an official luncheon at which he was made an *Officier* of the Legion of Honour. At the request of Harvey Wood I took him out to dinner that night. Ethel attended a different ceremony in November when all our old group of French friends met to talk of André Gide whose eighty-second birthday it would have been. Roger Martin du Gard gave Ethel a copy of the volume of *Hommages* that Gallimard had just published, dedicating it to her as '*l'incomparable amie insulaire*' as she was for them. The last exciting thing that happened to me during that visit was that at Julien Cain's suggestion I was introduced to Colette by her husband Maurice Goudeket. We had a charming little conversation and she gave me a special copy of *La Vagabonde* dedicated to me.

In 1953 we had many pleasant times. Ethel was then living happily at home and had rejoined the WVS for whom she had worked during the war. Their leaders all knew Nancy and so understood Ethel's position. They were very glad to have her back again. That was the year of the Coronation which we took Elsie to see on a huge television screen, set up in the Festival Hall. It was extraordinary to sit in a comfortable stall so close to the abbey where the ceremony was taking place. A special series of Honours was conferred at that time and I was lucky enough to be one of the Council officers chosen to receive an OBE. In that year also we had a particularly lovely holiday, spending the month of June in the village of Les Portes in the Ile de Ré in a house which Catherine and Jean had rented the year before. They had so loved the place that they bought an old wine-press for themselves to turn into a holiday home for themselves and their children and suggested we rent the house they had had. We passed our days happily in the stone-built old house which had a huge fig-tree growing in its garden and where one of the villagers cooked for us and looked after the house. The weather was perfect and we bathed all the time. Ethel painted happily many of the ancient local buildings and some old wrecked ships, while I sat happily translating Colette. It was a village much frequented by interesting French people. Jean Monnet had a house there, as had also Suzy Solidor, a retired nightclub queen who called her own house *les Hauts de Hurlevent* (which curiously enough is the way the French translate *Wuthering Heights*!). It was during our visit that the Mayor decided to have the dustbins collected as we previously all had to carry them to the local dump. During a party in the house of Jean Monnet at which Suzy was entertaining us with her sea shanties, suddenly one of the guests raised a cry of *les poubelles* because the mayor had said there would be a heavy fine to pay if we hadn't put them outside our doors by midnight. The party broke up immediately and fled to obey. One heard a clattering throughout the village of people dragging out their bins. Next morning we found that the dustmen had indeed done the job leaving a large fig leaf at the bottom of each bin.

Chapter Twelve

Slow Approach To Paris
1950-1954

One of the main events of 1953 was the holding of the Mixed Commission in Edinburgh, where we were able to impress the French by the barbaric splendour of the arrangements, especially on our last day, when, on returning at dusk from a drive round the surrounding countryside, we saw the Castle floodlit on its hill and had our final banquet inside it, in the course of which a kilted piper swirled round the table droning nostalgically away, and was rewarded with a large tumblerful of whisky which he tossed off neat. Although these meetings always entailed an extra load of typing for my charming and efficient young secretary, Katherine Price, she took it all in her stride, and even added to it, as I found when, on top of the finished pile of documents on my desk at the end of it all, there lay a poem beginning

> Last year they decided to meet in Provence,
> For the cooking, the climate, the sun of belle France.
> This year they're risking the inclement weather
> For tours in the Trossachs and tramps in the heather
>
> But whether in Aix or north of the Border,
> The meeting will follow the long-approved order.
> I don't need my crystal to foresee the way
> In which they will spend a small part of each day.

and going on for five more stanzas, each more ironically witty than the last. I had had no idea she had such a gift for satirical light verse, though I knew from our talks that she saw through it all.

The French team was led on that occasion by the Comte de Bourbon-Busset, a very cultivated man who had succeeded Louis Joxe as head of the Relations Culturelles department.

He was a writer of novels as well as an official, and when he and his wife came over again in November, on a private visit, we invited them both to dinner one night with the Kenneth Johnstones, so that we had a good chance to get to know them. I enjoyed the chance of talking of literary matters with him, for I had that year spent even more time than usual on my translations. Not only was I finishing my version of Colette's *La Vagabonde*, the volume she had given me, but I was also doing some of Supervielle's stories.

Strangely enough, I cannot remember exactly when it was decided that I should be the next Representative in Paris, nor whose idea it was, unless it was my own, because I could not see that any of my colleagues had better qualifications. But I feared it would be a tough job to persuade the Council to take this step, as they had never previously sent a woman as Representative anywhere, and Paris was their most important post. Fortunately for me Anthony Haigh, our liaison officer with the Foreign Office, and also I think a member of the Mixed Commission, was in favour of the idea; and our then Chairman, Sir Ronald Adam, a very wide-minded soldier with no prejudice against women, unhesitatingly approved the suggestion, a decision for which I feel I owe him much gratitude. So in February Anthony Haigh was empowered to write to our Ambassador in Paris, as was customary, to obtain his agreement to my nomination. As he was Sir Oliver Harvey, who remembered me well from the Ministry days, he gave his enthusiastic approval, although alas he had retired when I arrived in October 1954.

Although the Council had to await this formal approval before Personnel Department could announce my posting publicly, there was no reason why I should not tell my wonderful news to those nearest to me. One can well imagine the deep delight it was for Ethel to hear that the promise she had made me when we first met, over thirty years before, to help me learn more of France was now to be so richly fulfilled. It was thrilling for her too to know that she would be going with me to live again in that country where she was so much at home; for after the last nine years of shared daily life under the same roof it was unthinkable for either of us that we should ever live apart again. Unthinkable for me too to face this heavy new job without her help in all the practical matters that she was so much better at than I. My idea was to transport our whole household, Elsie and Honey included, if the idea of living abroad did not scare her. Far from it, she was as excited at the thought as we both were, and immediately began taking rudimentary French lessons from a French neighbour.

The next person I wanted to tell was my brother, who had recently been promoted for the last stage of his career with Shell-Mex and BP, to be manager of all the northern counties and had gone to live in Newcastle. So at the beginning of March I spent four days with him and his wife. From our childhood, in spite of his temper, he had always had a touching, brotherly, unjealous admiration for me, and was of course bursting with pride about Paris. I am glad, thinking back on it now, to remember how harmonious that visit was, for at the end of that year a great sorrow awaited him.

Almost immediately after I got back to London, the Council sent me to Paris for four days, so that I could myself tell those concerned about my appointment. Harvey Wood, who met me and installed me in the cosy little Hotel du Rond Point in the rue de Ponthieu, which I was to get to know well in the autumn, had been told my news himself and seemed pleased about it, but left me to tell the staff next day. I then went to see Sir Oliver Harvey, whose agreement I had to obtain for our moving from the Champs Elysées building. He introduced me to his Minister, Patrick Reilly, with whom, he said, I should probably have to deal, as he did not think his successor Gladwyn Jebb had much interest in Council affairs. Patrick Reilly was a very friendly man and I felt confident that he would help me. Lastly I called on Bourbon-Busset and the other main officials with whom I should have to deal. He said they would all be pleased to have me there and Julien Cain particularly said that he was glad Ethel was coming with me.

Then came one of the chief objects of my visit, which was to examine one or two of the buildings that Harvey Wood's Jewish contact, Bernard Chayette, (who had found us the house in the rue de Chanaleilles for our library, and who now coveted also our main offices in the charming little pavilion at the end of our courtyard) had discovered through his architect, M. Brillard. As the Ambassador agreed to our move, we felt the moment had come to find something that would house offices, a big reception room, library and all. And I privately hoped it might be big enough for my little household as well.

I returned to London on 20 March to find that my appointment to Paris had been announced in the office bulletin of the 18th. Almost immediately a stream of contratulatory letters began arriving from our European Representatives and some members of their staffs, and even some from Representatives in other countries too. I wondered if any Representative elect had ever received so many sincere-sounding, warm-hearted and sometimes almost delighted letters, some even from men who I knew were not very happy in their own postings and perhaps coveted mine, but who yet were all inspired by the same view, that here at last the right person was being sent to the right place. These congratulations from colleagues were supplemented by many others from friends in England. To drop their names would be as wearisome for me to write as for my readers to read, so I will quote only two. For Ernst Kris it was 'a dream come true', while Philip Hope-Wallace wrote 'This is history realizing itself'.

After that hectically full month, April was happily quieter and I remember only one Council event in it. Sir Ronald Adam was about to retire and he gave a cocktail party on the 13th for his successor, Sir Paul Sinker, where I had my first brief glimpse of him. At the end of that month, Ethel and I went for a week to Porlock Weir, where I wanted to tell Alice my news and to reassure her that, although we were leaving England, I should still visit her every year for a week, as I had always done since she left me, and would come at once if she needed me. I need not have feared that my departure from England would upset her for, as always, she never thought of herself and rejoiced as much as my other friends had done, and perhaps even more so, knowing what France had meant to me during all the years she had served us.

It was as well we went to Porlock Weir when we did, for very soon after our return there came an abrupt change in what had seemed an unbroken run of good fortune. In the middle of a meeting I was seized with such a violent pain that I could hardly get home. Ethel rang for our doctor and he immediately diagnosed gall-stones and said I must be operated on at once, wisely counselling me to get it over before going to live in Paris. It was easy enough to get into a hospital in those days so by mid-May I had had my operation in University College Hospital. It was not a serious or complicated one and I enjoyed the rest and the spoiling by streams of visitors. The last to come was my nephew Iain.

When I was up and about again, the Council gave me three weeks sick leave. As my visit to Eric in the north had inspired me, I thought it would be a good idea to get to know still more of England, so I persuaded Ethel to drive me slowly up the eastern side of the country, visiting chiefly cathedrals and abbeys. We stayed a few days in York and had the good fortune to be there during the performance of the Mystery Plays, where I vividly remember the fall of Lucifer backwards from the top of the black ruins of St Mary's Abbey against a glowing sunset sky. On our return journey we lingered at Fotheringhay, so haunted still by the spirit of Mary Queen of Scots on that thistle-covered mound where the place of her execution stood. After so much sight-seeing I felt I could indeed be proud of the riches and beauty of the country I was soon going to represent.

Almost immediately I returned to London, the Council interrupted my sick leave and sent me once again to France for four more crowded days, this time in connection with the British Institute in Paris, a much older foundation than the Council, which had links with both the Sorbonne and London University. Its main function in Paris was teaching English, chiefly to the French students of the Sorbonne. The new Director was to be Hilary Wayment, a Council officer who was to be seconded by the Council for that purpose. As they were holding their *Conseil d'Administration*, and as Hilary would be in some sort under me, I suppose the Council felt I should be present at this meeting too.

I then resumed my interrupted sick leave and this time I spent it quietly at home, working on my translations. I had already finished *La Vagabonde*, hoping to present Colette with it, but alas she died early in August. But I paid short visits to the Council office in London too, and I remember one small event which was to prove most useful in my future work. The Council had arranged a course for some of the locally employed staff of its offices abroad to familiarize them with its work. One member who came on this course was Madeleine Pablos, an outstandingly good secretary, with an excellent knowledge of English, who had been in the Paris office for many years and was the Representative's secretary. She and my London secretary, Katherine Price, came to dine with Ethel and me one night and so got to know each other, which made it pleasant for both of them when they became respectively the London and Paris voices of the private line which linked our two offices, and proved a tremendous time-saver in moments of crisis which occurred increasingly towards the end of my time in Paris.

On 14 July my annual leave began, but with so much travel earlier that year I spent this also at home, settling a few practical details. The chief of these was the letting of the house. By a great stroke of luck for us, my Dutch friend Jane de Iongh was at that moment waiting for a new flat. But it was uncertain how long this work would take, and she wanted a temporary refuge. She knew our house well and liked it and so we arranged that she should move in there as soon as we left. Another practical matter Ethel and I attended to then was the purchase of all the extra china and glass we should need for entertaining in Paris. It was also a month when we did a good deal of entertaining at home, giving final dinner parties for friends before the summer holidays began.

The most interesting and useful of these was when Sir Paul and Lady Sinker came, and with them the Varins. I had met Paul briefly in the office, but neither of us had yet made the acquaintance of his wife, Ruth. We took to her at once, finding her a most charming and cultivated woman, more of an intellectual in the field of letters than her husband, whose strength, although he had been a classics don and was a cultivated man, lay in his exceptional powers of administration. He was aware of this and we thought it very endearing of him to tell us that, when he announced his new appointment to his family, his teenage daughter Penelope said 'Don't they mean Mummy?' The other happy result of that party was that they both got to know Ethel and to realize what a help she would be to me in Paris (although the Council never gave her any official position or salary for the work she was going to do). Paul especially at once developed a great admiration for her, finding her the ideal English woman with her handsome looks, lack of any affectation in appearance or talk, and of course her simplicity and fun.

SLOW APPROACH TO PARIS 1950-1954

On 9 August I handed over my work as Controller of the European Division to Reggie Wickham, a rather dry official under whom the Division felt that life might be less jolly. As I was now free from the office, but still working, I spent a good part of the next six weeks in the Reading Room of the British Museum. I was not a specialist in any subject, and knew that lecturing to the anglophil societies and the English departments of the provincial universities would be part of my job, I thought it would be a good idea to read as many as I could of the accounts by early English travellers, chiefly of the seventeenth and eighteenth centuries, of their travels in France. This turned out to have been a good idea, since even university audiences like to hear historic descriptions of the places they live in, and the views of foreigners who visited them.

Early in September I heard from Harvey Wood that, in spite of his promise to find me a suitable flat, he had failed to do so. This was not altogether his fault, as at that moment furnished flats were in short supply. But my situation began to look more desperate when he soon after informed me that he had forgotten October was the month of the motor show in Paris, when all good hotels were fully booked, so the only place he had found for me was the little Hotel du Rond Point, which had a small room available. Thinking that this might mean that I would have to live out of my trunks for some weeks, Ethel left the WVS on 20 September and set immediately to work to pack for me - the first of her self-appointed tasks. It was a heavy one, both physically and mentally for she had to fold my whole wardrobe, down to the last scarf and ornament, arranging it all in separate groups in the nine trunks and suitcases they filled, putting in each a detailed list of its contents and providing me with a master-list of the whole, as well as with a complete bunch of numbered keys. My job was a different one: mooning about in our library, choosing what books I should want to take with me, and sorting papers and files that I might need, all ready for the next stage of packing, when I should have found a flat to put them in. It was not surprising that after this back-breaking job, Ethel felt so worn out that, after seeing me off on the night of 30 September, she went the next day to Cumberland for a rest with her friend Eileen Olsen who now lived at Threlkeld in Cumberland.

My arrival in Paris was anything but triumphal, although surprisingly I had no trouble with the customs. Both Hawkins the Deputy Representative, with his own car and Collins, the Council chauffeur, an old English soldier left over from the war, with the Council car, came to meet me and surprisingly managed to pile all my luggage into them and took me to the little hotel, where I found that even the small room I was to have would not be ready till the next day, and there was only a much smaller one for me to sleep in that night. As I could not yet unpack and felt at a loose end, Hawkins took me that afternoon to see two possible flats for Ethel and me which had suddenly become available, one of them, to my excitement, in my favourite *arrondissement*, the seventh. Hopeful by nature, I felt at once that this was going to be what I wanted. But my hope died when I found, on enquiring where the maid slept, that the servants' rooms were on the top floor, all giving on to an uncarpeted passage with a sink at the end of it and a tap with cold water. And the kitchen was in the basement. It was a situation that I subsequently found in almost every flat I saw in Paris, both ancient and modern; and it remains a mystery to me that, at any rate until that time, there appeared to be no shortage of domestic servants who took such accommodation for granted. What, I wondered, would Elsie's reaction be? The next Saturday I at last got into the room where I was to live for a month, and spent several hours arranging all those trunks and cases round the walls, leaving only a narrow passage between them and the bed, and unpacking such things as I knew I would immediately need. The evidence of the devoted care that Ethel had put into this first job she had done for me overwhelmed me with gratitude, and when I discovered in my pigeon-hole a letter she had found time to write to me in the midst of it all, full of encouragement to me in the loneliness she knew I should be feeling, I spent the rest of the day writing to thank her and hoping she was having the rest she deserved.

I duly turned up at the office on Monday morning, where, as there were few cultural matters to attend to, since neither the academic nor the social worlds of Paris had yet got into full swing, I was able to continue to inspect the various flats that were beginning to be advertised at the Embassy. Luck quickly attended me for after only four days I found something that, though far from being what I ideally wanted, had so many advantages that I thought we could put up with it for the four months for which it was temporarily to let. It was at 31 rue la Pérouse, near the Etoile, a quarter I did not much like, and it belonged to a nice Scottish couple. Their only condition was that we should keep on their servants, a married couple who lived in the flat, as they did not want to lose them. So I agreed provisionally to take it, if we could make some arrangement for Elsie, and wrote to ask Ethel to come over and see it.

My letter of course filled her with excitement and helped to take her mind off the cruel stroke that Fate had just dealt her. For she had only been in Threlkeld less than a week when Elsie sent a telegram asking her to return at once, as a burglar had broken into the house on her day out and, finding it virtually empty, had concentrated on Ethel's room and taken nearly all of her few precious jewels. Unlike me, she was no great wearer of jewels, but there was one, a ring made of a gold coin of the time of Philip of Macedon, showing his head on one side and his four-horsed chariot on the other, which she specially loved for its beauty and its rarity. She of course returned home at once to comfort Elsie and to see to all the tiresome business that a burglary entails, with the police, the insurance, and the builder who had to make good the damage the break-in had caused, before Jane took the house over. As there was no chance of going to Paris that weekend, she filled in what leisure she had by selecting the car we had decided we should need for our private enjoyment, a Hillman Minx, which the supplier said would be ready by 20 November.

So it was not until 15 October that she was able to come over to see the flat which she at once agreed would do temporarily. As for the servants, she thought it would be a help to her in her new duties to have two experienced yet simple and homely people to show her how things were done. So Maurice, who was the butler and did the marketing, and Odette the cook, were kept on. I signed the lease and we agreed to move in on 31 October. Ethel then returned to London to tell Elsie what we had had to agree to. She was of course greatly disappointed not to be accompanying us, but she bore it with her usual unselfishness. Jane was now installed and they had taken to each other, so all was well.

157

Ethel then began the last of her many tasks, putting together all our silver, glass, china, linen and blankets, that she had seen we would only eventually need as the owners of the present flat let us use theirs, and arranging for the Council to collect all that, as well as the big box of books and some pieces of furniture, such as my desk and one or two bookcases and pictures, which it was their business to pack, insure, store and eventually transport when we were able to house it. Characteristically she left to the last the packing of her own possessions, caught the ferry-train and arrived in Paris on the morning of 31 October, where I was waiting for her at the Gare du Nord. As 1 and 2 November are public holidays in France, we had plenty of time to install ourselves and take the rest that Ethel badly needed, and even to begin enjoying the fun of living in a continental but comfortable flat so unlike our own house.

But this happy idleness did not last long, for on 5 November we had to give our first official lunch party. The Council in London had arranged to send Dr Keith Simpson, the well-known forensic doctor, to Paris to meet some of his opposite numbers there. Beyond finding out who these were, and inviting them to a luncheon at which he hoped some plan for the visit might be worked out, Harvey Wood had only time to tell them that the name and address of their host was now changed. They all accepted but Ethel and I had the impression that they were not greatly interested, and were in fact a rather dull and stiff-looking bunch, especially the leader of them, Professor Piédelièvre, who looked both solemn and pompous. However we did our best over the aperitifs to break the ice when suddenly a miracle occurred. Ethel, who was talking to the Professor, happened to mention that she had known France a long time and had, among other things, been at the Scottish Women's Hospital at the Abbey of Royaumont in the First World War. At that magic word Royaumont, where he had been a *poilu*, he said '*Quoi, vous etiez la? Alors, vous m'avez sauvé la vie!*' (which she hadn't of course, having been an ambulance driver and not a nurse). His whole face and manner then abruptly changed and became warm and human, he hugged her and, beaming, turned to his three colleagues to tell them of his discovery, at which they too changed and shared in his pleasure. It was as if Ethel had suddenly become again the

Whity I first met, to whose easy and natural warmth the French had always immediately responded. After that there was no difficulty in arranging an interesting programme of discussions and meetings for Keith Simpson; and the legend that the French never invite you to their houses was disproved, for from then on we were always invited to the Piédelièvres' family parties. And I realized what a tremendous help Whity would always be to me on social occasions, and so indeed she was.

The only other entertaining we did that November was to give a reception for the professors of English from the provincial universities. This I did at the suggestion of one of them whom I already knew, Professor Talon of Dijon, who thought it might help me. He told me that every year the American Cultural Attaché invited them all for a few days refresher course in English and entertained them. But they had one free afternoon and Professor Talon thought they would be pleased to come to the Council and meet me. It all sounded to me harmless enough, but when the American Cultural Attaché heard of it he was furious with me, saying they were *his* guests and I ought to have asked his permission. I of course said I was sorry I had upset him. But when he learnt that the party was not my own idea but that of Professor Talon, he calmed down and never raised any objection when I repeated the event in subsequent years. Anyway, this meeting with the professors at the outset of my time in France proved a great help in the work I proposed to do in the provinces, as did also the annual conference of our Consuls in France for a week of discussions at the Embassy, when one morning was allotted to me to go and meet them and tell them also of my plans.

I had already paid two duty calls on our Ambassador, Sir Gladwyn Jebb. At the first he showed little interest in me or what I told him of my plans, merely asking me if I spoke French. As I knew that he knew that I did, I realized that this was teasing, so I took it in that spirit and simply replied 'I'm learning'. But when he repeated this question on my second visit, I first replied as before, and then made bold to say that this would get us nowhere, and that if he would only listen to the serious plans I had to work in the provinces, to try and compensate for the fact that our offices there had been suppressed in 1952, this work would supplement his own as I should be dealing with non-political people. This time he did listen. A few days later I got a message from his secretary, a friendly young man called Frank Barker, telling me that the Ambassador had to go to Lyon on his first official visit to the provinces, and wanted me to write a speech he had to give at an old and august academy of literature and the arts and sciences, about which he knew nothing; nor did he know what he should say. I pointed out to the secretary that to write the Ambassador's speeches was no part of my job, but he urged me to do it, saying that he thought it would help my relations with H.E. So during the weekend, when Ethel went to London to fetch our car, bringing her friend Eileen back with her to give her courage for her first encounter with the Etoile, I worked all Saturday in our library, and managed to turn out something that greatly pleased him. It was a mixture of comparisons between Lyons and London, both founded by the Romans, whose remains he knew they cherished as we, who that very year had founded the trace of a temple to Mithras, did too. There were similarities too between the characters of our citizens; and to top it all off I threw in some amusing quotations from my seventeenth- and eighteenth-century travellers. Madeleine Pablos turned some passages of my pedestrian French into her elegant variety. The speech was very well received in the Academy, who praised his unusual knowledge of their city. So I felt I had won my spurs; and indeed I had, for thereafter he supported me in every way he could.

By way of contrast to all this, I had a material matter to attend to that November. The furniture of my office, which was big enough to hold small meetings in, had been bought by Captain Howell when I dare say the choice was limited. But it was so hideous, being made of pale grey pickled oak streaked with white so that it looked like liver sausage, and the desk was so huge and clumsy that I felt I simply could not sit at it. Anything less English could not possibly be imagined, and I had dreamt of mahogany, of eighteenth-century or Regency design, reproductions if need be. I wrote so eloquently to the Council about this that they agreed to let me go and look for what I wanted in London in early December. Jane invited me to stay and I arrived on 10 December.

But it was a sad-faced Elsie who opened our door to me, for

she had just heard from my brother the tragic news that his only son, Iain, had died the day before. This young man, so courageous and eager, had contracted nephritis at the age of six and suffered from a terrifically high blood pressure ever after, which all the doctors warned my brother meant he would die young. He was therefore denied the public school and university education that my brother had dreamed of for him; but he was determined to lead a man's life as far as he could, and had married just the right sort of girl for him and fathered a child. Then a friend told him that there were better chances of a good life in Canada than in England, so he had sailed in the previous June, leaving a pregnant wife whose son, Alasdair, had been born in August, to follow him to Montreal, where he had found a house and a job, after Christmas. But it was not to be. He fell dead of a cerebral haemorrhage on 9 December aged only twenty-six. My brother heard of it from the police in the bleakest way, and I don't think he or his wife ever got over it. I too was shattered, as was also Ethel, who had greatly loved and admired the boy. I couldn't give my mind to my mission after that so I returned to Paris with the job not done.

The office was just about to close for Christmas and Ethel and I felt rather forlorn as to where we should spend it, cut off as we were from our families and England now, and living in a rather anonymous flat. And of course all our French friends had already made their own arrangements. Then a most unexpected thing happened. Monsieur Chayette, with whom I had had only business dealings over the possible exchange of our office, offered to lend us a charming little house he owned at Puiselet-le-Marais, in the Ile de France not far from Etampes. It was set in a little wood of a garden just off a very quiet road aptly called Le Chemin du Paradis; and he had a friendly village woman who would cook and look after us in general. We of course accepted this generous offer most gladly as it was exactly what we wanted. We went there on Christmas Eve and spent a week of utter contentment, wanting no other company than our own, resting, reading and walking or taking gentle drives around that enchanting countryside, which has remained one of our most loved parts of France.

Chapter 13

FEELING MY WAY
Paris 1955-1956

After that refreshing week of peace and solitude, we felt ready for what turned out to be a very busy year, largely because so many non-recurrent events happened in it in addition to the ordinary Council work. One of the first things we did on our return to Paris was to give an office party at our flat, chiefly so that Whity (as I more and more called her because so many of our old French friends did, and now new ones too) could meet the whole staff, as she had hardly had time to do before Christmas. It was only a small party because we were only a small staff, about a dozen in all at first. Three of us were London-appointed, myself, my deputy Bill Hawkins, who looked after all educational matters and musical ones too, as he was far more knowledgeable about music than I, and Milner the Librarian. The London post of the Fine Arts Officer, Frank McEwen, had been suppressed in the previous autumn, but as he lived in Paris anyway, on a boat on the Seine, he continued to help in art matters while wondering whether to accept a part-time contract offered by London. In addition to us three, there were some eight or nine locally appointed staff, the excellent secretaries of Hawkins, Milner and myself, who had all been there for years and knew their jobs backwards, the accountant Hobson, a filing clerk, and the receptionist Edith Atkinson, who dealt firmly and skilfully with all callers, and some two or three library clerks to cope with the massive student and other readership at our very large library across the river. And there was of course the chauffeur.

I had not only a small staff but a very small annual budget - about £150,000 I think it was. This had to cover not only the salaries of all the local staff (the London-appointed ones were paid by London), but all the everyday expenses and such things as my journeys to the provinces and expenses there. I remember feeling embarrassed by the contrast between my own salary and allowances, and what I felt was the meagre pay of our local staff, who yet seemed content because of their devotion to the work.

In addition to the staff I had two other great advantages. The first was that the 1950s were a time of ardent anglophilia in France, just as they were also a time of francophilia in England. This made the social side of my work in France, which consisted of putting eminent English visitors in touch with their French opposite numbers, very pleasurable, especially when I was able to do it by entertaining them at meals in my own flat or giving parties for them.

The other advantage was the fact that I was a woman, and this, rather surprisingly, stood me in good stead with both men and women. I never felt any antagonism among the masculine officials with whom I dealt, who treated me with a mixture of esteem for my efficiency, helpfulness when I needed their guidance, and in general a sort of amused appreciation, especially as I could never take things solemnly and tended to see the funny side of them. Nor did they apparently feel envy of me, for instance at the monthly dinners of the Cultural Attachés which took place in some modest restaurant, when it was the custom to invite some eminent Frenchman to be the guest of honour. As I was the only woman member I always had the privilege of sitting on the visitor's right and could thus have a sustained conversation with him before, when the meal was over, we all moved about and the others got their chance. It was in this way that I met Jean-Louis Barrault, Albert Camus and the witty and delightful Jacques Trefouël, director of the Institut Pasteur who, with his gifted wife, were to become great friends of ours.

As for the other aspect of that advantage, it happened that there were in Paris at that time many women who played a considerable part in cultural matters. The two most outstanding of these were the Duchesse de la Rochefoucauld and Madame Jenny de Margerie, particularly the former on whose presence I could count at anything I organized. These two and some others invited me to a small feminine gathering as soon as I arrived, partly to give me a good deal of useful information but chiefly to welcome me and to say how pleased they were that the British Council had for once chosen to appoint a woman as Representative. The fact that I held what was normally a man's post was made clear by the protocol department of the Quai d'Orsay, who decreed that my title should be Madame le Directeur du British Council.

Now to turn to the work, which began as soon as the office opened after the New Year break; and if I give an account of what I had to cope with in the first two months it will show the variety of tasks a Council Representative has to tackle. I had hardly sat down at my ugly desk before a man whose name none of my staff knew rang up to tell me that a plaque was going to be fixed at the entrance to the Hotel Voltaire on the Quai Voltaire, recording the names of three writers who had lived for a short time there. One of these was Oscar Wilde and the man asked me if I would give a short speech about him, standing on a little platform erected at the entrance and of course speaking in French. The mere idea of doing this in that very busy street, with buses thundering past, filled me with panic, but I felt that, as this was the first request made to me, I must accept. Fortunately in the course of a sleepless night I remembered that Oscar Wilde was Irish; so I rang up the organizer the next morning to say that I feared the Irish Ambassador would be upset if he heard that an English-woman was to speak on behalf of his countryman and suggested that he should be asked instead. He did as I suggested and I was thus able to join the listening throng when the event happened.

It was a relief after that to tackle jobs which I felt were more appropriately the Council's function. I had been asked by the very keen students' secretary of the Ecole des Sciences Politiques to try and find them an English lecturer. When I heard that Maurice Edelman MP, who was a member of the Council's Executive Committee and very keen on our work in France, was coming over, I wrote and asked him if he would do this. He immediately accepted and gave a brilliant talk, in fluent French, on the English Constitution. The students were delighted and when he agreed to answer questions, they couched them in what they thought was the proper English parliamentary style. This earned us the friendly acquaintance of Jacques Chapsal, the director of that famous school. Maurice also wanted me to meet Paul Reynaud in connection with a book he was then writing, so we invited them both to lunch at our flat, with their wives, and after the meal left the two men together.

One of my annual duties in January was to preside over the committee which met to interview the candidates for the full-term scholarships and short-term bursaries which the Council allotted to France. The chief of the seasoned members of this committee was the kindly Professor Bugnard, director of the Institut National d'Hygiène. He and the other officials, some of them scientists, all knew the right questions to ask while I merely tested the candidates' English, an essential condition of the awards. In January too we had our first house-guest, the artist Ben Nicholson, a retrospective exhibition of whose work had been arranged by the Fine Arts Department of the Council in London, and which lasted for two months. Frank McEwen helped to set it up at the Musée d'Art Moderne. The Ambassador asked Ben Nicholson to lunch, with Frank and me too, and there I had the opportunity to meet Georges Salles, the very distinguished director of the Louvre, who later did me a great favour. Also in January I gave my first lecture to the pupils of the well-known Ecole Alsacienne, were André Gide and many other French writers had been to school. I did this at the request of the teacher of English, Bichette Debû-Bridel, whom I had first met on my visit to France in 1944, for which her husband was partly responsible.

While all this was going on Whity was learning the art of marketing, which she had never done before, with the help of our experienced man-servant Maurice. For buying wines and spirits she had to go to the Embassy NAAFI stores and every time she went there she consulted the list of furnished accommodation available, for we were beginning to get very anxious as to where we should go when our present lease came to an end on 26 February. This watchfulness of hers was rewarded when she suddenly saw the announcement of a flat in the seventh *arrondissement*, just the part of Paris where we wanted to be. It was in the rue de Martignac and we immediately went to see it. This short and little-known street runs from the rue de Grenelle to the rue St Dominique, and half-way down it there runs into it an even shorter street, the rue Las-Cases, in which stands the large church of Ste Clotilde, whose twin spires form a marked feature of the Paris skyline. The corner house at the angle where these streets join belonged to the Comte de Coulombiers, an old aristocrat who now lived at Senlis and had turned the top two floors of his town-house into a flat, keeping only the ground and mezzanine floors for himself.

The first floor of this flat contained a very large drawing room, panelled and painted pale green, with five long windows and much beautiful, though shabby, genuine Louis XV and XVI furniture. Out of it led a good-sized dining room, and out of that a big though rather old-fashioned kitchen. On the floor above there were not only two bathrooms but four bedrooms, so as we only needed three for ourselves, there would be that great rarity in a Paris flat, a double spare-room where we could put up not only official visitors and Council staff but our own friends and family when they came on holiday. We naturally fell in love with the place at once and thought it exactly right for our purposes. But as it was extremely expensive and I knew the Council would take a lot of persuading, I rang them up immediately and they sent the official responsible for France over the next day. He so shared our enthusiasm that he assured me we would be allowed to have it, and on the strength of that, as our other lease was just running out, we at once moved into a room in the Hotel Lincoln, taking with us merely what we temporarily needed and sending all our other trunks and suitcases to the office. But as I still feared that the delay in communications might lose us this treasure, we both flew to London where, after much eloquence on my part, I secured the definite agreement I wanted. We then returned to Paris and on 4 March I signed the contract with the old Count. The rent was to be paid in a strange way, half each month by cheque to his man of affairs and the other half to be left in cash with the porter at the Jockey Club. I felt it wise not to tell the financial people in London of this, knowing that later when an inspector came out he would be certain to object, but it would then be too late.

The Council in London had immediately despatched our household goods which Whity had left with them. But meanwhile she had plenty to do because I was so immersed in office work that she once again had to undertake single-handed the job of getting all our trunks from the office to the flat, unpacking them and disposing their contents in the many cupboards and commodes. Our household goods arrived in time to enable us to sleep there on 11 March. The next day Elsie arrived by the ferry-train and Whity went to meet her. She didn't bring Honey the cat with her, as we thought this would be too much for her in her first experience of such a journey, and that it might be better for her to get used to her new work before he came. So it was not until April that he flew over in his basket, despatched by Jane from Heathrow and looking very proud, we thought, when he arrived. He took the change to this new gardenless abode as calmly as did Elsie, who, when we came down to breakfast next day, cheerfully said 'Here am I, dusting the V and A' and who soon got used to the rather peculiar arrangements of the flat, which I think I must describe.

The Count had arranged that it should have its own front door and be known as Number 1 *bis*. This tall and imposing door flanked the exactly similar one of Number 1, inside which sat the concierge, Madame Paul, a smiling friendly person. For Number 1 *bis* we had a key to let ourselves in, for we had no concierge, nor was there any room for one, merely a small space for clothes-racks when we began to give receptions, when Madame Paul came to help. So we went straight up a long curving flight of carpeted stairs which wound up past the two floors of our apartment, with a little landing outside each. Callers and tradesmen too had to ring our electric bell which by some hydraulic system communicated with a large rubber pear inside the passage leading to the kitchen. If squeezed hard enough the door would click open. But the power needed for this pressure was often beyond Elsie's and my feeble hands and only Whity's were strong enough. In any case the operation took some time, so we were often obliged to open the landing window and shout down *'Attendez un moment s'il vous plait; on presse la poire'*, a remark that surprisingly seemed to be understood by everyone, who replied *'Parfaitement; on comprend'*. But after a while this got too much for all of us and the landlord managed to install a more up-to-date system. Our drawing room had its oddities too. The house must have been about 200 years old and the drawing-room floor sagged slightly in the middle, so that people tended to enter at a brisk trot, until they came to the central chandelier, which ended in a large glass ball, against which tall guests risked banging their heads, until Whity managed to remove it. All this made for the amusement of our visitors, to receive whom we were now ready.

Our pieces of furniture arrived at last on 18 March and we had hardly arranged it all before we heard that Kathleen Raine, the poet, had just come to Paris and wanted to meet other writers. So we gave a little cocktail party for her, to which I invited many of the writers whom I had met when they visited London immediately after the war, as well as others whose acquaintance I had recently made. So it was quite an impressive gathering with such people as Philippe Soupault, Pierre Emmanuel, Raymond Queneau, Jules Supervielle and even Tristan Tzara, a survivor of the Dada movement. But we also started giving luncheons too. We had decided to give them rather than dinners, as we felt that neither of us, let alone Elsie, could cope with the very late hours of dinners in Paris, I in particular as I always had to be in the office by nine o'clock. I spent hours in choosing the guests to ensure an interesting mix. This was helped when I got to know the heads of the many international organizations then established in Paris, such as OECD and NATO, particularly the latter, and there were the foreign correspondents of English newspapers too, particularly Frank Giles with his wife Kitty and the erudite Darsie Gillie of the Guardian and his wife Cecilia. Our parties were nearly always cheerful, informal occasions where Elsie's cooking was much appreciated.

It was amusing too when eminent Frenchmen who did not know each other met for the first time under our roof. The most striking incident of this kind was when we invited our old friend Roger Martin du Gard, who had become something of a recluse but was longing to see our flat, to come to lunch. We invited another of our old friends, Jean Schlumberger, to come too, but Roger said he would only come if I would invite no one else. I made no precise promise but asked him to come early to see the whole flat before lunch. The tour of the rooms ended in the dining room and when he saw the table he exclaimed in dismay *'Il y a six places!'* I replied that he need not stay if he did not want to, but told him that the other guests were Julien Cain, the administrator of the Bibliothèque Nationale and his amusingly eccentric wife Lucienne. Hearing that completely won over Roger, who said he had always wanted to meet Cain as he was anxious to bequeath his papers to the library. It was one of our happiest luncheons and afterwards Cain remarked *'Comme c'est curieux qu'il faut deux Anglaises pour faire se recontrer deux Francais comme nous!'*

It was fortunate that Easter fell in the first days of April that year and the kindly Monsieur Chayette once again offered us the use of his little cottage in the wood at Puiselet-le-Marais. We were glad to accept because we were both very exhausted, especially Whity who had had all the heavy practical work to do once again. This time we took Elsie with us for she too was tired after the rush of work that she had had to face so soon after her arrival. The little wood was now full of wild flowers and we spent most of our time lying and reading in it. When we returned to Paris Whity was told that as she had no official position it was necessary for her to get a *permis de séjour*. For this she had to give the names of two sponsors so she asked her old friends Jean Schlumberger and Olivier Wormser, who was now at the Quai d'Orsay. She got it so quickly that she asked Jean what he had said about her. He replied with his dry smile *'J'ai simplement dit que vous êtes une personne inoffensive!'* This made us laugh as I am sure he had had to be much more eloquent than that.

As the main event of that April was not due to take place until the end of the month, I thought I could fit in some of these provincial visits which I had told the Ambassador were one of my principal aims. I had in my budget the small sum of £400, which had been included in it when our four provincial offices had been suppressed in 1952. With this I intended to offer a little financial help, either by gift or loan, and regular loans of English books, to the keener branches of the Association France-Grande-Bretagne (FBG for short), the sister Society of our Franco-British Society in London. To this end I made the acquaintance of Robert Wieder, the Secretary of FGB and suggested that he might like to accompany me sometimes when I visited the branches. To this he enthusiastically agreed, and either with or without him I visited no fewer than ten provincial towns in the course of that year. Not all were rewarding, but the two I saw in that April were outstandingly good. The first was at Nantes, where the branch was under the leadership of Robert

Guibal, an *armateur* (ship-owner, but it sounds more dashing in French!). He told me that he had just found a small room which could become a meeting-place for his members, and said that if I could pay the rent of this for two years, he was sure it would enable him to double his membership so that then they would be able to pay it themselves. I gladly agreed to his proposal, and his prophecy was to come true. After that I went to Toulouse, where the society was practically dead, so I wasted no time over it but went on to Bordeaux, where I found that the books from Toulouse and other former provincial offices had been sent and put in the kitchens of the Consulate. The Consul there, Pat Johnston, was quite the liveliest and wittiest of those I had met, and he suggested that he might be able to get Foreign Office permission to put up bookshelves in two ground-floor rooms that he did not need to make a small library there. Pat Johnston had a delightful wife too, Jean, and we were to become great friends. Professor Loiseau, who was president of the local FGB thought that this library was a splendid idea. I offered once again to pay part of the expenditure and to send them block loans of books when they were ready. Incidentally, these increasing block loans gave our library staff in Paris much more work to do and it was not long before we had to take on an extra clerk and an old man who did nothing but pack up books all day long.

But the main event at the end of that April was the regular meeting of the Mixed Commission of the Anglo-French Cultural Convention, and both the Sinkers came over for it. Paul had told me in advance that he wanted to use this occasion for a problem that was much on his mind; so as there were no cultural difficulties between our two countries he spent most of his time discussing this problem with our French opposite numbers. He knew that French teachers who went to work in schools or universities abroad did not lose their seniority, as ours did, and so were eligible for higher posts when they returned to their own countries. He wanted the same system to prevail in England and was anxious to learn how the French did it. Soon after he returned he introduced the system into England and I think that was in fact one of his major contributions to the work of the British Council.

In addition to these discussions with French officials he

had plenty of time to talk with me about a new building for the Council. I think I was beginning to feel that Harvey Wood's and Bernard Chayette's dream whereby we would cede the lease of our Champs Elysées building to him in return for the lease of a bigger building, which would hold both our library and offices, would never be realized, as I never saw a house that was remotely possible. I told Paul that I thought the Council would have to pay for a new building for itself and though he agreed he said there would be no money available until 1957 and I must in the meantime continue the search.

I cannot remember when it was that the Ambassador first asked me why the Council did not want me to be a Cultural Attaché. Every other country had such an official, even when it had no culture, and it would be easier for him to refer to me by that title. I explained that the Council's dislike (at that time at any rate) was due to their fear lest we should be thought to have any political bias. H.E. felt there was no danger of this, in France at any rate, and said that if I would take the matter up with the Council he would do the same with the Foreign Office. I had an opportunity to do this when in early May I went to England, taking a week of my annual leave, to pay my promised visit to Alice in Porlock Weir. In London I spent a few days hunting for the furniture for my office which I had failed to find in the previous December. This time I got what I wanted; antiques, alas, were out of the question but I got some good reproductions; a desk for myself, one or two cupboards, a long table for meetings and some nice regency-style chairs, to be upholstered in my favourite green. This was just the right moment to talk to Head Office about the Cultural Attaché affair, as I could point out to them that it would mean that these articles could be sent over duty-free to the Embassy. They naturally saw the advantage of this and it may have been a clinching argument. The Foreign Office also acceded to Jebb's request, so on 2 June I was accredited to the diplomatic corps, with the proviso by the Council that this concession was only to hold good while the present Ambassador and I were in Paris. Of course anyone with a flicker of foresight could have seen that neither of our successors would agree to give this title up and they never did.

While I was in London Whity went with Catherine to the Ile de Ré for a fortnight's breath of fresh air, for she was not by nature an urban person, and all she ever got in Paris was on our Sunday morning visits to Bagatelle, and the privilege of enjoying the gardens of the Musée Rodin on Sundays, which the museum's keeper Cécile Goldscheider gave us. While Whity was away the actor-manager A.-M. Julien invited all the Cultural Attachés and theatre critics to a sumptuous lunch at Le Vert Galant, to tell us of his plan to launch next year an annual season of what he called *Le Théâtre des Nations*, and of his hope that we would spread the news of this in theatrical circles in our own countries. I discovered in talking with him that he had been a member of Jacques Copeau's school of acting in Pernand Vergelesses which Whity and I had visited in 1929. When I told him that Whity had known Copeau long before that, when he ran the Vieux Colombier in Paris, Julien was thrilled and keen to meet her. So once again her old connections added warmth to our present work and made her very much part of it. He remained a faithful friend throughout our time in Paris.

Apart from the arduous job of having to write one's annual report in June, there was little office work at that season, for June was far and away the busiest social month in Paris, when every Embassy gave a cocktail party to which it was almost a duty to go and where one always met the same people. I found the endless standing on these occasions very exhausting as I always had rather tender feet. So that year I was glad I had decided to break the traditional leave pattern whereby the office was closed in August and the whole staff went on holiday, by taking three weeks of my own leave at the beginning of July. I fear that this threw the burden of the office on Hawkins at a busy time for him, for it was in July that he ran our annual summer-school for teachers of English. But fortunately he had a new member of our staff to help him, for he took on a young Scottish girl called Molly Walker, who had been a lectrice at Rennes University, where I had met her earlier in the year. She spoke beautiful French and was in general a great addition to the office.

Whity and I went to Majorca for our holiday at the eastern end of the island. We spent most of our time swimming in the aquamarine sea and going for endless walks. It was perhaps because of those walks that on the day of our return I got an acute attack of rheumatism in one foot. I went to see my doctor as soon as we got back to Paris. He could not understand what had caused the pain, and thought it likely that it would disappear as quickly as it had come. So I persuaded Whity to carry out her own plans and go and spend three weeks at Cabris with Beth. Incidentally she found that my dear friend Ernst Kris was also staying nearby. I was sad to miss him, for he died in 1956 and I never saw him again.

The main reason why I had broken the usual leave pattern was because I wanted to have our office rooms in the Champs Elysées building painted, as it was obvious we should be there for some time to come. Except for my own office and the one big salon on the first floor, which was all white, the whole place looked very dingy and badly needed a coat of paint. Of course it was not possible to find a firm of decorators in Paris in August to do this, even if we could have afforded it; but our accountant Hobson found me a Russian painter who said he could do it alone. I think perhaps I should emphasize that I was not instructed by London to have this done; I was merely obeying that instinct of mine which drove me to beautify as much as possible any office I worked in, as I had first done in my Camberwell days.

But I would have thought twice about it if I had remembered that our chauffeur was also on leave, and had realized how agonizing my rheumatic foot was going to be, as it meant that I had to limp painfully to and from bus stops four times a day. However, in three weeks the job was finished and Whity returned to Paris. Of course she was horrified when she learnt what I had had to endure, as I naturally had not told her; but she knew me well enough to realize the gratification I had got in seeing the job done. To make up for my labours I had ten delightful days at the end of August when the office was still closed; and as two of our friends, Alethea Hayter and Umberto Morra, came to stay, Whity drove us to some of our favourite haunts outside Paris, particularly the park of Ermenonville, with its lake and Rousseau's tomb and the extraordinary sand-covered hills nearby called the Désert de Sable. We took our friends too to what had become our favourite out-door summer restaurant - the Pavillon du Lac, at the Buttes Chaumont, where the local couples held their wedding feasts, which were great fun to watch. Then since as usual there was little work to do in

September when the office opened again, and I felt I could still do with a little more of my very generous leave allowance of sixty days, while Elsie too was in need of a change, we took her with us to the Ile de Ré, where we had been lent a house by a friend of Jean and Catherine, who were with their children in their own house.

We returned to Paris on 1 October, a year to the day since my first arrival, in time for our first musical event that month when the Hallé Orchestra, with Barbirolli, was sent over by the Council in London. I remember little of it so I think I must have left all the arrangements to Hawkins, both the press conference before it and the reception afterwards, which took place in the large gallery at the Théâtre des Champs Elysées. This I believe was the first occasion for which I used a new firm of caterers which my friend Bichette had recommended. The head of it, Madame Guillemard, was a very voluble lady and when she came to discuss matters with me and I asked her what her waiters were like, she replied ecstatically *'Mademoiselle, mes hommes ont tous le feu sacré!'* I found she spoke truly for her men were so utterly dedicated to their work that I never had any need thereafter to worry about the service. We used her firm too for a party which we gave for professor Anthony Blunt, famous then only, of course, as the authority on Poussin. The Louvre had invited him to give a talk about the Courtauld Institute whose head he was, preliminary to an exhibition of its pictures. This seemed to me a proper occasion to entertain the art world of Paris, which Frank McEwen had helped me to get to know the winter before.

Quite apart from my continuing rheumatism I had another misfortune that month. Our Italian friend Guglielmo degli Alberti had come to stay with us and I took him to see a film at one of the cinemas in the Champs Elysées. On coming out I failed to see the three sharp-edged marble steps which led to the street, so great was the crowd pressing in, that I fell down them and cut the shins of both my legs so badly that the manager insisted that I should go to hospital, otherwise he would be held responsible. I had always heard, from the French themselves, that their hospitals were bad. He called an ambulance which took me to the Laennec hospital, where I found this to be true. I was the only person in the out-patients department. When at last after an hour's wait a doctor arrived, he was horrified, because the flesh had so shrunk away from the bones that he had to draw it together with enormous stitches before putting on a dressing. He told me that he would arrange that a nurse would come and take out the stitches in a week's time. When she did I noticed that she had black fingernails and cut the stitches with a pair of un-sterilised nail-scissors before putting a new dressing on top. As after that I still felt a bit groggy I decided to go to England to consult my brother-in-law, Jack Ranking, Pat's husband, in Tunbridge Wells, a doctor in whom I had great faith. Whity came to England with me as it was a year since she had seen her family and friends. Jack found that both my wounded legs had gone septic. He managed to clear that up and threw away the drugs I had been advised to use for my rheumatism and told me to rely on aspirin.

I hoped that the change had done Whity good too, for in December she had the most exhausting of all the tasks she performed for me, and that was preparing for the visit of the Foreign Office inspectors. I do not know of any other profession that is subjected to this hideously exacting inspection, the purpose of which was alleged to be to discover whether our allowances were adequate. To prepare for it Whity had to keep throughout the year detailed daily lists of every item of expenditure, ranging from food and drink and the cost of large receptions, and including wages, electricity, gas and so on, down to small items like cosmetics and tips. She then not only had to add up these huge columns but to separate the totals under various headings. On the basis of these the Foreign Office Inspector assessed the rate at which I was living. She also had to add up the number of guests we had entertained and I think that when they saw that we had had 165 people to meals and 226 to cocktails in that first year alone they must have been satisfied.

But there was at least one bright spot in that month. The aspirin treatment had begun to work, with the magical result that on 19 December my rheumatism suddenly disappeared entirely. So Whity and I were able to enjoy the Christmas holiday free from official duties and being as deeply happy alone in each other's company as we always were. Then, as the French more and more tended 'to make the bridge', as they called it, over Christmas and the New Year, and as nothing much happened in the first days of January, we decided to take still another week and accepted an invitation from our friend Douglas Cooper. He was a man who had made many enemies by his outspoken art criticisms but he had always been niceness itself to Whity and me, ever since we met him at the end of the war. He now lived in a large square renaissance-looking house with big round towers at its four corners, called the Château de Castille near the Pont du Gard. This was really a kind of folly built in the eighteenth century. It stood back from the road and a long series of broken columns led up to it. We went to Avignon by the Mistral, the first of those wonderful high speed air-conditioned trains with which the French had replaced their rolling stock that had all been destroyed in the war.

On arrival we found that Douglas had had to go away on business, but the friend with whom he lived, John Richardson, was only too delighted to play host. There were two other guests, James Joll, the sub-warden of St Antony's College at Oxford, and a friend of his, John Golding, who was working for his PhD at the Courtauld. John Richardson had the use of Douglas's car and he drove us all over that wonderful countryside, which we knew far less well than the eastern part of Provence. Two things I remember particularly were visiting the delightful town of Uzès and seeing the little pavilion where Racine lived, and also of calling on the tenants of Cézanne's old house, Le Jas de Bouffan, where some of his earliest paintings still hung on the walls.

Although we had no particular cultural event planned for the spring, an outstandingly popular one did occur which, although we had no responsibility for it, provided more publicity for us than anything we had done ourselves. To explain the origin of it I must go back to my predecessor, Harvey Wood. Being an ardent Scot he had soon made the acquaintance of Gabriel Rémond, the Secretary of the Association Franco-Ecossaise, who had told him of a small Franco-Scottish exhibition he had seen in the Council's offices in Edinburgh, and said he would much like to organize a similar one in Paris. But nothing was done. When I in my turn made Rémond's acquaintance he told me too of his wish; but I soon saw he had no ability to organize this or indeed anything else, and as I knew that it was not the kind of thing the British Council ever undertook, I could only say that I also liked the idea and would see what could be done.

It then so happened that I spoke of it to Charles Braibant, the director of the Archives Nationales that are housed in the splendid Hôtel de Rohan on the fringe of the Marais. He at once pounced on the idea, seeing in it a successor to a series of exhibitions he had recently mounted there: *France-Brésil, France-Canada*, etc. He said he would organize the whole thing and immediately instructed a senior member of his staff, Bernard Mahieu (whom I had good reason to remember ten years later when he helped me on some research of my own) to begin working on it. He planned that it should cover the whole period of the Stuarts in France from the fifteenth to the eighteenth centuries, and said he would be able to borrow nearly everything he needed from French museums and private individuals, only asking me to get a few items from Scotland. They would also produce the very full catalogue for which they hoped I would write a short introduction. And when it appeared I saw that Braibant had been generous enough to put on the title page that the exhibition was organized *'avec le concours du British Council'*. When I told the Ambassador all this he thought it would be a splendid occasion to ask the Queen Mother to come over and open it, which she fortunately agreed to do, and very charmingly did.

Cynthia Jebb had a brilliant idea for this occasion. She was planning to give an early dinner party for the Queen Mother on the day of the afternoon opening and then to take the whole party, to which I was invited, on to a big reception for *le Tout Paris*, which Braibant wanted to give late that evening in the splendid suite of rooms where the exhibition was held. Cynthia thought it would be very dramatic if we could get a highland piper from the British army in Germany. She managed to do this and then asked me to leave the dinner before the rest of the guests and take the piper with me in an Embassy car to the Archives, where we would wait at the top of the magnificent staircase until the Queen Mother and her party arrived. When they were half-way up the stairs I would tell the piper to begin piping and to march slowly through all the rooms. It worked like a charm. The guests, startled by the unaccustomed noise, fell back, forming a natural corridor for the Queen Mother, who then entered with the Ambassador. I slipped in after them, joining Julien Cain in one of the rooms. It was then that I learnt what a royal memory is, for he was one of those who helped me, about whom the Ambassador had asked me to write very brief notes to give the Queen Mother, as he intended to present the guests to her. They stopped in front of Cain for this purpose, she immediately said, in the most natural way in the world, in her pretty French, how delighted she was to meet him, as she well remembered the wonderful exhibition, *A Thousand Years of British Books*, which he had organized at the Bibliothèque Nationale a few years before, and what a splendid occasion it was. After she had moved on he turned to me absolutely staggered that she should remember that.

That exhibition lasted until the early summer and was immensely popular with a far wider range of people than we ourselves ever reached. But I was able to help keep its popularity going among the more elegant Parisian world by inviting them to a concert in mid-April. A Scottish quartet from Edinburgh, called the Saltire Singers, were in Paris on tour and I asked them if they would give a concert of old French and Scottish songs at the Exhibition. They gladly agreed and it was a delicious evening, which I expect Janet Adam Smith, who was staying with us at the time, remembers as vividly as I do.

After all that was over I went on a short provincial visit to Bordeaux, accompanied by Reggie Wickham, Controller of the European Division, who wanted to see some of my work in the provinces. I chose Bordeaux as the liveliest centre, where Pat Johnston had already started on his plans for the library. The chief members of FGB, Professor Loiseau and Madame Bidault, entertained us and I gave a lecture for the first time under university auspices, which evidently gave Wickham a satisfactory impression. While I was away, Whity had had her friend Eileen Olsen to stay and driven her to see the Loire castles. When they returned Eileen stayed with us, so that I could not put up Wickham, who had remained a few days longer in Paris for talks with me. But we had him to lunch a few times, once with Eileen, and I remember feeling that it was somehow a doomed occasion, for neither of them was articulate and they had nothing to say to each other. A day or two later, Whity drove Eileen and me to the Gare du Nord, where she got out of the car, took a waiting porter and walked straight to the platform with him without once looking back and laughing and waving as she always had done. We felt quite stunned with surprise. A few days later, when we returned from a short Easter visit to Geneva to see our old friends we heard from Elsie that Eileen had been killed in a motor accident, when her husband was driving her home. It was only a few months later that we heard that Wickham too had died from lung cancer.

In May there occurred far the most important and exciting events that London had yet sent us, the English Opera Group's presentation of *The Turn of the Screw*. We were rather apprehensive about it because the last opera by Benjamin Britten which the French had seen was *Billy Budd*, which they had not liked. We also knew that they didn't like ghost stories. But Hawkins had taken a great deal of trouble in preparing a press conference, with gramophone records from the opera and plenty of information about Henry James and Britten. All the main music and theatre critics came and he plied them with whisky. The performance took place at the Théâtre des Champs Elysées and the large audience was so immediately gripped by the performance that after the interval, for the first time in my experience, they were all back in their seats before the *trois coups*.

A humbler event at the end of that month was when my faithful accountant Hobson had to retire and we gave a little party for him. He was replaced by an excellent young Channel Islander called George Lecocq, who was an equally great help to me during my remaining years in France. He saw, as Hobson had done, that I was not clever at understanding the Council's complicated book-keeping, which I was supposed to supervise every so often by a surprise check. When Lecocq saw that I had forgotten this he would gently say 'Isn't it about time you surprised me, Miss McLeod?' And then when I did he would carefully point out something that he thought might have puzzled me and explained it.

All this time our entertaining was getting heavier and heavier as I made the acquaintance of more and more influential people. But the party we enjoyed most was when in June an inshore mine-sweeper moored in the Seine, paying a courtesy visit on Paris. The Embassy asked us all to help entertain the officers and men, and Whity immediately begged me to choose what she called the Jolly Jack Tars. So we provided masses of beer and sandwiches, Elsie made some wonderful cakes and we invited some of our youngest staff to help us, putting Nicolas, the eight-year-old son of Catherine and Jean, in charge of the beer. He took this duty so seriously - it was almost a case of the *feu sacré* - that the moment a sailor had taken a sip or two from his glass Nicolas rushed to fill it up so that we soon had to restrain him, in case our supplies gave out. They were a nice simple bunch of sailors and after some initial shyness they talked freely of their lives. On leaving, the chief one made quite a speech, saying how much they had dreaded coming, but couldn't have enjoyed it more.

Mentioning Nicolas makes me feel that this is perhaps the moment to say something about our old original friends, whom we continued to see as much as we could when we had a moment of leisure. La Petite Dame was still at the Vaneau, aged ninety that year, and Beth, whose marriage was going badly, as we had guessed it would, was always coming and going between Cabris and Paris. Roger Martin du Gard had become very much of a recluse, as I have said, but Jean Schlumberger was as spry as ever. We were always welcome at weekends at La Mivoie, the house of Jean and Catherine in the Vallée de Chevreuse; but I fear that things were not going well between them either and that year they were divorced. In July of that year Jean sailed to America to make a new life. He sailed in the ill-fated Andrea Doria which sank 20 miles off the coast of America with the loss of all his possessions - clothes, books and all, - a cruel way to have to begin a new life in a new land. In spite of that he soon got a university post, and stayed with us in Paris every year during his summer vacation.

On 14 July Whity saw me off to England where I went straight to Tunbridge Wells, where I had decided to have my big-toe joints removed, as standing at parties was getting unbearable. I had a private room in the Kent and Sussex hospital and found it full of red roses which Whity had asked Pat to get for me. She then went down to Cabris, leaving our flat in the keeping of an old Polish dressmaker, because she loved cats and looked after Honey while Elsie returned to England for her own holiday. After Cabris Ethel went on to the island to stay with Catherine and her children.

The operation was successfully performed but turned out to be much more elaborate than the surgeon anticipated, so he told me that I would have to remain there some five or six weeks, and there could be no question of the Sicilian holiday which Whity and I had planned to make when it was all over. Except for the heavy weight of the enormous plaster boots from knee to toe-tips, which were very painful and caused me many sleepless nights, I thoroughly enjoyed the rest, with daily visits from my family, and from many of my friends who to my great surprise, came down from London to see me. I also had a pleasant job to keep my mind alert and prevent the days from seeming too long. Maurice Goudeket, the widower of Colette, of whom we had seen a lot, had written a book about her called *Près de Colette*. He had told Fred Warburg, who had agreed to publish a translation, which he asked me to do. The book had greatly impressed me, so I set to work as soon as I felt well enough, with the help of a young secretary whom Jack Ranking had found for me.

When at last I was allowed to leave the hospital I had the acute disappointment of finding, when the plasters were taken off, that not only were my legs very weak but once again I had agonizing rheumatism in one foot. Although I was able to stay at Eric's I had to return to the hospital for physiotherapy for another fortnight. Eric was extremely kind to me, helping me to buy soft summer shoes and taking me for country drives to pass the time. At last on 3 September the surgeon, Mr Bintcliff, passed me fit to travel to London. Whity wanted to come and help me there but I felt that although I had a good deal to do, agonizing though it was, I ought to be able to manage alone. After all that I was never more happy to get back to Paris and be met by Whity in early September. Since as usual there was little office work to be done, she and I had plenty of time to talk over a possibility that Catherine had put to her. This was that we should build a cottage at Les Portes, at the other end of the big field she had just bought behind her house and where she was planning to build an extra room for herself, so that we could use the party wall for ours. I could see how much Whity longed for this as she knew the place better than I did. I told Catherine I could only pay her small sums each month for the building of it, using money that I think the Council expected me to be able to save. She agreed and later that autumn her architect came round and we finalized plans.

On 18 September Hawkins came back from leave and as I felt I could still do with another fortnight of my own leave by that time, we decided to take a real little holiday before the work began again. I wanted to go to Italy and stay preferably by some lake where I could just sit. So we wired to our friend Guglielmo asking him to meet us in Milan and advise us. Once there he immediately telephoned and got us a room at the Albergo Grande Italia, Cannero on Lake Maggiore. We spent an enchanted fortnight there, either sitting in the little garden, separated by a rough path from the lake, or else taking lake-steamers in the little harbour below us to see such beautiful places as Isola Bella with its white peacocks. Every day I was able to hobble a little more eaily down the path leaning on Whity's arm until we returned to Paris on 3 October.

While I was in hospital she had written to ask me if this prolonged absence from work had lessened my enthusiasm for it. On the contrary, realizing that the first two of the regulation four years for a Representative abroad were now over and there was a lot more I wanted to do, I felt anxious to get back to it and was more full of zeal than ever. So I was glad when an occasion rose for me to give just the kind of party that I felt was our proper function. John Lehmann, who was a friend of mine, wrote and told me that he was bringing out a book of translations of French short stories by young writers, and that he was coming to Paris on a visit, and would much like it if I could invite them all to a party so that he could make their acquaintance, as he did not know them personally. I was delighted to do this as it gave me a chance to widen my own knowledge of the younger writers, all of whom came to the party. I added many of the older ones whom I already knew and some of the most important literary agents, Mrs Bradley for one, feeling that this would please and help every body.

The only other cultural event we arranged that autumn was when our Chairman, Sir David Kelly, and his wife Marie-Noële - who had sincerely rejoiced at my appointment - came to visit us. We gave a more or less official party for her with many Embassy guests. But one who wasn't there was Sir Patrick Reilly, who had retired in October. I felt quite lost when I heard he was going, as he had always been most kind to me. I hoped his successor would be equally so. I need not have doubted, for Sir George Young (always known as Gerry), an outstandingly warm-hearted and good-looking man, whom I met for the first time at that party, proved as helpful as his predecessor and I came to rely on him a great deal during my remaining years.

It was a good thing that I did feel full of zeal for although that autumn was a comparatively quiet one, in December we had a very full programme of events and meetings, some of them presaging exciting things in the following year. One of the most thrilling things from my point of view concerned the theatre which, as I said before, was a particular interest of mine. Ever since Whity and I had seen Peter Brook's production of *Titus Andronicus* with Laurence Olivier and Vivien Leigh at Stratford in 1955, I had been badgering the Drama Department of the British Council to try and send it to take part in the Théâtre des Nations where we had hitherto not been represented so when Stephen Thomas, the head of the Drama Department, said he was coming over on 6 December I felt sure that they were going to do something about it, and hoped that this would be the peak event of the theatrical year, which indeed it was. As a sort of curtain raiser the Council sent me on that same day a small exhibition showing a model Elizabethan playhouse, which was opened at the Théâtre National Populaire (always known as the TNP). This gave me a chance to meet Jean Vilar, the Director, who was always putting on Shakespeare's plays. He was also the director of the Avignon Festival.

I found that the Fine Arts Department in London too were going to be worthily represented next year, for now we had a new Fine Arts Officer, Roland Penrose, on the staff. His appointment had been a subject of a great deal of discussion in London, which now had plans for sending modern art abroad and felt we must have somebody who could handle this side of the work which Frank McEwen had done. The Council had no money to pay for such a post, but the problem was finally solved When Sir William Rootes, a member of our Executive Committee, generously offered to pay a part-time salary of £800 annually for three years. This sounds like chicken-feed now, but it was a good salary then. Roland Penrose accepted the post and arrived at the end of November with his wife Lee. They already knew everybody in the art world in Paris and had been able to get a beautiful flat in the Place Dauphine. So what with their art contacts and ours we were now fully represented in that world.

As little beyond this planning for the following year happened in December we had time to relax and see something of our oldest friends and some of those among our new French contacts who had become friends too and were to remain so thereafter. One of the chief of these was Jacques Dupont, the main Inspector of the Monuments of Paris, who was then working on the restoration of the old buildings of the Marais, a particular interest of mine. He was a man of great taste and a very witty conversationalist. He fell at once for Whity and always jokingly called her Number Two, realizing how very much more than that she was. As we were going to spend Christmas Day at the Mivoie that year we took Elsie out to lunch for a treat on Christmas Eve. On 28 December we both left for London.

Chapter fourteen

MISSION ACCOMPLISHED
Paris 1957-1959

We were only going to spend a week there. My reason for going was that the Anglo-French Mixed Commission was being held at that unpropitious moment of the year; I really don't know why, but I think there were two causes. The first was to inform both sides what we were planning to do for next year, the second and more important being to meet the new director of the Relations Culturelles. Jacques de Bourbon-Busset, who had recently retired to give himself to writing, had been succeeded by Roger Seydoux, a career diplomat who proved to be as pleasant a man as his predecessor. Whity's reason was to take advantage of the January sales for buying such things as bedding for the three beds in the cottage we were going to build on the island, all the furniture of which she had offered to provide. My meeting only lasted three days so I was able to help her with this.

I didn't want to stay any longer than the week as I was very anxious to get back to Paris for a party I had arranged before we left in December. I had heard that Peter Brook, the producer of *Titus Andronicus* was coming to Paris in early January, so I thought it would be a good idea to ask him to luncheon to meet Jean-Jacques Gautier, the theatre critic of *Le Figaro* and Robert Kemp of *Le Monde*. It was a very exciting party and I felt that I had now done all that I could to ensure that this long-desired event would be a success. For early February another big cultural event had been planned by the Fine Arts Department. This was an exhibition of work by Lynn Chadwick and Ivor Hitchens, which was of course held at the Musée d'Art Moderne and which fortunately Roland Penrose was there to organize.

As there was an interval between these two affairs, on

185

1 February I went with Milner by train for the official opening of the new library at Bordeaux. Pat Johnston had had a separate entrance made to it from the road, and Professor Loiseau thought he could arrange that one of his students would act as a part-time librarian. Another provincial visit that February was to Caen, where I had been invited by the delightful professor of English, Sylvère Monod, to lecture in the amphitheatre of the grand new university, which had been rebuilt after being destroyed during the war. Whity drove me there and we were given a *vin d'honneur* after it.

On returning to Paris in March I did the last practical job I still had to do for our office and that was the buying of new furniture for our typists, who were still using the battered old wartime stock. The Council in London had given me money for this purpose and although I didn't really like the modern office furniture of chrome and plastic that I was obliged to select because there was no other choice, it at least provided comfortable seats and adequate desks for their typewriters and papers, and I think they were all very pleased by this improvement.

Social entertainment began again in March and one of the guests at a very carefully chosen luncheon was that most intelligent actress Martita Hunt, an old and good friend of mine. She was in Paris making some film for a French company and I asked her if she would consent to give a poetry reading in the big room of our office, though I could give her no fee. She was delighted to do this and thereafter I spent many evenings with her, trying to decide the choice of poems she would like to give, for she was very well read and had a wide range to choose from, including the metaphysical poets of the seventeenth century. While she was making her choice I was always going to and from our library to get her books. I had invited a very special audience for her, including our Ambassador and all the other English-speaking ones, all the nine professors of English at the Sorbonne and many other officials and quite a few actors as well. There was just room for a hundred of them in our room. The recital was on 1 April and I was surprised to find that Martita had taken the trouble to learn all the poems by heart. She of course spoke them beautifully, and the audience was enthralled and crowded round her afterwards at the small *vin d'honneur* we had arranged in my office. She had certainly heralded what was to be a wonderful theatrical year.

But the outstanding event of that month was the visit of the Queen and the Duke of Edinburgh, which lasted for a whole week. The French had staged a splendid programme of events in which I, and to some extent Whity, was fortunate enough to share. One of the occasions to which we were both invited was the performance of a ballet, *Les Indes Galantes*, in the exquisite little Louis XV theatre in the palace of Versailles, which had been especially restored for the occasion and upholstered in deep-piled pale blue velvet. We had seats in the circle quite near those of the Royal couple and so I had the homely satisfaction of seeing Her Majesty unable to resist stroking the depth of the velvet on the edge of the balcony, as any woman would have done.

On the last night there was a monster reception at the Louvre, when many humble people, who had not been able to have invitations to anything else, had their chance. One of these was an old man who had called at our office and asked Hawkins if there was any possibility that he could see the Duke of Edinburgh who, as a little boy, had attended his school in Neuilly. The Embassy got an invitation for him and told Hawkins that he might present him when the Royals passed along the lines of people. This he duly did and though I am sure the Duke had not been prepared, as soon as the presentation was made he warmly shook the old man's hand and said 'Oh I remember you and I'm so glad to see you again. You always used to say to me that if I went on being as naughty as I was I would never get anywhere. And now look where I've got!' I am sure that the Queen knew that it was because René Coty was President at that time that there was such a homely atmosphere in all the arrangements that had been made for her, for he was the kindliest of men and took an almost fatherly care of her. When, a year later, I attended an investiture and told her, in answer to her question, that I had been in Paris on that occasion, she gave a radiant smile of happy recollection and said 'Oh, that *lovely* visit!'

After those very full three months Whity and I felt we must have a little holiday so we accepted an invitation from two of her old friends from her Luxembourg days, who had subsequently become friends of mine too. They had recently built a beautiful house in an oasis just outside Marrakesh.

We had ten splendid days there, enjoying the exquisite garden they had made, visiting that extraordinary city, which one felt had not changed since Bible times, and being taken for exciting drives to desert cities in the mountains. On our way home we stopped at Rabat, where Whity bought two beautiful green coverlets for our island beds, at the cottage we hoped would be ready for our summer holiday.

We got back to Paris just in time for the performance of *Titus Andronicus*, which took Paris by storm, both for the superb production and the excellence of the English actors of whom everyone had heard so much. As the Festival Ballet was also appearing in Paris at that time, I decided that we would entertain both companies at a morning reception from eleven to one, for I always thought this was the best time of day to give a party for actors, after they had had a good night's rest and no matinée to bother about. With all the members of both companies and all our French connections in the worlds of theatre and ballet, we obviously wouldn't have enough room for a party of this size, either in our own flat or our big office room; so I asked the Jebbs if I could borrow the Embassy ballroom. He at once agreed and she said I could if I didn't call on her servants for any help. I assured her I had marvellous waiters who would leave the place as they found it. The Jebbs themselves were nice enough to come to the party in their ballroom as if they were merely guests and I remember his secretary, Robin Johnstone, saying as he sauntered in 'Nice little place you've got here'. It was one of the most brilliant affairs of the season.

In July we received a very happy return for the contributions we had so far made to the theatrical life of Paris. Both Whity and I received an invitation to the annual festival at Aix-en-Provence. We went there by road, driven by the new young office chauffeur Talon, and made a leisurely journey of it. On arrival at Aix we found that we had been put up at the Riviera Hotel on the outskirts of the town, which had a charming garden and was a marvellous place to relax in. That night we had seats for *Le Mariage de Figaro* which was given in the open air in the courtyard of the Archévêche. On another night we went to a spectacular performance of *Carmen* in the Parc du Tholonet, where they made use of the whole hillside whose paths were full of lantern-carrying peasants. We spent our days wandering about the ancient city and its cathedral, and buying local pottery for the cottage. After leaving Aix we went to Menerbes in the Lubéron to spend a night with our old friends Tony and Thérèse Mayer whom we had known at the French Embassy in London. The next day we lunched with Dora Maar who lived in a frightening house on the edge of a cliff. Dora was a former mistress of Picasso's and a painter herself, and I think it was after this meeting that Whity began giving her English conversation lessons. I remember that she liked reading the Bible aloud. We then drove to Avignon, to whose festival I had been invited. Whity had not been invited, so I dropped her off at the Château de Castille to stay with Douglas Cooper while I went on to stay at the mosquito-haunted Hostellerie du Vieux Moulin on the river bank. One of the two performances I saw in the Palais des Papes was Pirandello's *Henry VII* and the other was *Murder in the Cathedral*, in French of course. Then I picked up Whity and we returned to Paris after nine fabulous nights away.

When I got back to the office in mid-July I was once more plunged into the everlasting question of the new building for which I had never ceased to look. Perhaps the urgency the Council seemed to feel now was due to the fact that I had recently told them that our lease of the Champs Elysées premises only had two years to run, and I had also informed them that I thought I had found a house which might do. I told the Ambassador this too and, late though it was in the season, both Richard Seymour from the Council and one or two men from the Ministry of Works, summoned by the Ambassador, came over to see it. All realized that it would cost an enormous amount to adapt and I don't think any of us really liked it, so they all returned to London with nothing done.

At last on 2 August Whity and I drove to the island, longing for the lovely, lazy, seaside life we thought we should have there. But alas we were doomed to disappointment. Although the young architect had come to see us two weeks before and had given us the *'clé en mains'* the traditional expression for the completion of a building, when we arrived we found that the door for the key was still lying in the middle of the field, the men were still painting the inner walls, the floor tiles had not been laid and there was no glass in the windows. It was a horrible shock and we were in despair. Fortunately Catherine had lent us her own house to sleep in and there was a café in the village where we could get meals; but we had to spend the first ten days of that holiday on the site urging the men to get on with their work. Finally we threatened them that we were going to bring in our furniture, which had been stored in an outhouse belonging to a friend in the village, the very next day. And this we did, pushing it on a handcart, beds and all, with the help of the young architect's charming mother, who was as upset by her son's conduct as we were. And that day it poured with rain. By this time the men had finished enough for us to put all the furniture inside so we managed to sleep for the first time in the house on 9 August. But the plumber and the electrician had not yet fitted in all the kitchen and bathroom equipment and I realized for the first time that I had no idea how to cook. However, Beth was staying with Catherine and gave me a few rudimentary lessons, after which I managed well enough. It was not until the 23rd, after much scrubbing and cleaning by ourselves, that we felt we were sleeping in a really orderly room with a door in place to shut us in.

But we were not long to enjoy the rest and peace that we desired, for the very next day I received a letter from the Council telling me they had turned down the house we had all seen and that I must immediately return to Paris and continue the search. I at once replied that there would be no point in doing this as everything in Paris would be closed that month. But it was a case of headquarters knowing better than the man on the spot, they did not believe me and sent fresh orders for my return, so I had to obey. Fortunately in Paris I found that Elsie had just got back from the Danish package-tour that she had bravely gone on from Paris, and I was able to find her the one little baker's shop in the rue Cler, the only one of the local provision shops open that month. I then went to the Embassy, borrowed a car and a chauffeur, made a list of all the house agents in Paris, called and found them all shut and returned to the Embassy to dictate a letter to a kind secretary there, reporting to the London office the result of my obedience to their instructions. As it was then nearly September it was not worthwhile going back to the island, so I stayed where I was until Whity returned too and the rest of the staff arrived.

I had no heart for more house-hunting at that moment and I had another matter to attend to, a staff one this time. Hawkins, who had been such a faithful and loyal employee to me during my many absences, had left at the end of July. I had said in my personal report on him that year that I thought he deserved to be promoted to a Representative's post; and as I knew that Belgium was ready for a new man I made so bold as to suggest that he should be posted there, and he was. In his place I was sent a man called Bob Hilton, an entirely different type. He had been a Representative himself in Bangkok, where he had also had some fairly high-grade educational duties to perform. Although he assured me that he didn't mind working under a woman, I never lost the feeling that he did. But as I felt he was capable enough to get the hang of things quickly at that not very busy time and as Whity and I were by then beginning to feel the need of a rest after all the exhausting events of the last month, we went for a week's holiday at the end of September to a charming little place in Switzerland, a walled town called Morat, where we were well fed, had long nights and lazy walks, and soon recovered.

One very sad thing had happened that summer while we were all away. Gerry Young's wife Elizabeth died, quite suddenly I believe. I hadn't known how ill she must have been for he never said anything about it and she had come to lunch with us as late as June. From then on Whity and I saw a great deal of him, inviting him as often as we could, and he increasingly relied on me to accompany him to official occasions when I also had been invited, and which he would otherwise have been obliged to attend alone. I remember especially how much his company meant to me when I had to stand in line with the Embassy staff at President Coty's next annual reception for the diplomatic corps. To stand in line in this way while waiting to be presented was one of those times when, as a single woman, I always felt awkward, but with him beside me all was well. It was on that occasion that, when I reached the head of the queue, René Coty, turning to me after a conversation with an old grey-bearded man and hearing me introduced by that important-sounding title, *'l'Attaché Culturel de Grande Bretagne!*, beamed at me with a fatherly smile and said *'mais c'est très bien! c'est très très bien!*

There was still little work to do when we returned from Morat, but I remember that in early October I went to Dijon, where I was a guest at the thrilling banquet of the *Chevaliers du Tastevin* at the Clos Vougeot, which lasted for four hours. The floor of the ancient building was made of little pebbles, so, as you weren't supposed to drink every different glass to the lees, you simply poured what you didn't want on to the floor.

In the autumn, as though I hadn't already enough to do, I thought of bringing out what I called a cultural bulletin. The idea was that I should keep an eye on French events in Paris and whenever I could find some connection with England in them we should write short articles emphasizing this. For instance when the famous bookshop Gallimard filled its windows with the works of Conrad on some particular anniversary, we would have an article on him. Or if there was an English play in translation, or some English music being performed, we would have a piece about that. The articles would be short and sometimes one of us would write them. Otherwise I would ask the London Feature Articles Department to provide what I wanted. They were delighted to do this because they were just about to be suppressed and this gave them a new lease of life. I always wrote the editorials myself, and decided that one bulletin every two months would be enough and we would make a hundred copies of it to send to our main contacts. As we had so little money they would of course have to be typed and roneod on my favourite green paper and Hilton designed a charming cover-page. It would mean a great deal of extra work for the staff, not only the translating of it all into French by Madeleine Pablos, but the roneoing, collating and pinning together of the sheets, when everyone would have to lend a hand from myself down to the chauffeur. So I called a staff meeting and said that if they thought this meant too much work I wouldn't do it. On the contrary they were all enthusiastic and I must say that everyone who got copies was delighted, particularly Roger Seydoux, who wrote me a letter saying that this was exactly the sort of thing that people in our kind of job ought to do.

Mid-November also brought the last of the theatrical productions which had made such an impression that year. Gielgud's agent, a Dutchman called de Blieck, had called on me earlier in the year saying how much Sir John would like to give his Shakespeare performance, *The Seven Ages of Man*, in Paris, where he had previously been known only for his parts in films. Sir John was at that time a member of the Royal Shakespeare Company at Stratford, so that he could only spare a Sunday and a Monday; but he was so keen to come that he would do it for only £100. I asked the London Office if they would give me this money but they refused and said I would have to make the performance pay for itself. Gielgud said he could come on 17 and 18 November, so I arranged a Sunday night performance at the really beautiful theatre at the Cité Universitaire, and the other on the following night at the Théâtre des Ambassadeurs in Paris, where theatres are always closed on Mondays. The woman director of this theatre told me that I should have to pay the rent of it for that night and I was involved in endless work getting the programme printed, advertising it in all possible ways, including on the *vespasiennes* (street urinals) and even having to pay authors' rights, although I didn't see what Shakespeare would get out of it.

To my horror on the evening of the 17 November there was a very thick fog so that the director of the university theatre was doubtful whether students would want to turn out on a foggy night (especially as they had to pay for their tickets and programmes) and he felt he had better close the balcony in case few came. He need not have feared, for though Whity and I arrived about an hour before the performance we found they were already pouring in, so that the balcony had to be opened after all. I noticed amongst the audience Jacques Lemarchand, the critic of the *Figaro Littéraire*, who told me he had particulary come that night so that next morning he could give what he hoped would be a good review to bring the public in. Sir John's performance certainly deserved this for it was such a tremendous success that the student audience crowded on the stage to hug him afterwards and he as usual could not restrain his tears. No doubt as a result of Lemarchand's review the performance was an even greater success the following night. I had given away many tickets to the kind of important persons who always expected them, and many to the actors of the Comédie Française and the TNP, but I could have filled the paid seats many times over, for in the foyer I was besieged by people whom I had to turn

193

sadly away. The French made Sir John a *Chevalier de la Légion d'honneur* so I think he was well pleased. Certainly for me this set the crown on that theatrical year and established forever the reputation of our English actors. I am sad that he does not mention this occasion in his autobiography.

After the strain of those last weeks it was a relief that there were no more official engagements, so that we could concentrate on seeing something of the many English friends who came to Paris at that time. But I did have one very pleasant occasion which might be called semi-official, when Jean Schlumberger, who had had his eightieth birthday that year and was now doing a good deal of writing for *Le Figaro*, asked me to lunch at the Ritz to meet his editor Pierre Bresson and five other journalist-writers. When Pierre Bresson asked him how long he had known me, Jean amused me by saying, with that characteristic French expression to indicate a long acquaintance *'je l'ai vue naître'*. The only other person I knew at that luncheon was Gerard Bauër whom I had first met in 1944 and whose delightful columns in *Le Figaro* I used to enjoy each day. It was a very agreeable introduction to the world of journalism, a new one for me.

On 16 December Whity and I left to spend Christmas in London. So I was there when my CBE was announced in the New Year's Honours. I went straight to the Council to thank Paul for having included me in their list. I had written to him a week or two previously to say that I knew my time in Paris would be up in the following September and to ask if I could have a further six months. On 3 January he wrote to say that I could have a full year. The reason I had given him was that I was still hoping to find that new building and also that there were great tracts of France I had not yet visited.

I fear that in my pleasure and self-absorption about all this there was one thing I had forgotten. Roger Hinks was a friend of mine and at some moment when I was writing to him I had asked him whether he would like to succeed me in Paris, as I felt sure he was the best person I could think of for the job, and I knew that his present Representation in Athens was due to end at the same time as mine was. He was delighted with the idea, and as we both then communicated it to the Personnel Department in London, who approved it. Roger asked them if he couldn't leave Athens rather earlier, as he was very unhappy there and be given some job in the London office while waiting. They had agreed, but it must have been a blow to him when he subsequently learnt that he would have to wait another year to succeed me.

The first few months of 1958 were comparatively easy going, rather to my relief. The only artistic event was when the Council sent the young Julian Bream, the lutenist and guitarist, to give a recital at one of those two comfortably-sized concert halls in Paris, the Gaveau and the Pleyel, I can't remember which. What I do remember was the charming modesty of Bream himself. I took him to the hall and left him in the artist's room to prepare himself, but I forgot to warn him that evening affairs in Paris always started very late, often after the scheduled hour of nine o'clock. I then went back to the entrance and when I had satisfied myself that all the critics and the audience had arrived I went to tell Bream that we were now ready for him. It was then about 9.15 and he jumped up in panic saying 'Oh, I was afraid you'd forgotten me!' He was a great success.

A memorable event in Paris in early March was a lecture on Matisse given by Douglas Cooper. He had a great desire to lecture in the big hall in the Ecole du Louvre, which held 700 people. This was always reserved for talks by museum directors, but I pleaded with Georges Salles, who knew Douglas well, to break the rule for him. He good-humouredly agreed and of course Douglas was delighted. It was to be an evening lecture and on the night in question, as I looked through the curtains while Whity and I were having dinner, I saw to my horror that it had begun to snow thickly. I felt panic-stricken at the thought that no one would venture out for a talk even though Douglas was a well-known art critic. I need not have feared for when we got there in good time people were already beginning to stream in and altogether 500 turned up. Georges Salles himself took the Chair, which was a great honour. After the lecture we gave a party for Douglas in our drawing room, which many famous artists attended, among them such as Giacometti, Hayter and that rather mysterious painter Balthus, as well as Dora Maar and the sculptor César.

Although I can't remember exactly when it happened, I must relate a mission that the Ambassador had imposed on me sometime in the year. Oxford University had written to both Braque and Picasso to say that they would like to confer honorary degrees on them. Neither had replied and so the Ambassador said it was my job as Cultural Attaché to get answers out of them. I wrote to Braque who civilly asked me to tea in his Paris flat and, while I was admiring both his pictures and his own magnificent head, for he was wonderfully handsome, he explained to me that he could not accept this honour because he was asthmatic and never knew from one day to the next whether he would be able to speak, let alone travel. He did not of course explain why he had not answered the letter, a not uncharacteristic habit of painters I think, but I said I would explain and all would be well. As for Picasso, I had asked Douglas Cooper what I should do, for he claimed great friendship with him and said it would be quite simple. He himself would write to him and say I would call at five o' clock on a specific day in April (a day when I was to be in Aix), telling him why and asking him to see me then. When I arrived at the iron gate of his house at Mougins I rang the bell and after an interval a very grumpy-looking peasant woman crossed the garden from the house to open it. When I explained that I had an engagement with Monsieur Picasso, which made her look at me with the darkest suspicion, she said she would go and see, clanged the gate in my face and left me standing in the road. When she returned she said he was busy working with his wife and as I was five minutes late he could not see me. It was in vain that I explained that I had an official mission; I had to leave defeated.

On 28 April I went, by plane this time, to England for my annual visit to Alice. While I had been away Whity had taken her two sisters to stay in the now finished cottage, where all the purchases she had made at every possible opportunity, in London, Aix, Paris, Rabat and La Rochelle, were in place and the whole thing, she said, looked delightful. A comic incident which I forgot to mention had happened when she went to the Bon Marché in Paris to buy the three divan beds we needed. They had asked her if she had some French decoration, such as the Legion of Honour, because if so she could get the goods at a ten per cent discount. She had the quickness of mind to say she was buying them for someone who had, and they replied saying they must see the Citation. I had of course left this in London but I rang up Michel

Fontaine, my old friend from the French Embassy days in London and now at the Quai d'Orsay, to ask him if he could get me a copy of it. I remember his laughter when he heard what I wanted it for, as he had never heard of such a thing, but he got it for me all right, and it saved Whity much of her scanty funds.

June that year was unusually full of events, one of them quite unlike anything we had done before. At the beginning of the month we joined a delegation from the Franco-British Society in London, led by the charming and efficient secretary Marion Coate, which was visiting first a police school at Sens, where the policemen were trained to give first aid immediately to human victims of car accidents. After that we went on to Vézelay, where we stayed and saw an unforgettable *Son et Lumière*, when the whole country was floodlit. It was so arranged that, after listening to the great speech of Peter the Hermit as we stood on the terrace above the church, we heard the voices of the pilgrims singing as they set off from the surrounding hills on the first crusade, growing fainter and fainter as they marched away so that we really had the sense of the journey on which they started.

We returned from that visit just in time for what was to be the most practically satisfying event of all my time in Paris. I had quite recently discovered what I was convinced would be the ideal building for the British Council. It was a medium-sized commercial hotel in the rue des Ecoles opposite the Collège de France, exactly the right position, at a corner with the little rue Jean de Beauvais which runs down to the Boulevard St Germain. It was for sale at a much more modest price than anything we had previously seen. I had asked to look over it and found that it consisted of five floors of about fifty-six small rooms. I rang up Paul at once and asked him if he could come over for a week and get the two Ministry of Works men to come too. As the weather was so lovely then Whity and I suggested that he and Ruth might come two days earlier to spend the weekend with us. They gladly accepted and when they arrived we found that the next day was their Silver Wedding day; so we took them off for a picnic to our favourite Vaux-le-Vicomte, where we had got permission to see the inside of the house as well as the marvellous gardens. It was a memorable day for us all. On the next day work began in earnest. I took Paul and the

Ministry men to see the building, which by then was not occupied and they examined it thoroughly and agreed with me that we would only have to remove the partitions on the first and second floors to house the library. There would be enough office room on the floor above and the two above that would make a perfect flat. It was to be sold with the whole of its contents. So Paul signed a document to say that the British Council would definitely buy it at the price asked.

All this was concluded in a week and on the night they left we gave them dinner at the Mont Blanc, the excellent restaurant in the rue Las-Cases near our flat. It was one of those restaurants where in summer they have tables on the pavement outside, with a little green hedge in tubs to protect them from the road. It was there that the first of two little incidents occurred which were to have a bearing on my constantly repeated request to have a new car to take the place of the battered old machine we had had to make do with so far. As we were dining, Talon the chauffeur looked over the hedge and said he could not get the car to start. Paul, who knew of my wish, laughed and said 'That was very well arranged, Enid'. I said I had done no such thing and urged Talon to get a nearby garage to help him start the car, which they did in fact manage to do. But when they got into it to drive to the station Whity and I followed in our own car, in case the other broke down. On the way we ran into a mob of rioting students in a narrow road. They let Talon through all right but then turned on us and began trying to open the doors and pull us out. Talon saw this in his mirror and immediately ran back to beat them off, which greatly impressed Paul. When we got to the station he asked if it would be right to call this incident a brouhaha, a word he had always wanted to use. We assured him it would, and I think these two little affairs may have been partly responsible for the fact that we did get a nice new car, a Humber Hawk, in the next financial year.

This had been such a high point in the season that it was difficult to remember that we were still in the middle of it and that more celebrations at the Théâtre des Nations were yet to come from England. The first of these was a visit by a company which included Edith Evans and John Gielgud in *Henry VIII*. What I chiefly remember about that was the extraordinary modesty of Edith Evans who seemed quite overcome that Whity and I should have gone to Le Bourget to meet her. I don't think the whole performance was a very good one but then neither is *Henry VIII* a very good play. Next came John Neville from the Birmingham Repertory Company playing *Hamlet*. This was certainly not an outstanding event so I think the French applause was more for Shakespeare than for him. As it was now mid-July and the season was virtually over, I went off to Mulhouse to visit the FGB society there and Whity, rather exhausted by all the theatre-going, took herself off alone for three days to Royaumont, where she could take solitary walks in her long remembered woods.

To return to the new building, there was one condition before we were allowed to buy it. The French authorities said we must put up on the front door a notice to say that the intention was to change the use of the building from tourist accommodation to offices. This had to remain in place for a month and if anyone objected they must say so within that time. But as it was now nearly the end of July, we decided that it was not a good moment to put up that notice as there would be no one in Paris during August to see it. So instead we closed our own offices for August and went off for our usual holiday on the Ile de Ré, where we found all our old French friends. This time we concentrated on having a large terrace of rough island stones built with a low stone wall on which one could sit enclosing our little property. The only sad thing that marred our undiluted pleasure of that month was that our dear old friend Roger Martin du Gard died. Although we had seen little of him latterly, this left a sad gap in the ranks of our oldest friends.

We returned to a September quite unlike those idle ones we had previously known. Although we then had that notice put on the door, it raised no objections apart from one student, who had scrawled over it *'Merde pour les Anglais!'* which shocked the concierge very much but made us laugh. The first thing we had to do now that the building became ours, was to make an inventory of those contents of the hotel which we had to sell, including the toilet arrangements in each room. I remember that the well-known Sam White, the Evening Standard reporter, got wind of this and made great play in his column about the Cultural Attaché selling bidets.

Only when the building was empty was our nice Polish architect, Boleslav Eber, with whom I had already had some dealings in our library, able to look over it and begin making plans for its conversion. Of course all the staff wanted to see the place but the two most interested were Beatrix Collingham, who had just been appointed librarian to replace Milner, and Roger Hinks, who was to be my successor, who came to see it.

The only items we had not sent for sale were the stair carpet and some of the bedroom carpets as well as the large quantity of bed-linen, as we felt we knew many people who might like to get this cheap as it was good solid material. This was a job which Hilton thought it would be fun to organize so he spent a day there in sweltering heat, returning at the end of it absolutely worn out, for the cautious and thrifty French housewives, who had flocked to the sale we had announced, insisted on his unfolding every single sheet, sometimes several times over so that they could compare those which had weak places. Tiring though this was I think he enjoyed the job. Several of our staff, including Whity and myself, were among his customers.

As all these activities fully occupied the staff, Whity and I decided that it would be a good moment to fit in that little holiday in Sicily we had not been able to take the year before. So on 23 September we set off for a marvellous three weeks. Whity remembered much of it from a holiday she had had there thirty years earlier, and had always longed to show it to me. Little had changed and when we were in Syracuse she discovered that the old man who rowed us across the harbour, to go up the little river Cyane to the fountain where the nymph was supposed to dwell, was the same man who had taken here there on that first visit. Thinking back to it all, I remember it with such vividness that it is sad not to have space to describe it; but I must include one story of a dumb American girl on the CIT bus. After seeing the superb lonely temple of Segeste she said at dinner that night 'The guide said that it was never finished even in the old days. What I can't understand is why they ever began it!'

As the coast was now clear for Eber to examine our new building thoroughly and make plans, and as the season was not yet in full swing I had plenty of time to visit him there whenever he wanted to consult me. A curious fact he discovered when the plaster was taken off the inner walls which had to be demolished was that they were only really thin partitions composed of slender tree trunks encased in plaster. This astonished me but Eber said that this was quite an accepted way of building inner walls in the mid-nineteenth century.

On 6 November I was invited to a very moving ceremony when de Gaulle decorated Churchill with the much coveted *Croix de la Libération*. The ceremony took place in a room at the Hotel Matignon. I don't know why de Gaulle had waited so long to confer this decoration on our old wartime leader; perhaps he had wanted to do it when he had himself become head of the Government, which he had in the previous June. I can think of no reason why I should have been invited except that I was English. Churchill was now a very old man and it was pitiful to see him shuffling along as he reviewed the guard of honour that had been provided for him.

In November we had one of the finest art exhibitions which the London Department had yet sent us, of the works of Henry Moore, Armitage, Scott and Stanley Hayter. The show opened on 21 November and as it continued on its triumphant way for some time it seemed to me to be a good time for another provincial visit. I had been invited by Professor Martin, the very nice professor of English at Poitiers, who was a great contrast to his uncooperative namesake at Montpellier, to go and give a lecture there. He had assembled a good crowd of gay and enthusiastic students and I had a wonderful reception at the end of which they presented me with one of their typical student caps of black velvet, covered with little gold ornaments, and were delighted when I put it on at once. I stayed the night there and he had set aside time the next day to take me on a sightseeing tour of the neighbourhood, one of the most exciting places he showed me being the actual field of the Battle of Poitiers. I then went on to Tours to participate in the opening of a splendid new branch of the French archives. I was the only Cultural Attaché there and I feel sure I owed my invitation to Charles Braibant.

At the end of that December a small sad event occurred in our personal lives. Our beloved Honey, now twelve years old, had taken to hiding under cupboards and refusing food.

We had for some time been worried about what we would do with him when the time came for us to leave France, for we thought he would never be able to stand the six months quarantine. But one day an old French schoolmistress we knew, who loved cats, said she would take him and look after him well. When we told Elsie this she said in her dry way, 'Oh I don't think you need worry, I'm sure he'll die before we go, he's always been so considerate.' She was quite right, for when we took him to the vet he told us that he had cancer and it would be better to put him to sleep at once. So after a last stroke and kiss we watched him have an injection and as those huge golden eyes gradually closed we said goodbye and left him there. Elsie never expressed her grief at losing the companion of her solitary days though I think he was the only thing she ever loved. Fortunately we stayed in Paris that Christmas which must have helped to comfort her, though we were all sad to feel that we were no longer 'four in family' as we always described ourselves.

Immediately after Christmas I had to go to London for a few days. Eber had finished his plans and estimates for the reconstruction of the building so I took them to the Council for approval. This they were given but Oxbury, the Controller of Finance, told me that no work must start until we had written authority from the Treasury. When I returned to Paris Eber told me that he had got together a complete team of the workmen he would need but would not be able to keep them unless they started at once. He also said that unless they did he would not be able to guarantee that the job would be finished before I left Paris. I immediately telephoned Oxbury to tell him this but, sensing my panic, he said he was quite sure he would get this written authority in a day or two. Knowing something of the dilattory ways of the civil service I was less sure. But as the risk of not getting the building finished seemed to me worse than the risk of anything the Treasury might do to me, I decided for myself that the former was more important and told Eber to begin at once, which he did. When later that afternoon Oxbury telephoned to say that he hoped I hadn't taken his assurance as authority to begin, I replied that I had, the men were already hammering away and it was too late to stop them. It was in fact fortunate that I had acted as I did for the Treasury approval did not arrive until the following May!

Soon after this, Elsie's remark that she was sure Honey would show his consideration by dying before we had to leave Paris, became only too true as far as she was concerned. For a few weeks later she received a letter from a Mrs Coles for whom her sister had worked, telling her that that sister was dying of cancer and begging her to go at once to help look after her. Elsie had never liked her sister and even disliked her, but she never hesitated for a moment. Though she was happier with us in Paris than she had ever been, she had a very strong conscience and felt that it was her prime duty to go to England. So we saw her off as soon as she could get ready. This left us in somewhat of a quandary as we didn't know where to find another maid; but this was solved by the Ambassador's private secretary, a young man called Geoffrey Shakespeare. He and his wife generously offered to lend us their maid Jeanne whenever we needed her. She was an excellent cook.

But we did not give many of our luncheon parties just then, partly because I was busy overseeing the work in the new building, and partly because I was awaiting the arrival of an exhibition which I planned to call *The Age of Elegance*, which I had been begging the British Council for years to send me, and which the authorities at the Musée des Arts Décoratifs were keen to have. I wanted it to be an exhibition of the most simple and elegant English furniture of the seventeenth and eighteenth centuries, with emphasis on the beauty of the wood. I knew this was not the kind of thing in which the Fine Arts Department took the slightest interest, as they cared only for modern art. They appealed to Trenchard Cox of the V and A, but unfortunately he sent, to head their committee, a member of his staff called Molesworth, whose taste I knew was for the flamboyant and ornamental. Dreading what he would do I begged to be allowed to go over and tell the committee what I wanted, but this was refused. When eventually the exhibition arrived at the end of February, I found my worst fears were realized. My feelings about the objects were well expressed by John Russell, who came to report it for the *Sunday Times*. He said he knew that I had hoped that this exhibition would be the climax of what he kindly called my 'notably happy appointment in France', and then went on to comment on the emphasis that had been laid on the elaborate and the ornate so that one hardly ever heard what he called 'the music of pure proportion'. This was exactly my feeling and when the French press as a whole echoed it, frankly saying that France could do this sort of thing better itself, I am afraid I took a malicious pleasure in sending the cuttings to London, which did not acknowledge them.

When I had swallowed my disappointment over all this, I felt that the time had come for me to make the last of those combined lecturing and sightseeing provincial visits for which I had asked extra time. So I set off by myself for quite a prolonged tour beginning at Orleans and Blois (I lectured at both places) and then going on to Bordeaux to collect Pat Johnston, who took me to various places in the area of his consulate, partly to show me them and partly so that I could give a lecture at Bagnères-de-Bigorre. While I was away on this tour Whity went to Cabris rather than remain in our empty flat, as she was anxious to see as much of Beth as she could in our last year.

But she returned as soon as I did, in time to go off to England in April for a ten-day visit. I spent the first week of it in Porlock Weir where I was saddened to find my dear Alice was now suffering badly. But her spirit never flagged and she was as usual entirely interested in my affairs. Back in London I spent a good deal of time with Muriel Rose, the officer who was responsible for furnishing offices abroad, and with Roger Hinks. I felt that as he was going to occupy the flat in the new building, I ought to let him choose the furniture and decorations. Fortunately he had excellent taste so we were able to agree over everything. It was at that time that I suggested to the Council that he should come over for a whole month in May and June, partly to make up for his having had to wait for so long, and partly because I thought it would be useful for him to get to know the main officials with whom he would be dealing, both in Paris and in the provinces, since I remembered how useful it had been for me to have this foreknowledge when I first came.

Before Whity and I returned to Paris we had asked Elsie to come and have tea with us at the Charing Cross Hotel, when we told her that June was going to be our most important month and asked her if she thought she could get back for it. She promised to think it over and let us know, but when her letter came it was to say that, although she felt 'quite sick' not to be able to help us in June, one look at her painfully suffering sister made her decide that her own feelings didn't matter and so she couldn't come. As soon as we got back to Paris I went off yet again, this time on a very short lecture tour to Marseilles, Toulon, Cannes and Nice; but the whole tour was very brief because we both had to be back in Paris on 1 May which was to be a very full month, beginning for Whity with another visit from those Foreign Office inspectors, although now that they knew how lavishly we spent my entertainment allowance they did not cause her too much trouble.

The whole of the rest of May was almost entirely social. On the first weekend of it my niece Pat and her husband Jack came to stay with us, the only two of my few relations who came when I was in Paris. We wanted to give them as good a time as possible so we took them out to lunch on both days, the first time to the Pavilion Henri IV on the great terrace at St Germain-en-Laye, and the second to one of our favourite outdoor restaurants, the Moulin at Forges-les-Eaux, where one had lunch by the stream. On the day that they returned to London we were delighted to receive the new car, which had at last arrived. That year Whitsun was in mid-May, so Whity and I were able to accept Douglas Cooper's invitation to go and stay with him for the bullfights at Nîmes, which were one of the great social occasions of his year. On the evening of the first fight he gave a splendid supper at his house, to which came Picasso, Cocteau, and Chanel among many others, as well as the bullfighter Dominguin. Before the next afternoon's fight we were the guests at lunch of Picasso himself in Nîmes and of course met all those people all over again. This time the bullfighter was Ordoñez.

On the day after we returned Roger Hinks arrived from London, and two days later he, Whity and I set off in the new car for a provincial tour which lasted a fortnight and enabled me to say goodbye to all my acquaintances there and at the same time introduce him to them. He naturally enough did not take much interest in the FGB branches, but it was certainly useful to him to meet the consuls and some of the dignitaries in the larger towns. When we got to Aix Whity left us to go by train to Cabris once again, and Roger and I returned to Paris. In Paris Roger took up his quarters in the delightful Hôtel de Bourgogne et Montana, midway between our flat and the office, where he then spent a fortnight reading past files and finding them, I fear, rather overpowering. But at the same time he enjoyed meeting a good many of our Paris contacts, especially the museum officials as he was an art historian himself. He left Paris on 18 June. I was rather relieved that he was not able to stay for the two farewell parties that I gave on 23 and 26 June. We had to give two parties because there were so many people, nearly 200 in fact, of whom I had to take leave. The faithful Jeanne, who had returned to her master some time before, came to help with these.

As there was a feeling of anticlimax after that and I thought there might be need for me to be on the spot in August to oversee the finalizing of the building, we decided we had better take our island holiday in July. We now felt that we were really accepted by the villagers, who had christened our house la Maison des Anglaises. It was a lovely lazy holiday, the foretaste of many like it to come.

We had to leave on 1 August as we had let the cottage but we travelled slowly back to Paris where, to our great surprise and delight, we found Elsie waiting for us at our flat. How she managed to get away I don't remember – perhaps her sister was having one of those remissions that often happen with that disease. However it was, Elsie was able to remain with us till the end of our stay. The office was shut, as always in August, so we spent a very pleasant month, having many French and English friends to stay, including an old Council friend of mine from Spain, Marjorie Simpson who was to do me a great service with Spanish publishers later on. We were able also to visit a few of our French friends in their country houses, such as the Duponts at Eaubonne, the Cains at Louveciennes, and Bichette, who had always longed to show me her country cottage. We saw some of our greatest friends in Paris too, like the Wormsers who invited us for 'champagne and conversation'. And of course we took Elsie for many treats to compensate for her long and dreary absence and she took us to lunch one day at our favourite Pavilion du Lac.

When the staff returned at the beginning of September those from the Champs Elysées had at once to begin going through the masses of old files and other papers, together with their personal possessions to get ready for the move. But the library staff went on with their normal work, for we had had to decide that they would remain in the rue de Chanalailles for at least another year because, although the two library floors in the new building were already cleared there would not be time that year to have the new shelving and other furniture made. But the offices were being painted and carpeted and work was going ahead on the new flat for the Representative which was obviously going to look delectable. So as there was no need for my services I decided that I might as well take the remaining ten days of my leave allowance. Whity and I therefore left on 3 September for a ten-day tour of Burgundy, in our own car, driving slowly along the little roads, seeing many places still new to us, such as Tournus, Cluny and Monréale, as well as old favourites. The weather throughout was mellow and golden and the sight of the white cattle browsing among mauve autumn crocuses in that peaceful countryside lent a lyrical charm to that last little holiday we were to have in France.

During the remaining twenty days of September much happened. Roger arrived on the 20th to take possession of his new flat and every day we received more and more letters, both from friends and officials, expressing their deep regret that we were so soon to leave Paris. Even Douglas Cooper wrote a letter, raging against the folly of our having to go and even our landlord the Comte de Coulombiers expressed his sadness, saying that he had never had such pleasant tenants, who had never complained about anything. The letter I liked best of all was one from Paul Sinker, praising my work not only in Paris but during the fourteen years I had served the Council, and his regret that I was now about to retire. But what pleased me most in his letter was its final paragraph, in which he said how deeply he had appreciated the part Ethel had played in France doing so many dreary tasks as well as making her own contribution to the social side by her character and personality. He mentioned too all she had done for the Council in London when she had run the Student Welfare Department so he felt they owed her a double debt and begged me to tell her so.

During those days I gave a staff party in our flat at which they presented me with the traditional present that was always given to departing Representatives. Mine could not have been better chosen for, knowing my passion for France, they gave me a set of the famous Guides Bleus, which they hoped would bring me back again to see more of it. That was a nice homely party, but there was homeliness too in the atmosphere of the farewell dinner that the Ambassador gave me, when he asked me to choose the twenty-eight guests I would like to come to it. Whity of course was invited too and the others were the friendly heads of all the departments I had worked with. Louis Joxe spoke for the French, hinting at an honour that was to come to me, and the Ambassador spoke so glowingly of my character and services that I found it very difficult to give a speech in reply to both of them, which I had to.

On the morning of 1 October Whity set off in our car with Elsie. I spent the whole of that last day with Roger who, after a good dinner, drove me to the Gare du Nord where I found, waiting outside my carriage on the ferry train, a little group of people who had come to say farewell: a few of the staff with Wieder and Eber. At the last minute dear Gerry Young dashed on to the platform, saying in his characteristically nonchalant way that as he happened to be dining in the neighbourhood – as if anybody ever did! – he just thought he would come. As the train moved out I don't think I felt sad at the sight of those affectionate faces, as I knew I could always see them again on future visits to France. But there was one whom, alas, I should never see again: Gerry, who died during an operation for a cerebral haemorrhage six months later. Instead I had a deep sense of satisfaction that I had managed to accomplish what I had set out to do. And after all I was going to the home I loved to live there again with Whity, who I knew would be at Victoria next morning to meet me, as indeed she was.

But I hadn't quite finished with the Council. In the following week I had to meet the Executive Committee and the new Chairman, Sir Edward Bridges. Paul had obviously mentioned my wickedness, as he called it, about getting the new building started, for he introduced me by saying that I had done so 'by fair means and foul', and then going on to say complimentary things about my work in France. I then had to give a brief summary of that work but chiefly about my labours over the building. When I confessed how I had broken the Treasury rules to get it started Sir Edward, who had himself been the Permanent Secretary of the Treasury for very many years, said 'Good, that is the kind of thing I like to hear' whereupon all the Committee relaxed and joined in the compliments. So I left the Council without a stain on my character.

Chapter Fifteen

A RICHLY VARIED RETIREMENT
1960-1979

We had barely had time to settle into our house before we heard a tragic piece of news. Just as my own and only nephew, Iain, had died young at the beginning of my time in Paris, so now at the end of it, my niece's husband Jack Ranking, the consultant who had been so good to me during my illnesses while I was there, died suddenly too of heart failure at the equally untimely age of forty-nine. He left his childless wife, much younger than he was and trained for no job, to face her life alone, which she did with the utmost courage, thankful that she could at least return to her parents' house just across the road from the one she had now lost.

We were unable to help her immediately, though we did what we could later on, for we were just about to embark on a major reconstruction of our house, including the installation of central heating. We had been surprised to see not only how woefully shabby it had become, but how impossibly old-fashioned and difficult to use all the kitchen regions were, and how inadequate the spare room above. So we applied to our friend, the young and imaginative architect Dom Burns, who at once planned just the sort of alterations we wanted, and got approval for them. The work was to begin in January but the problem was what we should do with Elsie while it was in progress, since she would have nowhere to live and work. By a stroke of our usual luck, though it seems heartless to call it so, she was once again called to the bedside of her now definitely dying sister; and once again she felt she must go, leaving Ethel and me, whose quarters were untouched, to manage on our own, since we had to be present to answer the many practical questions which arose every day. It wasn't a comfortable or warm winter but at least we could spend the weekends with friends; and during such leisure hours as we had I could get on with my translation of *La Naissance du Jour*, which I had begun in Paris, while Ethel went to painting classes at which she met a fellow painter, Ellen Miles, and her husband Ashley, the head of the Lister Institute, who were soon to become some of our greatest friends.

At last towards the end of February all the heating engineers, plumbers, builders, electricians and carpenters disappeared, their work finished, and we were able to install the new kitchen equipment. Then again our luck held, as Elsie's sad sister died at the end of February, so we were able to go and fetch her in the first days of March, longing to begin cleaning the new quarters with which she was delighted. Ethel and I were then rewarded for those months of discomfort by getting an invitation from our friends the de Wintons to stay with them from the 15 to 25 March in Rome where Charles was then the Council's Representative. They had got to know all our old Italian friends, Guglielmo degli Alberti, Umberto Morra, the Ruffinis and Carandinis, and invited them to a luncheon to meet us, after which they all also invited us to their houses so we had a very happy time.

When Roger Hinks heard that we were leaving Rome on the 25th he invited us to stay for a few days with him on our way home, so that I had the pleasure of living for a moment in that flat that I had helped to create and decorate. He also gave a party for us, inviting many of our main French contacts. This was generous of him because we received such a rapturous welcome from these people whom he himself had hardly had time to get to know. They in turn invited us and it was difficult for me not to feel that I was still the Cultural Attaché, especially when we visited our dear old concierge and Whity called on the shops in the rue de Bourgogne which had served her so well and we went on Sunday morning, as of old, to Bagatelle to see the sheets of hyacinths in the grass.

Immediately we got back we started on the decoration not only of the new parts of the house, but of the older rooms which needed new wallpaper, paint and curtains, as did the staircase. For it was one of our main aims to make the house a place of comfort and beauty where we could entertain at meals, or invite to stay, both our English and foreign friends whom we hoped would come and share the fun and gaiety of our own happy daily lives, which they gladly did. With that done Ethel was free to get into the neglected garden and start what was to be one of her principal occupations in the years ahead. But now all she could do was to tidy it and fill the borders with as many glowing flowers as she could choose to prepare it for a garden party which we wanted to give in early June.

For me the problem of filling my time was more complex. Ever since the days of *Héloïse* I had dreamt of a literary life, so I felt very gratified when Chatto and Windus suggested I should write another biography. But I had no particular subject in mind. I merely knew that I would like to find some historical personage with connections in both France and England. In the meantime I had plenty of translations. And by way of practical things I accepted the invitation of Lord Harvey to rejoin the Executive Committee of the Franco-British Society, of which I had been a member since the end of the war. I was also asked by John Lehmann, who was President of the Alliance Française to become a member of their Council. Both these institutions felt that my recent experience in France would be useful to them when the lecturing season started in the autumn and they hoped I would be able to suggest possible people for them to invite. The Alliance too had many branches in big provincial towns where I sometimes gave lectures for them myself.

By mid-June we both began to feel the lure of the island again; and as Alethea Hayter, who was now Deputy Representative, had asked us to spend a few days in her delightful flat on the Quai d'Orleans, we thought we would go to Paris first, taking with us Ruth Atkinson, who also had friends in Paris and whom we had invited to be our first visitor at Les Portes. While we were with Alethea something very exciting happened to me, for on the morning of 14 June the announcement of my promotion to the rank of *Officier* of the Legion of Honour was announced in the *Journal Official*. I was not unprepared for this as Louis Joxe had hinted at such a thing during the final dinner which the Ambassador had given me. But naturally I felt very proud of it because the rank of *Officier* was a rare honour even for a Frenchwoman and much more so for a foreigner.

So I was in an elated mood when at last we arrived on the

island to whose spell Ruth immediately succumbed, as did Alethea who came later for a weekend and was followed by Madge Wallace, a beloved cousin of Ethel's since childhood and full of wit and fun. The island was indeed a magic place with its wonderful light, clear as that of Greece. Yet its pleasures were few and simple. Whenever possible we had our meals out of doors at the stone table on our little upper terrace or on the large lower terrace where we passed the hot afternoons reading or just lazing and watching the lizards darting over the old walls. An unusual surprise for our visitors were the oysters, which Ethel's capable hands soon learnt to open, and which were so cheap that a dozen each for supper was almost a daily treat. Then there were the bathes from the huge sandy Conche des Baleines, after which we would enjoy a picnic lunch in a grove of ilex trees behind the sand dunes which encircled the bay. For days when we were feeling energetic there were walks in the marshes behind the village where one could see rare birds like the stilts and avocets. And in the evenings we would walk to the sea wall to watch the sun going down over those huge Atlantic waters. Sometimes too we would go for meals to the one or two good restaurants of the island, especially one in the village next to ours which was called Ars. So much did our visitors enjoy sharing these pleasures that we evolved a plan whereby each year we would invite three to share our stay, which generally lasted about six weeks; one at the beginning, one in the middle and one at the end, each for about ten days, leaving a week or so between each when we could be by ourselves and see something of our island friends like Jacqueline Regreny, who looked after our cottage in winter. For us these months on the island felt as though we were living at home in another country rather than having a holiday, so much did the villagers make us feel one of themselves. This habit we were to keep up for sixteen years, and about ten of our friends took advantage of it, eagerly asking when their next turn would be. It was a great pleasure for us to be able to share our French home in this way with friends who loved a foreign seaside holiday but couldn't otherwise have had it. We could only have one at a time as our spare room was tiny.

Another pleasure the island gave us was the drive home, over which we never hurried. During the years when one could fly from Cherbourg to Hurn by that now vanished Silver City Line, we always drove up the west side of France. On the first journey we went to St Malo and Dinard, where I had an odd experience. While we were waiting in our car for the ferry to cross the Rance I suddenly noticed that the woman who was driving the car next to ours was an exact double of myself. The shape of her head, the colour of her hair, her features, eyes and even, when she turned and smiled, her teeth. I asked Ethel to look at her and see if she agreed and she said yes, it was so. Then the woman obviously saw it herself and when she asked her passengers to look at me, they clearly agreed too and laughed. At that moment we had to drive on to the ferry so I couldn't speak to her but it gave me rather an uncanny feeling to have seen a mirror-image of myself. We spent the last night in the homely and simple Hôtel du Vieux Château at Bricquebec, twenty miles from Cherbourg, which became one of our favourite ports of call on our journeys either going or coming.

During the autumn, as I still hadn't thought of a subject to write about, I first took a course of cooking demonstrations at the Cordon Bleu. This amused Elsie a good deal but she was generous enough to praise my efforts to improve our menus on the island. Later on the experience I gained was to be a great help to me in London too. In addition to the lectures for the Alliance Française I used some of my still abundant energy by giving others for the National Trust. I was in any case a life member of it and, as I said in the first chapter of these memoirs, I always had a great love of old buildings and architecture in general. So when Ruth Dalton gave me an introduction to the Trust's secretary, Jack Rathbone, he gladly enrolled me in their team of lecturers, gave me a set of their booklets and showed me the slides I could borrow.

Ethel also began then a new pastime which occupied her, together with her painting, when the gardening season ended. This was tapestry. She was always a bird-watcher and on the island had seen that there lived in the trees between our cottage and Catherine's house that beautiful bird the hoopoe with its pink body feathers, broad black and white striped wings and elegant crest; so she drew one on canvas and made a charming tapestry of it with a background of the little white pyramids of salt, the collecting of which was in our early days so characteristic of the island. This was the first of a long series of tapestries she was to make throughout the coming years, sometimes inventing her own designs or taking them from objects which had struck her fancy. Friends also asked her to do one for them of something that they particularly liked, and those for me always had frogs on them, particularly one fat laughing frog-face peeping out from strange leaves. She was gifted enough to be able to draw the designs herself directly on to the canvas.

In the following year, 1961, we both paid a short visit to Paris. I saw a great many of my former contacts with one sad exception. My dear friend Bichette, who had been so helpful to me in my Paris days, had a stroke on the very day I was going to see her, never regained consciousness and died a week later. I think it was during that visit that I told Robert Wieder that I was now lecturing for the National Trust. He at once asked me whether I would go on a provincial tour of the branches of FGB and give them a lecture on that subject. I hesitated about this, as I feared Roger might not like me to go in this way on what was now his stamping ground; so we asked him and he said he didn't mind; I don't think he really cared much about the provincial towns himself. So I promised to go on that tour a year later.

As soon as I got back from Paris, Ethel and I felt that we ought to be a little more adventurous than always going to France. I had met a woman who organized an annual festival in Baalbek, so we planned a journey to various places in the Lebanon, Syria and Jordan, especially Palmyra and Petra which we had always wanted to see. As there were no package tours in those days we went to a good agent who knew that part of the world well and quickly planned a most enjoyable tour for what nowadays seems a trifling sum. Tom Morray, the Council Representative in Beirut, was a friend of us both and he and his nice wife took us for a few charming drives in that now war-torn country which was then such a pleasant place. Then we left Beirut with a car, chauffeur and a courier of our own and sped up to the Krak of the Knights, the most impressive of the huge Crusader Castles, before we travelled across the desert, shimmering in the heat, to where the oasis of Palmyra suddenly rises behind some low hills, the golden stone of its temples and colonnades and strange tower-like tombs, with the stone images of the dead sitting in them, glowing in the green setting of the surrounding palm trees. The next high point for us after Damascus with its great mosques, and lovely Gerash, was Petra glowing rose-red. In the Holy Land we stayed in Jerusalem and saw Jericho and many more places, finally returning to Beirut whence we went at last to Baalbek. The whole journey had taken only three weeks, but left unforgettable memories.

When we returned in May we went to Porlock Weir as usual to see Alice and visited various National Trust properties on the way there and back, as I wanted to see as many as I could, to make my descriptions of them in my lectures livelier. The work of preparing these lectures kept me very busy that autumn and winter. I then had an accident and slipped on the frozen ruts in the unmade lane beside our garden and fell with my left arm behind me, breaking the wrist. Fortunately our vicar happened to come along, and helped me up and then conducted me home on his arm. When Ethel opened the door and saw the situation she cheerfully remarked 'Hello Vicar, I see you have taken to picking up fallen women'. But that broken wrist was a great handicap to me, especially as I had an engagement to fulfil in February, giving the annual prizes at my old school, Redland High School. I larded my talk with funny stories and it seemed to go down well with both the staff and the girls. I met there Alison Dobbs, a fine-looking Irish woman who had taught me French sixty years before and thereafter she became a dear friend of us both. Ethel had come with me and we spent the weekend in Bristol, where my brother, who was not in very good health at that time, asked me to go and look over his old school, Clifton College, and tell him of any changes I noticed there. I was soon to be glad that I did this for him.

On 1 March, my wrist now healed, I set off on the promised lecture tour. I gave my first lecture in Paris and then set off by train by myself to lecture at Blois, Nantes, Bordeaux, Tarbes, Marseilles, Aix-en-Provence and Nice. The weather was still snowy and the contrast between those lonely journeys and the way such tours had been arranged in the past soon put an end to my feeling that I was still the Cultural Attaché. I remember only one funny incident. In Blois, where the head of the Society prided himself on his English, which he insisted on speaking to me, I had a very small audience. When I asked him why this was so he said it was because I had come on the cinders. For a moment this puzzled me until I remembered that les Cendres was the usual French word for Ash Wednesday! When at last I got to Nice I went to stay with Jane de Iongh, now living at St Paul-de-Vence, for the night before I was to give my lecture. I was very tired and went early to bed. When she came to waken me next morning she told me that Ethel, who was staying with Beth at Cabris, had rung up the night before to say that Pat had telephoned to tell me that my brother had died. Ethel and Jane had agreed not to waken me as there was nothing I could do that night.

She came next morning and together they managed to get me on a night plane from Nice. Somehow I managed to give my lecture there before the plane left and I then flew back to London and went straight down to Tunbridge Wells where I hoped my presence would be of some comfort to Pat and her mother. But they were both wrapped up in all the sad tasks one has to do at such times and had everything in hand; so after the cremation I returned to London. As Elsie saw I was feeling rather lost she suggested I should go to Paris where Ethel and I had arranged to meet. This I did and Alethea put us up for three days and gave a most enjoyable party, inviting a list of some of my old friends which I had given her, thinking she would like them and that they would become her friends too, which indeed they did. I think it must have been at that time that I talked to her about my search for a character for a biography.

It was fortunate that I did so, for in the following August when we were on the island she wrote to tell me that she thought she had found the perfect subject I wanted, in the course of some reading on the Tower of London she was doing in preparation for a lecture she was writing herself. It was Charles d'Orleans, nephew of Charles VI of France, a young prince who had been captured at the Battle of Agincourt and spent the next twenty-five years as a prisoner in England. She mentioned a few of the lovelist of his poems which one found in every anthology and said she didn't think there was an English life of him.

This excited me greatly, but it was to be two months before I went to the British Museum to look him up, for as soon as we got back from the island we had planned to go for three weeks' holiday in September to Yugoslavia, staying at Split, Dubrovnik, and on the Island of Hvar before sailing up the Adriatic to Venice. On the boat that took us there we liked the look of a solitary woman, Hanna Kelly, who it turned out lived not far from us in Hampstead. We parted in Venice where we were to meet Alethea for a final week of that holiday. It was Ethel's and my first visit to Venice since that long-ago experience in 1926 and we saw much that we had not then seen, Torcello for one thing. We took a trip down the Brenta too and had many meals out of doors in the mellow September days. After we returned home we got in touch with Hanna again. Ethel realized at once that she was desperately lonely and felt, as she had with Eda, that she must do all she could to help. So she became one of our circle of friends and a devotee of the island, where she stayed no less than eight times in the following years.

Even when we returned from Venice I had a good many lecturing engagements to put in and so it was not until October that I was able to go to the British Museum and look up Charles of Orleans. I found that it was true that there was no English life of him, but there was an immense volume on his life in French by Pierre Champion, in the bibliography of which I found a mass of books which I should have to read myself. I found too that in addition to the two or three well-known poems the Prince had written, there were a great many more. I felt a little daunted as to whether I could tackle this obviously large subject, but it wasn't long before I fell under the spell of research and began making endless cards as I started reading. At the end of each day I hurried home to pour into Ethel's ears all my discoveries. She of course was delighted that I was beginning a new book, in which her interest never flagged. Not that she herself was empty of new occupations at that time, for at the request of a neighbour she had become a governor of North London College in the Camden Road. When she was asked to do this she protested that she knew nothing about education, but I subsequently heard that her fellow governors gladly welcomed her for the sake of her personality, her calm and wide-minded commonsense and her shrewd judgment on selection boards. She dutifully attended all their meetings and other functions. But of course her gardening, painting and tapestries remained her favourite occupations, as did other occasional country pursuits such as badger-watching, which she used to follow with Paul Sinker.

I went steadily on with my research during the winter and early spring months, but in June we accepted an invitation from Beth to go to Cabris where we hadn't been for some time. We stayed a month with her. But it was a sad month for our friends in Paris for Roger Hinks, who was due to retire at the end of it, had a stroke at the beginning of it and died, never having regained consciousness. This threw the whole burden of the work on Alethea until the Council sent someone out to help her. So we didn't see her when we returned to London, where we only stayed for three weeks before we set off for the island again, where this year we remained for two and a half months. By now I had enough cards filled with my research to be able to start writing on the island and as soon as we returned in the middle of October I began my regular visits to the British Museum again, to which Ethel used to drive me every morning. By the end of February 1964 I felt sufficiently sure of myself to go to Chatto and Windus and tell them of my proposed biography. Both Ian Parsons and Norah Smallwood thought it sounded an exciting subject and gave me a generous contract for it.

Happy though I was to have the contract, I did not want to give up everything else for it, particularly not the many journeys we had planned to take. The first of these was to Egypt, and in March 1964, as soon as I had got the contract we set off, taking Madge and Hanna with us on what was to have been a package tour but turned out to have only one other person on it, a quiet little man. Our greatest wish was to see the temples at Abu Simbel while they were still on their original site on the banks of the Nile and this we achieved, going up the river in an old-fashioned paddle steamer. Of course we saw all the other main temples too and had the luck to stay in those delightful old hotels, the Cataract at Aswan and the Winter Palace at Luxor. We went to the Fayoum too, where the pharaohs used to go fishing and shooting, and naturally we saw the pyramids. Travellers' tales without details are boring, but as I have no space for those I think perhaps it would be as well if I here give a mere list of the countries we visited each year for the next eight or nine years, just to show how rich and full our happy retirement was, and after that to relate the other events that took place in those years.

In the spring of 1965 we took Ruth Dalton with us to Morocco, having discovered that it was one of the two places she had always longed to see. We were glad afterwards that we did for she died in the following year. Once again this was an individually arranged tour and we had our own car and chauffeur. We went to Tangiers, Chauen, Volubilis, Meknez and Fez, but not Marrakesh as Ethel and I had gone there when we were in Paris. The next and much more important journey was to Russia in 1966 and this really was a big package tour, arranged for members of the National Trust, which took us to Moscow, Leningrad, Novgorod and many other places and palaces and museums and churches. But here I must allow myself to tell one comic incident. We were given a big banquet by the Leningrad University at which a member of its teaching staff sat between each English guest and proved amusing and pleasant company. But Ethel, who was sitting on an armless chair whose two front legs sloped outwards, Regency fashion, found they were slightly groggy, and her weight made them slide slowly under the table, taking her seat with them so that she slowly disappeared from sight and could only feebly call for help. Not a single Russian moved, no Russian face registered any emotion and there she lay until one of our fellow-travellers came and hauled her up. I can only think that the Russians had always been taught that English people often drink themselves under the table and thought they were seeing it happen. That visit is memorable for me because in the interval of a performance at the Bolshoi Theatre Ethel found her way to an underground café where she toasted my seventieth birthday in champagne.

In 1967 Tom Morray, who had done so much for us in the Lebanon, invited us to stay with him and his wife in Carthage, as he was now the Representative in Tunisia. We saw much of that beautiful country with them, and then flew on to Lybia, where again the Council's Representative helped us to see both Leptis Magna and Sabratha (nearly always wrongly pronounced Sabarthra). I was too busy with Charles to go anywhere in 1968 except to the island, but in 1969 came what I think Ethel enjoyed most of all, a Safari which started in Nairobi and then took us through Kenya where we spent a night in the Treetops Hotel and then on through Tanzania and Uganda, mercifully at a time when those countries were still peaceful. There could not have been a greater contrast to this than the ten-day package tours to Italy, arranged by an excellent firm called Specialtours, on one of which we went in 1970 first to Naples, Paestum and Caserta, and then to the less well-known places on the Adriatic coast, with their beautiful romanesque churches, Frederick of Hohenstaufen's great Castel del Monte, and on to the golden baroque city of Lecce. Our fellow-travellers on these little tours were pleasant companions of like tastes with our own.

It will probably be wondered how with all our absences during those years I ever found time to write that life of Charles of Orleans. But our travels abroad rarely filled more than four weeks in any one year, leaving me the remaining eleven months to spend chiefly on long days of research in the Reading Room and the Manuscript Department of the British Museum, where I remember my excitment on finding literally 600 exquisite lyrics which tell so much of his life and feelings that I wanted to incorporate them in my text. I was able to procure a copy as they are still in print, so that I could take them with me to the island and study them there. With all this gathered material I finished the text early in March 1968 and took it to Chatto's to read. They took a long time over it, as Cecil Day Lewis had to read it first and then Ian Parsons. Both found it too long, so Ian asked me to cut it by 10,000 words. This laborious and painful task took me another five months; but I was able to hand the completed manuscript to Ian in early September 1968. Printing started at once, but again that and the proof reading took an inordinate time and was so exhausting that when it was finished and had got to the binding stage I felt I needed a holiday. So I joined Alethea and we went first to see the extraordinary stone creatures of Bomarzo, then on to Orvieto and Viterbo, whence we saw the famous Renaissance Gardens of Lante and Caprarola.

The book immediately received glowing reviews in the main papers. In November 1970 it was awarded the Duff Cooper Memorial Prize which I was given by the French Ambassador, Geoffroy de Courcel, at a glittering party which took place in 1971. When I think back to that time now, although

I don't suppose it ever crossed Ethel's mind for an instant, I feel that that whole occasion was the fulfilment of her unwavering belief, first expressed nearly sixty years before, that I would one day become a writer, and the result of her promise to help me learn as much as I could about French literature. It was as a consequence of that book that in the following April I was made a Fellow of the Royal Society of Literature. Incidentally, and rather strangely, Chatto's could never persuade any French publisher to bring out a translation, although there existed no comparable up-to-date biography of Charles d'Orleans in French. But a Spanish version appeared, owing chiefly to the efforts of my friend Marjorie Simpson, of the British Council in Madrid.

While I was absorbed in all this work and pleasure several sad events had been taking place in our personal and domestic lives. In 1964 our earliest and dearest Italian friend Guglielmo Alberti, who had stayed with us so often in London and Paris, came to a most untimely end aged only about 60. The next to go was my dear old Alice whom we had continued to visit every year and who was mourned by all the children in her village and many important persons in the countryside for her great wisdom. In 1968 my sister-in-law Winnie died while we were on the island. She had been suffering from a slow cancer for a long time, but managed to write me a cheerful letter just before Pat summoned me home.

A different loss that took place in 1966, but not through death this time, was when on our return from the island, Elsie told us that her arthritis was now so bad that she felt she must leave us as she could no longer earn her wages by doing her work. We begged her to stay on as a friend and let us get some outside help, but that conscience of hers would not let her accept and she felt she must take advantage of an offer from her one and only school friend to go and live with her at Abinger. We could not but agree that this seemed an ideal solution for her so we took her there. But the friend turned out to be a cold and heartless woman as we found when we went down each month to see her. Unable to bear it any longer Elsie herself found an admirable home for a few arthritic people not far from us, where the heads of it, Mr and Mrs Blake, gave her a warm welcome. It was so near us that we often went to see her there, while we struggled to do without her ourselves with the help of assorted Sicilians who lived in our neighbourhood. But there came a sad day in December 1971, the year which had begun so happily for me, when Elsie died, as quietly and unobtrusively as she had lived. We missed her sorely not only for her devoted help but for her wit and remarkable character.

As for me, after having tasted blood with the success of *Charles of Orleans* I immediately plunged into research for another biography, a study of the life and works of Christine de Pizan, whom I had first heard of many years before but who came back into my mind during my research on Charles, when she was mentioned many times, chiefly because she had written the life of his uncle King Charles VI. I found that there was no full biography of her in English but many studies, chiefly American, of her books which fortunately printed the text of those difficult, largely allegorical works. There were several striking events in her life but when I told Ian Parsons about it he was far from enthusiastic, since he had never heard of her, but he had enough faith in me to give me a contract at the end of April. Although I started work on it at once, I again worked in a very desultory fashion, never letting it interfere with any other plans we had made.

So although I actually managed to finish it in the spring of 1974 I even then put off sending it in till August because we had accepted two invitations for June and July from Roger in Geneva and Beth. She was by then too old to do more than a little gardening so as we both wanted to see as many of our old haunts as we could in that wonderful country, we hired a car and drove through the lovely inland villages, taking only the briefest of looks at those coastal places, once so lovely, now so overbuilt. Returning from these drives it was lovely to sit on the terrace in the warm nights and listen once again to the nightingales and the croaking of the frogs in the swimming pool, that voluptuous sound that had always enchanted me. Had I but known it, I was never to hear it again for this was our last visit to Cabris.

When we got home I took my manuscript to Chatto's. But once again Ian wanted some alterations. I was able to tackle this straight away and finished it by the following January, and the book finally appeared in January 1976, to be received by a smaller but on the whole favourable press for, as Norah had foreseen, it was too academic a subject to have a wide appeal. As Christine de Pizan was largely unknown I called the book *The Order of the Rose*, the name of one of her poems.

There were several reasons which made me so slow in writing this book, some pleasurable, some less so. The pleasurable ones were, as always with me, travel. For it was then that we went on another of those Special tours, this time to visit the hill towns of the Abruzzi. This ended at Spoleto, after which we spent a few days with Nina Ruffini in Rome. When we got home I was delighted to learn that Chatto and Windus had decided to reprint *Héloïse*, inspired I suppose by the success of *Charles of Orleans*.

I did a certain amount of work on Christine during the summer, but in September we went on a long tour of Scotland with Joy Behrens, one of the friends I had made in the Franco-British Society. Herself a Scot, she planned it all and what was more did all the driving. We met her in Perth and our first port of call was Oban from whence we sailed to Iona, which both of us had long wanted to see. On our return journey from this tour we went to St Andrews, not far from which Ethel got the chance to visit Charlton in Fifeshire, the beautiful Georgian house with superb gardens where she and Beth had worked in the First World War, gardens now sadly abandoned, but full of memories for her.

Immediately we returned to London, my great-nephew Alasdair, the only son of that young man Iain, came to stay with us for three months while he attended a crammer for the entrance exam to Cambridge. He was a very pleasant guest but feeding a tall and hungry boy of eighteen didn't leave me much energy or time for my research. The final travel which made me default on the finishing date of the book was a journey we took in the autumn of 1973 to Turkey, a journey on which our old friend Basil Amulree joined us. I had always had a great longing to see the city which I could never call anything but Constantinople, and at last I realised that dream. After we had explored all its wonders we flew over the Bosphorus (it was the year before the building of the bridge which has taken the poetry out of that crossing); and on the other side we saw not only Iznik (Nicaea), Troy, Pergamon and a few of the great Greek cities further south. The one that enthralled me most was Ephesus.

And now I must mention the less pleasurable reasons which slowed down my writing, and our lives in general, and that was health. I don't want to turn this part of my narrative into an organ recital, but I must at least mention, as briefly as I can, the various ailments (not I think important enough to be called diseases) that began to attack us in those years, not surprisingly as we were both in our late seventies. My main complaint came on our return from Turkey in 1973. I thought at first that it was lumbago but the pain was so violent that, on being x-rayed, it turned out to be something called osteoporosis, a thinning of the vertebrae. This caused me excruciating pain for many months but then settled into a dull ache. Ethel too had had her share of pain beginning earlier with a fierce attack of sciatica in 1970 followed by a heart attack after bathing in the autumn of 1971, after which she never bathed again and was frequently exhausted. Then came for her the beginning of a persistent rheumatism.

But all these things never for an instant affected the fun and gaiety of our lives, nor our work in the house and garden, both of which we now kept up to the mark and even beautified still further. The chief thing we had done in the garden was to turn the far end of it into a stone-paved terrace, with a small statue of a little boy hugging a dolphin, where we could sit, not overlooked by neighbouring gardens or houses. In the house I added an extra bathroom to the guest-room, to the great pleasure of the many friends who continued to come and stay. Because of that we had a stroke of our usual luck. One of the young men who built it asked Ethel one day if she would like his father-in-law to help her with the heavy work of the garden, as he loved gardening and had only a small patch of his own. Of course she jumped at that and a tall, soldierly-looking man called Victor Millwood appeared at the weekends. When the summer was over I asked him if he would be able to come and do some house-work for us. He said he loved polishing and cleaning. So with his help we were able to go on entertaining friends as usual. A time came when he retired from his job and was able to give us more time. He was never to leave us during our remaining years. So with his help we could go on entertaining as lavishly as ever, so constantly in fact that when every now and again we found ourselves without guests on Sundays, alone with each other in the solitude that continued to be our chief bliss, we called them Selfish Sundays.

That journey to Turkey was the last of our more important foreign travels; but since as usual we longed to go abroad, in 1976, we followed the advice of several friends and went at the end of May to Corfu, staying at the well-known Hotel Castello, whose owner, the charming Madame Bouas, at once took to Ethel and gave us one of the best rooms. The hotel was not by the sea but was set in a huge park and one of the pleasures of it was that a part of this park by the house was used as an outside dining room under trees which were lit by lanterns at night. We had been given by our friend Basil Amulree an introduction to two friends of his, Elizabeth and Christopher Glenconner. They at once drove over to make our acquaintance and invited us to lunch at their ravishing house at Paleocastritsa at the other end of the island and came again to fetch us and bring us back on the appointed day. In our old age it was a pleasure to all four of us that we had made a rare new friendship. We returned to London in time to go and see Alasdair get his degree at Cambridge.

As that was such a blazing hot summer we felt that, although swimming could no longer be one of our pleasures, we must go to the island just once again, so we went for a short three-week visit in September when Hanna drove us out and Daphne Fullerton brought us back. It was while we were there that I had my 80th birthday and on our return I was greatly touched to be invited in early October to a celebration of that event, which two of our old Council friends, Yvonne de Pury and Rosamund Day, organised. I had told them I only wanted a simple cocktail party, held in Alethea's charming flat in Montagu Square and they let me suggest the list of guests. It consisted not only of some of the most senior officers under whom I had first served but many of the humbler ones who had been my staff when I was there and others more junior still. The Sinkers came from Shrewsbury to go to it and stayed with us overnight.

In 1977 we repeated the Corfu holiday in May and June, but the day after we arrived Ethel told me in the morning that she didn't feel at all well. Madame Bouas immediately summoned an excellent Greek heart specialist from the town of Corfu, who ordered Ethel to stay in bed for nearly a week, came again that same night, and seemed satisfied. By the second week she was up and about again and we once more saw our new friends the Glenconners. We realised by now that we should never be able to go to the island again and in September we told Catherine this and she said she would buy the house from us. She didn't want the furniture so this we gave to Jacqueline who was building a new house for herself, to let. In that same year Ethel's long driving career of more than fifty years without an accident came to an end and we sold our car cheap to our devoted Victor.

But once again we felt it impossible to accept that we should no longer be able to go abroad so when we found that the Specialtours Agency was offering a week's holiday in Vicenza, with daily journeys to Palladian villas, we were delighted to find that they still had two places for us. I enjoyed this enormously but Ethel found some of the day-long trips too exhausting, even the one to Padua where she longed to see the Giottos again. We returned to find that, on the afternoon of the day we got back, our house had been badly burgled, but though we lost a great number of our dearest treasures, the burglars had fortunately not damaged the house in any way.

To cheer ourselves up after this we found a young painter and asked him if he could possibly paint the white wall of an outhouse between the house proper and garden. I had been longing to have this done for years but could find no-one to do it. I had seen his name advertised in *The Times*, and although he said he was not an experienced mural painter he thought he could tackle it. I wanted a kind of Douanier Rousseau design with lots of wild animals peeping through a leafy background. He drew a design which we liked and thereafter came for several weeks when the weather happened to be fine, and produced something which has given us and our guests pleasure ever since. We had arranged that it could be floodlit from the side and it certainly looked extraordinary on snowy nights and seemed at all times to bind the house and garden together.

In 1978 we had to realize that we could no longer go abroad but must be content with country weekends with our friends and holidays in English hotels, of which we fortunately found two good ones. Ever since *The Order of the Rose* had been published Ethel had been worrying lest I should miss the act of writing and get bored. Then one day Marianna Traub, who for years had been teaching me Italian, but who never really cared for my historical biographies, suggested that I should write the story of my life. Ethel was delighted with this suggestion so, after thinking it over, I began on September 21st of that year 1978 and by Christmas finished the first two chapters which Ethel read and liked.

The winter of that year was a particularly cruel one and we were snowbound for weeks so that she could only sit and look out at the garden. As soon as the Christmas festivities were over I told her I was about to write the chapter describing our first meeting, saying she would then know what it meant to me. But she was never to see it. On a Sunday at the end of January we both woke up with terrible coughs, but thinking they were nothing worse than that we didn't call the doctor. On the following Wednesday, 31 January, she suddenly fell to the ground, unable to speak. It was two hours before I was able to get Dr Bunn, who at once sent her off to the Royal Free Hospital, assuring me that they would make her well in three days and send her back home where I could nurse her. It was a case of virus pneumonia, which I also had in milder form. Because of his assurance, which he sincerely meant, I was not frightened. But early the next morning I learned that, after a good night, she had suddenly and quietly died, her beautiful face unchanged, taking my life's happiness with her.

There is a passage in *Middlemarch* where George Eliot says: '"The theatre of all my actions is fallen" said an antique personage when his chief friend was dead; and they are fortunate who get a theatre where the audience demands their best'. That quotation had always lingered in my mind, for I knew that throughout my life I had had that good fortune. But there was something else as well. On going through her books after her death, I found a massive Bible which her mother had given her for her seventh birthday in 1901. She had obviously used it mainly for pressing the wild flowers she loved; but even at that early age, she must have read the Book of Proverbs, for in it there were several wobbly pencilled underlinings. One of these was 'A friend loveth at all times'. She had proved that to me too.

INDEX

In this very unorthodox index of persons I have listed all the characters mentioned in the text in the forms in which they appear in it: Christian names, nicknames, surnames with or without initials or titles, a few with their professions or jobs. Everyone has one page reference, some have more according to changes in their lives or characters which affected mine. I have given page references to members of my own family in a small separate section. For obvious reasons there are no page references to either myself or Ethel Whitehorn.

Adam, Sir Ronald, 150
Adams, Bridges, 13
Adam Smith, Janet, 178
Ady, Cecilia, 19
Alberti, Guglielmo degli, 65, 78, 174, 211, 222
Alice, 9, 49, 53, 66, 76, 77, 125, 126, 132, 143, 152, 204, 222
Allen, Dr Hugh, 24
Amulree, Basil, Lord, 224
Aragon, Louis, 131, 133
Armitage, 201
Aron, Raymond, 122
Ashton, Leigh, 118
Askwith, The Hon. Betty, 121
Atkinson, Edith, 162
Atkinson, Ruth, 212, 213

Balfour, Michael, 114
Balthus, 195
Bamford, Sir Eric, 134
Barbirolli, 174
Barker, Frank, 160
Barrault, Jean-Louis, 163
Bauër, Gérard, 130, 194
Bedot, Madame, 68, 69
Behrens, Joy, 224
Berenson, Bernard, 41
Bernac, Pierre, 133
Bernhardt, Sarah, 12
Bernstein, Sidney, 118
Beth, 44, 49, 81, 92
Bintcliff, 181

Bizanis, Constantine, 91
Blake, Mr and Mrs, 222
Blieck, de, 192
Blunt, Antony, 174
Bouas, Madame, 226
Bourbon-Busset, Comte de, 149, 185
Bracken, Brendan, 117
Bradley, Mrs, 182
Braibant, Charles, 177
Braque, 196
Bream, Julian, 195
Bresson, Pierre, 194
Bridges, Sir Edward, 208
Brillard, (architect), 151
Brook, Peter, 185
Brooke, Rupert, 92
Budberg, Baroness Moura, 122
Bugnard, Professor, 165
Bussy, Dorothy, 58, 137
Bussy, Simon, 58, 137

Cain, Julien, 143, 168, 178
Cain, Lucienne, 168
Camus, Albert, 163
Candolle, Madame Augustin de, 68
Candolle, Raymonde de, 68
Candolle, Roger de, 68
Caramello, 44
Caramello, Madame, 51
Carandini, Elena, 211
Carandini, Count Nicolo, 138, 211
Carey, Clive, 13
Carlyle, Dr A. J., 22
Carrington, Murray, 12
Cary, Father Lucius, 26, 29, 47
Catherine, 53
Cathrall, Alice, 28, 36, 67
César, 195
Chadwick, Lynn, 185
Chanel, 205
Chapsal, Jacques, 164
Chayette, Bernard, 151, 161, 169
Churchill, 201
Clark, Kenneth, 117
Coate, Marion, 197
Cocks, Miss, 10
Cocteau, Jean, 205

229

INDEX

Coles, Mrs, 203
Colette, 147
Collingham, Beatrix, 200
Collins, (chauffeur), 156
Connolly, Cyril, 133, 140
Cooper, Douglas, 176, 195, 205
Copeau, Jacques, 47, 60
Copeau, Maiène, 41, 76
Copeau, Pascal, 76
Coty, René, 187, 191
Coulombiers, Comte de, 166
Courcel, Geoffroy de, 221
Cox, Sir Trenchard, 203
Crichton Miller, Dr H., 37, 64
Curtius, E. R., 62

Dalton, Ruth, 214
Day, Rosamund, 226
Day Lewis, Cecil, 118
Debû-Bridel, Bichette, 165, 215
Debû-Bridel, Jacques, 130
Delisle Burns, Ann, 145
Delisle Burns, Cecil, 84, 85, 96, 110, 111, 121, 124
Delisle Burns, Dom, 145, 210
Delisle Burns, Margaret, 96, 110, 111, 124
Desjardins, Madame, 61
Desjardins, Paul, 59, 60
Dobbs, Alison, 15
Dominguin, 205
Du Bos, Charles, 62
Duff Cooper, 117
Duggan, Polly, 67
Duhamel, G., 133
Dupont, Jacques, 184

Eber, B., 200
Edelman, Maurice, 164
Eden, Sir Timothy, 123
Edinburgh, Duke of, 187
Einstein, 75
Eliot, T. S., 147
Elizabeth, Queen the Queen Mother, 177
Elsie, 142, 151, 168, 202, 203, 206, 223
Eluard, Paul, 131
Emmanuel, Pierre, 168
Entrèves, Alexander d' 138
Evans, Sir Arthur, 22
Evans, Edith, 199
Evans, Ifor, 118
Evans, Joan, 22

Felkin, Elliott, 38, 67, 145

Felkin, Joyce, 38, 67
Fontaine, Michel, 137
Forbes Robertson, 12
Fullerton, Daphne, 226
Fullerton, David, 123

Gallimard, 56, 63, 64, 109
Gautier, Jean-Jacques, 185
Giacometti, 195
Gibson, Miss, 30
Gide, André, 41, 46, 47, 57, 58, 60, 62, 64, 81, 93, 94, 111, 147, 165
Gielgud, Sir John, 193, 194
Gilbert, Stuart, 138, 140
Giles, Frank, 168
Giles, Lady Kitty, 168
Gillie, Cecilia, 168
Gillie, Darsie, 168
Ginn, (gardener), 126
Glasgow, Mary, 118
Glenconner, Christopher, Lord, 226, 227
Glenconner, Elizabeth, Lady, 226, 227
Golding, John, 176
Goldscheider, C., 172
Gombrich, Ernst, 112
Gombrich, Ilse, 112
Gott, Dr Arthur, 128
Goudeket, Maurice, 147, 181
Green, Dorothy, 12
Greene, Graham, 118
Greig, Miss, 30
Grey, Sheila, 141
Griffith, Kate, 62, 69, 97, 98, 99
Griffith, Sandford, 69, 79, 81, 88
Guibal, Robert, 170
Guillemard, Madame, 174
Gwyer, Barbara, 85, 105, 106
Gwyer, Sir Maurice, 85

H., Miss K. I., 25, 28, 30, 31, 35, 36, 47, 48, 49, 55, 57
Hadden, Mrs, 67
Haigh, Anthony, 150
Hamilton, Guy, 123
Harrison, Jane, 61
Harvey, Sir Oliver, 118, 150
Hawkins, Bill, 156, 162, 174, 179, 191
Hayter, Alethea, 141, 212, 217, 221, 226
Hayter, Stanley, 195

INDEX

Herbart, Pierre, 92, 93, 94, 146
Heurgon, Jacques, 62
Hilton, Bob, 191
Hinks, Roger, 194, 204, 211, 219
Hitchens, Ivor, 185
Hobson, (accountant), 162, 179
Hodson, H. V., 118
Holroyd, Michael, 34
Honey, 142, 201, 202
Hope-Wallace, Philip, 152
Howards, The, 90
Howell, David, 138
Humbert, Hélène, 29
Hunt, Martita, 186
Hunter, Mrs, 29
Huxley, Aldous, 16

Illitch, Blaguigna, 77
Iongh, Jane de, 141, 154

Jeanne, (cook), 203
Jebb, Cynthia, 177, 188
Jebb, Sir Gladwyn, 159, 171, 188, 208
Johnston, Jean, 170
Johnston, Pat, 170, 186
Johnstone, Kenneth, 135, 141, 145, 146
Johnstone, The Hon. Robin, 188
Joll, James, 176
Jourdain, Eleanor, 18, 19
Joxe, Louis, 139
Julien, A.-M., 172

Kelly, Sir David, 182
Kelly, Hanna, 218
Kelly, Marie Noële, Lady, 182
Kemp, Robert, 185
Kersey, Eda, 110, 121, 128
Keyes, H. S., 146
Kirkpatrick, Ivone, 119
Kris, Ernst, 106, 112, 121, 152, 173

Labarthe, André, 122
Lambert, Catherine, 143, 180
Lambert, Jean, 143, 147, 180
Lambert, Margaret, 108
Lambert, Nicolas, 180
Lansel, Pierre, 83
La Petite Dame, 45, 81, 143, 180

Lecocq, George, (accountant), 179
Lee, Laurie, 118
Lehmann, John, 182, 212
Leigh, Vivien, 183
Lemarchand, Jacques, 193
Loiseau, Professor, 170
Lostende, Maggy de, 140
Lowe, Phyl, 30, 36, 43
Lowes, Dickinson, 74
Lvovna, Tatiana, 66

Maar, Dora, 189
Macadam, Ivison, 72, 74, 75, 114, 115
McEwen, Frank, 165
Macmillan, Lord, 117
Macnaghten, Angus, 141
McNeile Dixon, W., 91
Madan, Falconer, 28
Mahieu, Bernard, 177
Malik, H. S., 46
Malraux, André, 94
Margerie, Jenny de, 163
Martin, Professor (at Montpellier), 201
Martin, Professor (at Poitiers), 201
Martin du Gard, Roger, 56, 57, 60, 62, 63, 64, 65, 93, 112, 147, 168, 199
Massigli, René, 137
Mauriac, F., 131
Maurice, (butler), 157
Maurois, André, 62, 119
Mayer, Thérèse, 189
Mayer, Tony, 189
Mayrisch, Andrée, 51 (then see Viénot)
Mayrisch, Emile, 42, 50, 51, 80, 82, 83
Mayrisch, Loup, 50, 51, 52, 61, 66, 80, 119, 142
Miles, Ashley, 211
Miles, Ellen, 211
Millwood, Victor, 225
Milner, R., 162
Mirrlees, Hope, 61, 65
Mirsky, Prince, 66, 69, 95
Molesworth, H., 203
Monnet, Jean, 148
Monod, Sylvère, 186
Moore, Henry, 201
Morra, Count Umberto, 78, 173, 211
Morray, Tom, 215

INDEX

Mortimer, Raymond, 120
Murray, Gilbert, 34
Murray, Lady Mary, 34
Murray, Rosalind, 34

Neveu, Ginette, 133
Neville, John, 199
Nicholson, Ben, 165
Nicolson, Harold, 117

Olivier, Sir Laurence, 183
Olsen, Eileen, 129, 142, 155, 179
O'Neill, Con, 116
Ordoñez, 205
Oxbury, 202

Pablos, Madeleine, 153
Parkinson, Nancy 124, 137, 143, 144, 145
Parsons, Ian, 108, 109, 219
Paul, Madame (concièrge), 167
Pavlova, 12
Penrose, Lee, 184
Penrose, Roland, 183
Perham, Margery, 21, 87
Picasso, 196
Pickles, Dorothy, 118
Piédelièvre, Professor, 159
Poulenc, Francis, 133
Powicke, F., 107
Pratt, Muriel, 13
Price, Katherine, 149, 154
Pury, Yvonne de, 226
Pym, Dora, 37
Pym, Canon Tom, 37

Queneau, Raymond, 168

Radcliffe, Cyril, 117
Raine, Kathleen, 168
Raleigh, Sir Walter, 19
Ramsay, Elizabeth, 74
Ranking, Jack, 140, 175
Rathbone, Jack, 214
Rees, Dr John, 64, 65, 66, 69
Regreny, J., 213
Reilly, Sir Patrick, 151, 183
Reith, John, 117
Rémond, Gabriel, 176
Rendall, Elizabeth, 11
Reynolds, Eileen, 118
Richardson, John, 176
Roché, Louis, 137
Rochefoucauld, Duchesse de la, 163

Rogers, Miss, 20
Rose, Muriel, 204
Rowe, John, 39
Royal visit, 187, 188
Ruffini, Edoardo, 90, 138, 143, 145, 211
Ruffini, Giorgia, 90
Ruffini, Nina, 90, 138, 224
Russell, The Hon. Bertrand, 33, 34
Russell, John, 203
Rysselberghe, Théo van, 40, 81

St Denis, Michel de, 76
Salles, Georges, 165, 195
Saltire, Singers, 178
Sayers, Dorothy L., 16
Schlumberger, Jean, 41, 60, 89, 169, 194
Schlumberger, Monique, 41
Scott, (the artist), 201
Scott, Sir Oswald, 123, 130
Seydoux, Roger, 185, 192
Seymour, Richard, 132
Shakespeare, Geoffrey, 203
Simpson, Marjorie, 206, 222
Simpson, Dr Percy, 28
Singer, Dr Charles, 28
Singer, Dorothea, 28
Sinker, Sir Paul, 154, 170, 197, 207, 208
Sinker, Penelope, 154
Sinker, Ruth, 154, 170, 197
Smallwood, Norah, 219
Solidor, Suzy, 148
Soupault, Philippe, 168
Southwell, Lorna, 37
Steel, Anthony, 124
Storey, Miss, 67
Supervielle, Jules, 168

Talon, (chauffeur), 188, 198
Talon, Professor, 159
Taylor, Mrs, 37
Tennant, Peter, 136
Thomas, Stephen, 183
Thomson, 74
Tizac, L. d'A. de, 109
Tolstoy, Tanya, 66
Toynbee, Arnold, 34
Toynbee, Philip, 133, 134
Traub, Marianna, 228
Trefouël, Jacques, 163
Tschiffeli, Madame, 68, 71
Tzara, Tristan, 168

INDEX

Varin, René, 138
Vercors, 131
Viénot, Andrée, 89
Viénot, Pierre, 89, 124, 125, 127, 128
Vilar, Jean, 183

Waddell, Helen, 85, 96, 97
Walford, Norah, 108 (see Smallwood)
Walker, Molly, 172
Wallace, Madge, 213
Wardale, Miss E. E., 19
Wayment, Hilary, 153
Whitehorn, Mr, 90
Whitehorn, Mrs, 40, 42, 105, 111
Whitehorn, Peggy, 42
Whitehorn, Roger, 42, 111
Wickham, Reggie, 155, 178, 179
Wieder, Robert, 169, 208
Winton, Charles de, 135, 141
Winton, Enid de, 211
Woodburn, D., 123, 134

Wormser, Olivier, 125, 169
Wright, Dr Joseph, 19, 21, 23, 27
Wright, Michael, 118

Young, Elizabeth, 191
Young, Sir George, 183, 191, 208

Zernov, Nicholas, 95, 96
Zimmern, Professor, 73

My Family

Father, 27, 53
Mother, 53, 54, 55, 121, 125
Brother (Eric), 15, 26, 50, 181, 217
Brother's Daughter (Pat), 140 (see also under Ranking)
Brother's wife (Winnie), 222
Iain (son of Eric and Winnie), 161
Alasdair (Iain's son), 161, 224, 226